49

AMAZON TOWN
A Study of Man in the Tropics

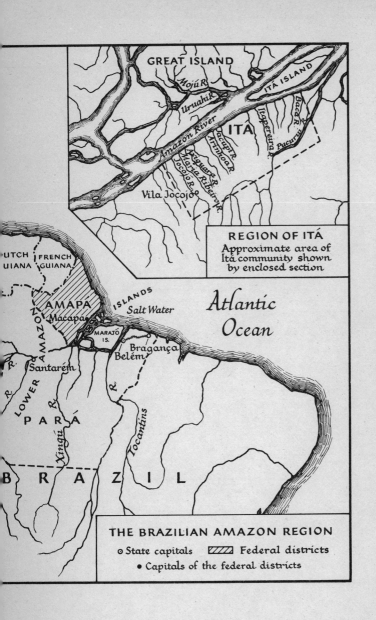

GREAT ISLAND

Mojú R.

Uruahú

ITÁ ISLAND

Amazon River

Iacupiri R.

ITÁ

Itaguari R.

Arúhoar

Itapereira R.

Baca R.

Pucurú

Jaguari R.

Gloria R.

Jocojó R.

Gloria Ribeira R.

Vila Jocojó

REGION OF ITÁ
Approximate area of
Itá community shown
by enclosed section

Atlantic Ocean

DUTCH
GUIANA

FRENCH
GUIANA

AMAPÁ

Macapá

ISLANDS

Salt Water

AMAZON R.

MARAJÓ
IS.

Bragança

Belém

Santarém

LOWER

R.

Xingú R.

Tocantins

PARÁ

B R A Z I L

THE BRAZILIAN AMAZON REGION
  ○ State capitals   ▨ Federal districts
  ● Capitals of the federal districts

AMAZON TOWN

A Study of Man in the Tropics

by

CHARLES WAGLEY

with a new chapter by

DARREL L. MILLER

illustrations by

JOÃO JOSÉ RESCÁLA

OXFORD UNIVERSITY PRESS

London   Oxford   New York

TO

Cecilia

My own guess is that our age will be remembered chiefly neither for its horrifying crimes nor for its astonishing inventions, but for its having been the first age since the dawn of civilization some five or six thousand years back, in which people dared to think it practicable to make the benefits of civilization available for the whole human race.

—ARNOLD J. TOYNBEE, in "Not the Age of Atoms but of Welfare for All," *New York Times Magazine*, October 21, 1951.

PREFACE TO THE
1976 EDITION

This is a new edition of a book which appeared first in English in 1953 and was published in Portuguese translation in 1956. But it is in a sense a "new book" because the entire situation of the Brazilian Amazon has changed as I shall indicate in this preface. It also is a "new book" because Darrel L. Miller, a graduate student at the University of Florida, has contributed a chapter on Itá in 1974. He was able to restudy Itá in 1974 after many months of discussion with me and after reading with care both the earlier edition of my book and Eduardo Galvão's *Santos e Visagems* (Companhia Editora Nacional, São Paulo, 1955), a study of the religion of the same town. This edition is based, then, upon the 1953 edition of my book which was published by the Macmillan Company; an epilogue which I wrote for a later edition which is no longer available (i.e. 1964, Borzoi Latin American Series, Alfred Knopf, New York) has been omitted.

Brazil has embarked upon a gigantic program for the "conquest of the Amazon." This involves the construction of over 13,500 kilometers of roads throughout the Amazon Valley including the East-West Trans-Amazon Highway, the North-South road from Cuiabá to Santarém, and finally the great Perimetral Norte (the Northern Perimeter Highway) which will encircle the Amazon Rain Forest in a broad horseshoe-shaped arc along the borders of the Guianas, Venezuela, Colombia, and Peru. With these roads, the last great world frontier will be open to automobile and truck transportation and will be connected to the main arteries of Brazil. It also must be said that one of the world's most delicate ecological systems, namely, that of the Amazon rain forest, will therefore be threatened. The whole emphasis of life in the Amazon region will be shifted from the great river system to roads. Now the uplands (*terra firme*) of Amazonia will be occupied rather than the river lowlands (*várzea*). As lands which annually receive silt, the *várzea* provide the good soils of the Amazon region while the uplands are generally poor. It is through the less fertile *terra firme* that the new highways penetrate.

Brazil has also embarked upon a program of colonization of the Amazon region, principally along the new roads. At first, it was planned to bring hundreds of thousands of people to occupy the uninhabited regions opened up by the roads. Now there seems to be some doubt whether this great program is economically feasible, although *agrovilas* (planned villages) and at least one *agropolis* (planned town) and a half completed *ruropolis* (planned city) already exist along the Trans-Amazonian Highway. There are people not only from Northeastern Brazil, but also from Minas Geraes, Santa Catarina, São Paulo, and from Rio Grande do Sul among the migrants. Not since the migration of the *nordestinos* to the Amazon in the late nineteenth century and the migrations of the *soldados de borracha* (soldiers for rubber) during World War II have so many people arrived. I could not count them but I have seen them in their new settlements and in old settlements such as Altamira and Itaituba. Not only are there colonists financed by the government, but there are many who came voluntarily at their own expense to find a new life in a new world. Never again will the Amazon be the same; for these Mineiros, Gauchos, Goianos, and even Paulistas are modifying Amazon culture and in turn they are learning from the Amazon people.

Even old river towns, off the highways, such as Itá are feeling the impact of the Brazilian surge to finally "conquer" the Amazon. This can be judged by Darrel L. Miller's last chapter in this book. I must confess that Itá has changed more than I could ever imagine—in my life time—but not in the way that I had hoped that it would change. It has *movimento;* it has automobiles; it has some roads opening up the backlands of the municipality; it has grown in population; it has more schools; and it has more State and Federal agencies—but it still has a dubious extractive economy. It seems to me that neither the highway system nor the very old river system of transportation will ever be successful until they are connected. The natural river "high-ways" can transport goods which then can be transferred to the new highways. If the energy crisis of the end of the twentieth century continues, then it would seem natural to connect the river ports by roads to the main artery of the Trans-Amazon highway.

I have not changed this book except for this new preface and the new chapter written by Darrel L. Miller. I want the description of "traditional" Amazon society and culture to stand as it is. Combined with Eduardo Galvão's excellent book *Santos e Visagems*, it is a monument to a people at a particular time and place in Brazilian history and cultural development. Even more, both books are important to an understanding of modern development of the Amazon because they describe the basic culture upon which Amazon social and economic development must ultimately depend. A new society is not fabricated out of a vacuum. It must be built upon historical anteced-ents. The new society which Brazil hopes to create in Amazonia will be built from the knowledge which the people of that region have accumulated over centuries from aboriginal times to the present. Over these centuries the Indians and the Luso-Brazilian caboclos who followed them in time learned to coexist and to exploit the Amazon-ian environment. They know the soils, the flora and fauna, the rise and fall of the great rivers, the epoch of rains and of relatively dry weather, the dangers of insects and of endemic disease, and many other aspects of their own milieu. And, out of this experience they fashioned their own Amazonian culture with its own social system, cuisine, forms of recreation, and mythology. This is a rich heritage which should never be ignored in the modern conquest of Amazonia.

However, this traditional Amazonian culture and the social and economic system which supported it has also been a barrier to change and to the formation of the new Amazonian society and culture which Brazilians hope to develop. The exploitative economic system which resulted from the extractive system of collecting wild rubber and other products of the forest and the system of debt servitude which tied the rubber collector to the owner of the trading post—the so-called patron-client system or *seringalista-seringueiro* system—

which are described in this book, have been definite barriers to development. Under the impact of the modernizing Brazilian economy both are disappearing in the Amazon valley. But even in the 1970s, these systems have not disappeared entirely; sometimes the old *barracão* (trading post) of the traditional patron exists side by side with a modern building of the Bank of Brazil. In Itá, as we will learn in the last chapter of this book, the recent surge of extraction of hardwoods for export was organized by the extension of credit by large companies to local entrepeneurs who, in turn, extend credit to local extractors in a manner reminiscent of the traditional system of rubber extraction. The traditional system dies slowly and as yet a more modern commercial and productive system has not taken form.

Furthermore, the new economy of Amazonia trends toward the continuation of extractivism but in a new form. Despite the efforts of the Brazilian government to establish small farmers on the land, huge tracts of land are being granted to large corporations both Brazilian and international. These lands are being devoted to the raising of cattle on enormous ranches on which forest is cleared and pasture grass is planted. Cattle raising requires little labor, so few people are required. Such ranches will not populate the Amazon Valley but they may increase beef production. Other large land concessions are made for the purpose of planting rapidly growing trees whose ultimate destiny is paper pulp; again there may be developmental and temporary benefits as these large companies raise some food crops (such as rice and sugarcane) on portions of the land. But the long-term aim is to produce export products, not to occupy the land. In addition, there is a fervor of exploration and development of mining for bauxite, iron ore (one of the largest deposits of iron ore in Brazil, if not of the world, has been discovered at the Serra de Carajas), and other minerals. Again, Brazil runs the danger of developing an essentially extractive economy in Amazonia—a system of exploitation of the gigantic area which will benefit little, or not at all, the people of the region. It will produce raw materials for export to the bulging industrial system of South Brazil or the mass of consumers of Japan, the United States, and Europe.

In this preface I do not want to sound overly pessimistic about the future of the Amazon Valley. Yet, at this time I must admit I am discouraged if not somewhat frightened. Brazil seems to be attempting to change Amazonia more with patriotic spirit than with true scientific planning. Long ago (and in the first edition of this book), I asked for a "tropical science" and a "tropical technology" distinct from that developed for the temperate zones of the world, which has always been copied in the tropical Amazon. It is true that the government of Brazil has restored some Amazonian scientific institutes such as the Museu Paraense Emilio Goeldi, the Institute Evandro Chagas (Belém); and it has supported strongly the National Institute of Amazonian Research in Manaus. The government has supported other educational and research institutions including the relatively new Federal University of Pará in Belém which now has a Center for Amazonian Advanced Studies. Even a new scientific center called the Cidade Von Humbolt is planned for the state of Mato Grosso. But these are as yet, to speak frankly, weak scientific institutions compared to those in South Brazil. There is a group of devoted scientists, but they are small in number and weakly supported. If Brazil sincerely wishes to develop Amazonia, then it must invest in scientific manpower and funds equal to those invested in the highways. In fact, I can only quote the eloquent and sincere words of Paulo Almeida Machado, who spent some years as director of the National Institute of Amazonian Research and in doing so came to understand Amazonia and to have a sincere affection for that region of his country. In 1974 he wrote:

> The history of the Brazilian Amazon contains a serious warning and an eloquent example of confusing economic prosperity with development. It does not matter how great the volume of circulation of money is, development will take place only when one knows the environment and the natural resources better and when man changes his behavior accordingly. Only education and research can guarantee the perpetuity of the new surge of progress that exists in the Brazilian Amazon. If man in the Amazon can develop and establish a partnership with the environment, the Amazon will take off definitely from its underdeveloped stage (In

Man in the Amazon. Charles Wagley, ed. Gainesville: University of Florida Press, p. 330).

In this short paragraph, Paulo Almeida Machado caught the spirit and perhaps the essence of the thought in this book, which I wrote many years ago. It is rather sad to say that this message is more up-to-date today than it was 20 years ago.

For this new edition, I have a few people to thank and acknowledge. I want to thank first Darrel L. Miller (and his wife), who went to Itá in 1974, for his excellent new chapter which documents the changes that have taken place in my little Amazon hometown. My wife, Cecilia Roxo Wagley, and I returned for a two-day visit in 1961 and I wrote a brief note for the second edition of this book. Darrel L. Miller's new chapter makes that short epilogue superfluous. I also want to thank the many students both in the United States and in Brazil who after reading this book in its early editions wrote letters of appreciation and warmth about the people described and the town. In fact, a group of secondary students from the American School in Recife (Brazil) made an excursion to Amazonia; they discovered the real name of the town and they spent a whole day trying to find personages who are described, and interviewing them. They wrote a series of reports which was mimeographed in two volumes which I shall always cherish. Furthermore, I want to thank Mercio Gomes who has translated this preface and Darrel L. Miller's contribution for a new Brazilian edition of the book.

It should be clear that my book on Itá (Amazonas) is not a study in the vein of modern social science, although it uses the framework of social anthropology. As I look back, I know now that I am essentially a humanist; and I realize that this was a humanistic book with a humanistic message.

Charles Wagley
Gainesville, Florida
1975

PREFACE

When I went to central Brazil in 1939, it was but one of several possible areas of the world that might have been selected for research among primitive peoples. For almost eighteen months I lived and studied among the Tapirapé Indians, an isolated tribe who still followed, in the main, their aboriginal way of life. They provided an excellent field of research for a social anthropologist, but living among them I learned little of modern Brazil. When I left Brazil in 1940, I knew that I would return. My casual acquaintance with the country during my passage from Rio de Janeiro through São Paulo and Goiás to and from the Tapirapé village convinced me that Brazil was one of the world's most exciting laboratories for research in social anthropology. Since that time I have devoted myself in one way or another to the study of modern Brazil.

In 1941 I returned to do research among the Tenetehara Indians, a tribe which was in close contact with rural Brazilians and which was being gradually incorporated into the nation. Then, in 1942, world events brought me directly into contact with the problems of modern Brazil. That year, as part of their common war effort, the Brazilian and United States governments established the cooperative public-health program which came to be known as SESP (Serviço Especial de Saúde Pública). SESP was first conceived as a wartime measure, and one of its principal programs was to provide medical protection to the producers of strategic raw materials—the rubber gatherers in the Amazon Valley, the migrants from the drought-stricken northeast who were moving into the Amazon to collect rubber, and the mica and quartz miners in the mountains of central Brazil. Since so many of these people lived in the backlands, a social anthropologist with experience and knowledge of these Brazilian hinterlands could be useful to the program. During the three and a half years that I was a member of the United States field party of the Institute of Inter-American Affairs connected with SESP, I served in several capacities: as a member of the SESP field staff in the Amazon Valley, as director of its migration program giving medical protection to the thousands of people who left their homes in the arid northeast to work in Amazonas, as assistant superintendent of the SESP, and finally as director of its Educational Division. During these years I learned about Brazil both as an anthropologist and as a practical administrator. My anthropological perspective was of tremendous help in the work of administration and planning, and in return my growing familiarity with practical problems helped to sharpen the focus of my scientific interest in Brazil. In traveling over a large part of the Brazilian hinterland, and by living with rural Brazilians, I became aware of rural problems as viewed both by the people themselves and by the planners and executives from the city.

The small Amazon town of Itá was first visited in 1942, on a survey trip made preliminary to the planning of SESP's Amazon Valley health service. It was on this slow trip by launch down the Amazon River, with my young Brazilian assistant and companion Cleo Braga, that I first became aware of the richness of Amazon culture and of the need for a study of a life of man in the Amazon. As we visited the towns and trading posts of the lower Amazon River and as we talked with people of all classes, I came to realize that the exotic grandeur of the tropical scene had drawn attention away from the activities of man in the Amazon Valley. The classical accounts of H. W. Bates, of Alfred R. Wallace, of Lieutenant William Herndon, of Louis Agassiz, and others who describe the great valley have devoted astonishingly little attention to man and to human affairs. The little town of Itá seemed to be an excellent locality for such studies.

After 1943, when a health post of SESP was established in Itá, I was able to follow events in the town from a distance by reading the physicians' reports, and to collect considerable data on the community. In 1945 I visited Itá again. On that occasion I was accompanied by Edward Cattete Pinheiro, a specialist in health education and a native of the region, and by Dalcidio Jurandir, a well known Brazilian novelist who was writing the text for educational materials to be used in the Amazon Valley by SESP. In his earlier years Dalcidio had lived in Itá and served as the secretary to the town's mayor. His intimate knowledge of the life of the town and the large circle of friends into which he introduced me made it possible to learn more about Itá in a month than I might have learned in more than twice that time without his help. Both Cattete Pinheiro and Dalcidio Jurandir taught me much about the Amazon out of the fabric of their own lives.

This book is mainly based, however, on data collected from June to September, 1948, during the United Nations Educational, Scientific, and Cultural Organization Amazon survey for the International Hylean Amazon Institute. During these months of research and residence in Itá, I had the assistance and the collaboration of Eduardo and Clara Galvão and of my wife, Cecilia Roxo Wagley, who had also accompanied me to ·Itá in 1942. Our research group rented a house in Itá where we lived and worked. We took our meals in the home of a local merchant. We visited with people in their homes and they returned our visits. We attended parties and dances, gossiped in the streets and in the stores, accompanied friends to their gardens, and traveled by canoe to rural festivals and to the trading posts where rubber collectors brought their products. We participated as much in Itá life as it is possible for outsiders to do. There was no linguistic barrier, for three of our research group were Brazilians and I have an adequate command of Portuguese. Each of us had long interviews each day with a number of people from all walks of life, and we wrote down copious daily notes. Case studies of 113 families, which covered details of their diet, expenditures, income, personal possessions, and much other specific economic and social information were carried out in the community by our research group with the help of two local assistants. In addition, the SESP also made available the results of a household survey in Itá which was concerned mainly with diet. In 1950 Iris Myers, who is trained both in anthropology and in psychology, spent several weeks in Itá at my suggestion. The results of her psychological tests are unfortunately not available at this time, but her letters and field notes provided me with additional data and many insights into Itá society. All of the sources mentioned above have been at my disposal during the preparation of this book.

The illustrations for the book were drawn by the well known Brazilian artist João José Rescála. For his "Tour of Brazil," a travel prize awarded annually to a Brazilian artist, he traveled through the Amazon Valley. He saw and visited people similar to those described in this book, and his drawings are based both on his memory and upon innumerable sketches made during his travels in the Amazon.

I wish to express my great indebtedness to all those mentioned above. In varying degrees, all of them have participated in the research which led to this book. I particularly want to thank, however, my research companions on the UNESCO mission in 1948, for they have allowed me the use of the wealth of information in their field notebooks. And, above all, I wish to thank our many friends in Itá whose hospitality and cooperation, and whose patience with the anthropologist's constant questions about every aspect of their life, made this study possible. Unfortunately, they must remain unnamed; it is the responsibility of the anthropologist to protect, as far as possible, the people who open up their personal lives to him and give information about others. In this book many of our Itá friends appear, but their names have all been changed. For the same reason the town itself has been given a fictitious name.

I wish to acknowledge the financial support of UNESCO and of the Council for Research in the Social Sciences of Columbia University for our studies in the Brazilian Amazon. UNESCO has granted permission to make use of the information collected during the Hylean Amazon survey, but the opinions expressed in the book are entirely my own and do not reflect UNESCO policy. Some of the data presented have been published elsewhere in different form. A chapter on "Race Relations in an Amazon Community" appeared in *Race and Class in Rural Brazil* (UNESCO, Paris, 1952), and a lecture given at the Brazilian Institute at Vanderbilt University, which summarizes some aspects of Itá culture, was published under the title "The Brazilian Amazon; the Case for an Under-Developed Area," in *Four Papers Presented to the Brazilian Institute* (Vanderbilt University Press, Nashville, 1950). The data on Itá religion have been elaborated by Eduardo Galvão in his doctoral dissertation The Religious Life of an Amazon Community (Columbia University Library, microfilm, 1952); Chapters VI and VII of this book owe much to his study of this aspect of Itá culture.

Finally, I am grateful to Alfred Métraux, of UNESCO, who has done much to make possible my continued study of Brazil. I wish to thank Carl Withers, Gene Weltfish, and Cecil Scott of The Macmillan Company, all of whom read the manuscript before its final revision and who offered numerous suggestions for correction and improvement.

CHARLES WAGLEY

New York, 1953

CONTENTS

Illustrations by João José Rescála

AMAZON TOWN
A Study of Man in the Tropics

1. THE PROBLEM OF MAN IN THE TROPICS

This book is a study of a region and the way of life of its people. The region is the Brazilian Amazon where a distinctive tropical way of life has been formed by the fusion of American Indian and Portuguese cultures during the last three centuries. In a larger sense, the book is a study of the adaptation of man to a tropical environment. It is also a case study of a "backward" and under-developed area.

There is an awakening interest in the economically marginal regions of the world. Vast quarters of the globe, inhabited by non-industrial under-nourished peoples, once seemed of little importance to our own welfare. It has gradually become clear to us that the plight of these people is the world's concern. In 1949 President Truman placed before the public the problem which such areas offer both for the peoples who inhabit them and for the more fortunate inhabitants of the technically advanced nations. "More than half of the people of the world," he stated, "are living in conditions approaching misery. Their food is inadequate. They are victims of disease. Their economic life is primitive and stagnant. Their poverty is a handicap and a threat both to them and to prosperous areas." [1]

Yet the improvement of the condition of life of these people need not await new scientific advances. Mankind possesses the technical knowledge, the result of an accumulation over many centuries of the contributions of men of many nations, to improve their lot. The problem is the extension of the knowledge and the technical skills which the world already possesses to the half of the world which has not acquired them. This is one of the crucial problems of our time.

Most under-developed areas are found in tropical and semi-tropical zones, although the tropics obviously have no monopoly on misery. In general, it is the tropical portions of Africa, Asia, the Pacific Islands, the Middle East, and the Americas which are the most retarded economically. And it is especially the hot and humid tropics, such as Equatorial Africa, the Amazon Basin, and New Guinea, in contrast to the hot but arid tropics, which up to the present seem to have provided the least favorable habitat for man. These hot and humid tropical areas cover about 38 million square

[1] Inaugural address of Jan. 20, 1949.

kilometers of the earth's surface and contain a population of almost 700 million people. Three-fourths of this population, however, live in tropical Asia, which has an extension of only 8 million square kilometers. With the exception of Asia, then, the hot and humid tropical areas are relatively sparsely populated. The "wet" tropics of Africa, Oceania, Australia, and America contain only about 170 million people in some 30 million square kilometers. Outside Asia the "wet" tropical regions have an average of only five to six people per square kilometer, while the United States, for example, averages almost seventy per square kilometer.[2] These less populated tropical areas, like the Amazon Valley, are, in effect, frontiers. They attract our interest not only because of the plight of the people who inhabit them but also because of their unexploited resources, their new land, and their potentiality for future settlement.

The Amazon Valley, almost as large as continental United States, is one of the most extensive of these modern tropical frontiers. It is also, perhaps, the most sparsely inhabited of them all. The drainage system formed by the great Amazon River and its many tributaries reaches into six South American nations—into Brazil, Bolivia, Colombia, Ecuador, and Venezuela. The major portion of the great valley is Brazilian. The total population of the Brazilian Amazon region, about one and a half million people, is lost in an area of three million square kilometers. The region is only half as densely populated as New Guinea and contains but one-twelfth as many people per square kilometer as the hot and humid areas of Africa. Though the Brazilian Amazon contains but a small portion of the "backward" peoples of the earth, its immense territory, its unexploited lands, and its unknown resources may some day play an important role in relieving world problems which result from hunger and misery.

Present conditions in the Amazon Valley certainly qualify it without any doubt as an under-developed area. Approximately 60 per cent of the people who inhabit the Brazilian Amazon are illiterate.

[2] Cf. Pierre Gourou, *Les Pays tropicaux* (Paris, 1948), pp. 5 f.

Although vital statistics for the region are admittedly deficient, it is recorded that in 1941, of 1,000 infants born in Belém, the capital of the Amazonian state of Pará, 189 died before reaching one year of age. In Manaus, the capital of the state of Amazonas situated in the heart of the Valley, the infant mortality rate per thousand in the same year was 303. In eight rural communities in the state of Pará from which statistics were gathered in 1941, infant mortality during the first year reached 304 out of each 1,000 born. It is the opinion of public-health authorities, however, that these figures are lower than the true index. Typhoid, which accounted for only 1.3 deaths per 100,000 people in the United States in 1937–1941, had a rate of 28 per 100,000 in Manaus. Tuberculosis caused 242.5 deaths out of 100,000 in Manaus in 1941 as against 45.8 in the United States; and malaria, a so-called tropical disease, had the rate of 334.9 in Manaus in 1941 as compared with only 1.1 in the United States. Yet health conditions in this Amazonian metropolis were superior to those of most small communities in the Valley in 1941.

In addition, the people of Amazonia do not have enough to eat. A study of the diet of working-class families in Belém carried out a few years ago showed an average daily consumption of food per person equivalent to only 1,800 to 2,000 calories. While the universal need for human beings doing heavy work is calculated at 3,000 calories, there seems to be a lower necessity in the tropics, which was estimated by one student of tropical diet at 2,400 calories.[3] Still, the average diet of the Belém families studied was deficient in calories and even more so in vitamins and minerals. It is the general impression of all observers that dietary deficiency and even semi-starvation are general throughout the Valley.

The economic life of the Valley is clearly "primitive and stagnant." The agricultural techniques used in Amazonia are mainly those inherited from the native Indians, "fire" or "slash-and-burn" agriculture. In 1939 only less than one-half of one per cent of the total area of the state of Pará was reported to be under cultivation, and that is probably somewhat high for the Valley as a whole.

[3] Josué de Castro, *Geografia da fome* (Rio de Janeiro, 1946), p. 67.

Transportation is by slow river boats, most of which are fueled by wood. There are only 1,600 miles of automobile roads and 238 miles of railroad in the entire valley. Industry is primitive and almost non-existent. The commerce of the region is based on the collection of forest products such as wild rubber, palm oils, pelts, and tropical hardwoods. Public facilities such as waste disposal, electric lights, and water supply are minimal. A few small towns have electric lights, and a few others once maintained electric plants but they have allowed them to fall into disuse. Until quite recently only Belém and Manaus had public sewerage and water-supply systems, and these systems were clearly antiquated. In Belém, after World War II, the public tramways had ceased to run and the electric-light plant was so rundown that the city was thrown into total darkness several times each night. In view of such conditions it is quite understandable why the Amazon region of Brazil did not increase in population from 1920 to 1940, while Brazil as a nation had an increase in population of 36 per cent. Only in the arid region of northeastern Brazil, where living standards are almost as low as those in the Amazon, is the Brazilian population static.

Do this sparse population, these wretched health conditions, the deplorably low standards of living, and the lack of industry mean that the Amazonian environment is an insurmountable obstacle to development? In other words, does a hot and humid tropical environment impose limitations upon human development that make it next to impossible to raise living standards in such areas? This is a critical question for all tropical regions. In the specific terms of the Amazon, is it a frontier to be populated and developed for the benefit of the world's hungry or is it doomed to be forever a "green desert"? Opinions regarding the potentiality of the Amazon have been mixed. On the negative side it has been described as a "green hell," and because so many grandiose dreams have centered on the region it has been called "green opium." In the same vein an agronomist once suggested, in half serious jest, that the only solution for the problems of the Amazon Valley was to fence it off and slowly remove all of the people. Yet, since the time of Alexander von Humboldt and even before, men have dreamed of great cities, rich agricultural lands, and thriving industries in the great Valley. One of these optimists was Alfred Russel Wallace, the famous English naturalist who visited the Amazon in the nineteenth century. "I fearlessly assert," he wrote enthusiastically, "that here the primeval forest can be converted into rich pasture land, into cultivated fields, gardens and orchards, containing every variety of produce, with half the labor, and, what is more important, in less than half the time that would be required at home." [4] Similar opinions, both pro-Amazon and anti-Amazon, might be cited at length, for writers have taken one side or the other with considerable fervor.

In recent years the pessimistic school of thought regarding the future of the Amazon Basin has found support in scientific data which tended to show a greater prevalence of disease in the tropics, indications of retarding of human growth caused by the excessive heat, the inferior quality of tropical soils, and other supposed barriers to human welfare in a tropical environment. A few writers have even maintained not only that the latter is a barrier but that living in the tropics actually leads to human degeneration. An extremist of this group is Ellsworth Huntington, who has stated absurdly that tropical environments lead to "weakness of will" which manifests itself in lack of industry, drunkenness, irascible temper, and sexual indulgence.[5] Other extremists fall back on racial arguments. These "tropical racists" argue that tropical climates may only be inhabited by races with dark pigmentation, that is, the Negro, the Mongolian, or mixtures of these stocks with Caucasians. These darker races or mixtures are inferior, they state, to white Europeans, and thus tropical regions are doomed to a lower level of cultural development. According to such theories, whites must miscegenate in order to survive, and thus lower their cultural potential.

[4] *A Narrative of Travels on the Amazon and Rio Negro* (London, 1853), pp. 334–335.
[5] *Civilization and Climate,* 3rd ed. (New York, 1939), pp. 68 ff.

Darker skin may well be a positive aid to acclimatization to the tropics and a lighter skin to the northern regions, for darker pigmentation seems to serve as a protection against the rays of the sun. The distribution of the three main racial stocks in the year 1500 seems to indicate that over many centuries such factors may have been at work; but there is no evidence that skin pigmentation has ever proved a serious barrier to acclimatization to any known habitable climate. The most northern of all peoples, the Eskimo, are Mongoloids; the American Negro has adapted quite well in the northern United States; and European whites live in Northern Queensland and in the Panama Zone, to cite only two examples, without any degeneration that has functional importance.[6] More important, all research to date in anthropology and related sciences has shown that all racial groups and all mixtures of racial groups have the same capacity for cultural achievement. In other words, all men are members of the same species and have approximately equivalent native intelligence and the same capacity to secure a higher standard of living. Those who warn of the dangers of race mixture and racial barriers to cultural development, in or out of the tropics, are simply making dangerous social propaganda.

What about the enervating effects of constant heat on man? Man is without doubt the most adaptable of all animals to varying temperatures. This is due not only to the fact that he is a warm-blooded animal, an advantage he shares with other mammals, but also to the fact that he is a culture-bearing animal. Through the use of cultural devices, he has been able to inhabit all known climates. Clothes and fire have made arctic climates habitable. Man builds protection against the searing heat of the tropical sun, goes about nude, or wears a protective covering, and adapts his habits to high temperatures. Without involving centuries of physical modification of the species, man can overnight don a white outer garment such as the clothing of the Hindus, which cuts down

[6] See Grenfell Price, *White Settlers in the Tropics* (New York, Geographic Society Publication No. 23, 1939), pp. 52 ff. and pp. 146 f.

his absorption of the radiant energy of the sun by nearly two-thirds.[7] Furthermore, the lack of body hair or fur makes man among all mammals the most adaptable to heat; he has a larger area than all other mammals for perspiration—the mechanism by which the body throws off excessive heat and adjusts to temperature.

Yet hot and humid climates seem to have given man more trouble than the temperate ones despite his remarkable physical and cultural adaptability. In hot moist temperatures the dissipation of excess body heat is more difficult. After a prolonged exposure to heat, regulation of body temperature can be maintained only through compensation within the body by a reduction of cellular combustion and a lower activity of the endocrine glands. In addition, high temperatures seem to call for greater Vitamin-B requirements (especially thiamin, pantothenic acid, and pyridone), and foods which are important sources of these vitamins, such as lean pork, have been found to contain only half as much Vitamin B in the tropics as in temperate zones. Thus the difficulty seems to be twofold: more Vitamin B is needed and foods contain less of it in the tropics than elsewhere. These physiological difficulties seem to result in a retardation of growth and in slower sexual maturity—at least, this has been shown under experimental conditions on animals, and one study seems to indicate that it is also true for man.[8]

Perhaps the best living conditions in the tropics are found in Panama, where the canal workers eat imported food, where tropical infections and parasitic disease have been kept to a minimum, and where housing conditions are good. It was found that "Americans born in Panama are roughly 10% heavier and 3% taller than Panamanians of similar age; they are at the same time about 3% lighter and slightly shorter (less than 1 inch at 17 years of age) than are the American-born children who have lived in the zone less than

[7] See Gladwin Thomas, "Climate and Anthropology," *American Anthropologist*, Vol. 49, No. 4, Part I (1947), p. 605.

[8] C. A. Mills, "Climatic Effects on Growth and Development with Particular Reference to the Effects of Tropical Residence," *American Anthropologist*, Vol. 44, No. 1 (1942).

a year." [9] It was also found that the onset of sexual maturity came about a year later for girls in Panama than for girls in Richmond and Cincinnati—contrary to the common belief in early maturation in the tropics. The difference between the Panamanians and the Panama-born Americans can be explained on the basis of parental stock of smaller average stature and on the basis of the inferior diet of the Panamanians. Yet the difference between the American-born and Panama-born Americans, slight as it is, seems to indicate that, as for experimental animals, there is for man a "tropical depression of growth and development under living conditions almost ideal except for tropical heat." [10]

Yet we may still ask what significance smaller stature has upon man's adaptation to tropical environment. Despite inferior diet and living conditions, at seventeen years of age Panamanian boys were only 3.18 inches shorter on the average, and 17.09 pounds lighter on the average, than American boys who had lived in Panama less than one year. Equivalent diet and other higher standards of living for the Panamanians would obviously reduce the difference between the Panamanian and American boys significantly. Furthermore, the average height of the Panamanian boys was 65.85 inches at seventeen years of age—well within the range of individual variations for the same age in any Mediterranean (Latin) group within the temperate zone. Neither height nor body weight has any correlation with mental capacity and cultural achievement. There have been exceptionally dominant and energetic men who were exceedingly short and who were excessively tall. The Egyptians, a people with many cultural contributions to their credit, evidently were short and physically slight. All racial groups are subject to some modification by environmental influences, just as the children of immigrants to the United States are taller than their parents. Such modifications do not correlate with their culture achievements. The significance of these studies in tropical biology shows that tropical climate, like

[9] *Ibid.*, p. 8.
[10] *Ibid.*, p. 12.

any climate, calls for certain special man-made devices and habits for human habitation and for cultural development. It would seem, for example, that in the tropics man needs less calorie intake, a different dosage of vitamins, special clothes to protect him from the sun, and other equipment analogous to that which we use against the cold.

The climate of the Amazon is most certainly hot and humid. On the map the equator seems to bisect the area. Yet there are many misconceptions regarding the Amazonian climate. The heat is not unbearable. The average temperature at Manaus is only 78.1° F., and the record heat in Manaus over a thirty-year period was 97.1° F.— about equal to a summer heat wave in New York City and not an unusual high for the North American Midwest. The difference between day and night temperatures is often as much as fifteen degrees in Amazonia. Along with a steady breeze, the lower temperature makes the nights quite comfortable. The humidity, however, is high; at Manaus it averages 78 per cent. The humidity and perhaps the lack of seasonal variation in temperature are perhaps the most uncomfortable aspects of the climate. There is only a four-degree difference between the "hottest" month and the "coldest" month. To the Amazon inhabitant seasons are marked by the amount of rainfall rather than by variation of temperature. Although rain is abundant throughout the year, averaging more than eighty inches on the upper rivers and slightly less on the coast, the period of January to June is the "rainy season" and is called the "winter." During these months it rains almost every day, and the streams overflow their banks. The remaining months of the year comprise the "dry season" or "summer." During the summer there are many days without rain, and the waterfall is generally in the form of brief, violent thundershowers. During these months the water level in the river drops and the water drains out of the low floodlands or *várzea*.

The tropical seasons of the Amazon, despite their lack of contrast in temperature, affect the life of man as do the seasons of the temperate zones. While freezing temperatures of the winter in the temperate zone call for heating of homes and special clothes, the steady rains of the Amazonian winter and the flooded lowlands which cover land trails restrict people to their homes. Fishing is not productive during these months and rubber can not be collected. The summer, on the contrary, is a period of activity—of garden making, of rubber production, of fishing, of visiting, and of festivals. In towns the streets are dry, and in the rural districts the overland trails are passable. On the main tributaries of the Amazon River system, sandy beaches are uncovered where turtles deposit their eggs. Clear days make travel more comfortable. The local expressions "summer" and "winter" have connotations analogous to the equivalent terms used in temperate climates; they refer to marked differences in the yearly cycle which break the monotony of life and with which man associates his various activities. The Amazon climate has its great disadvantages, but in many respects it has advantages over the great extremes of temperature found in many North American areas. Climate is not a barrier impossible to overcome.

A strong case against tropic regions has also been based on the prevalence of disease, especially the so-called "tropical diseases," as a primary deterrent to future progress. The fact that hot and moist zones contain not only most of the ailments common to temperate zones but also a series of local diseases is seen as an impossible obstacle to overcome. Leishmaniasis, a tropical ulcer; filariasis, which leads to the monstrous condition known as elephantiasis; [11] onchocerciasis, caused by a larva which burrows into the skin of the scalp; trypanosomiasis, caused by a minute parasite which enters the blood stream and even the tissues; [12] and *fogo selvagem,* a ringworm infection which quickly covers the entire body, are certainly horrible enough. Such exotic diseases, however, have limited distributions, and only rarely, as in the cast of trypanosoma in Africa, do they have an incidence high enough to form a serious barrier to the health of a total population. The most widespread and deadly of the

[11] A chronic condition caused by lymphatic obstruction and characterized by enormous enlargement of the parts affected.
[12] African sleeping sickness is a result of a form of trypanosoma.

"tropical diseases" is malaria, although its distribution is not strictly tropical. The ravages of malaria in the past and in the present in the tropical world are well known. Intestinal parasites, including amoebas and the bacilli which cause dysentery and the Ancylostoma (hookworm), thrive in moist and warm climates. It has been estimated that almost 90 per cent of the rural population of the Brazilian Amazon is infected with one variety or another of intestinal parasites. Tuberculosis and syphilis, certainly not limited to tropical environments, are also serious problems in the Amazon. Yaws (frambesia), a contagious disease resembling syphilis, is common, especially in the lower Amazon Basin.[13]

The prevalence of most of these diseases cannot be charged to climate alone; they are more a reflection of the backwardness of the region than its cause. Tuberculosis, it is well known, is related to low standards of living and to malnutrition. The prevalence of intestinal parasites is due primarily to the lack of adequate sewerage and water supply. The installation of sanitary privies and of modern water-supply systems by the public-health service of the Amazon has already reduced the rate of intestinal infections. Syphilis and yaws are social diseases. Neither is difficult to treat nowadays, and the prevention of both is a question of public education. Malaria, the "tropical disease" with the highest mortality rate in the Amazon, is today giving way to powerful drugs and to new preventive measures.

The SESP (Serviço Especial de Saúde Pública), the Amazon sanitation program maintained in cooperation with the Institute of Inter-American Affairs, a United States Government agency, has been spraying homes and public buildings with phenomenal success against the malaria mosquito, using a solution of 5 per cent DDT, the new wonder insecticide, mixed in kerosene. Among the 146 communities covered by the SESP spraying service in the Amazon, the small town of Breves situated in the delta region served as a "test case." Breves was notorious for almost annual malaria epidemics. A survey in July of 1943 showed that 45 per cent of the

---

[13] Yaws cede easily to treatment with arsenic lead.

population of the town had enlarged spleens caused by malaria and that 22 per cent had malaria parasites in their blood. The DDT spraying in Breves began in May of 1946, and one year later a survey showed the spleen rate to be only 16.8 per cent, while only 1.6 per cent of the people had malaria parasites in their blood. By May, 1948, the rates had been reduced to 8.3 per cent and 0.3 per cent respectively. After the third month of spraying with DDT, no specimen of the species of anopheles mosquito known to be the transmitter of malaria in the region was found in the Breves houses. After the first six months of spraying, only sporadic cases of malaria occurred among the residents, and the doctors consider most of these to be relapses or infections incurred during trips outside the community.[14] Results from the use of DDT in other Amazon communities are just as successful, and it is being used throughout the world for the same purpose, with excellent results.

The control of malaria no longer poses a serious problem to the development of tropical regions. The control of other diseases with high mortality in the Amazon is primarily a question of better living conditions, a better diet, increased education of the population, and full use of the scientific knowledge and equipment already available to mankind. A few diseases may defy control for many years to come, just as infantile paralysis has in the temperate zone, until new medical discoveries provide man with new tools to govern his environment.

But the health of the Amazon population depends as much upon improvement in nutrition as upon better medical facilities. A better diet for the majority of the Amazon population depends in turn upon increasing agricultural production in the region. Here again the tropical environment would seem to set a limit to cultural development. Although it is commonly thought that tropical soils, with their lush and luxuriant covering of vegetation which grows with such rapidity, are exceedingly rich, this does not seem to be

[14] L. M. Deane, Freire Serra, W. E. P. Tabosa, and José Ledo, "A Aplicação domiciliar de DDT no controle da malária em localidades da Amazonia," *Revista do SESP*, Ano 1, No. 4, pp. 1121–1139, Rio de Janeiro.

true. Tropical soils have been judged by soil scientists to be in general of poor quality. The vegetation grows fast because of the warm and moist climate during the entire year; yet the root systems of even the largest trees are surprisingly shallow. The humus is thin. Rapid decomposition of organic matter in the tropics makes for slow deposition of humus even in the thick forest, and when deforestation takes place for plantations or for settlements, erosion and leaching soon waste the earth. The heavy tropical rains dissolve the nitrates in the soil, leaving the insoluble irons and aluminums exposed. The hot sun bakes these into laterite—rock-like nodules. Such lateritic soils are not productive agriculturally, and the foods produced on such land are said to be weak in mineral salts, such as calcium, iron, and sodium chloride.[15] Laterite underlies the extensive sandy soils of the Amazon, and it actually lies exposed in many localities. Amazon soils are clearly inferior to those of more favored temperate areas.

Yet the poverty of the soil can easily be exaggerated in an effort to correct the popular misconception of the fertility of the tropics. One soil scientist estimated that, despite the mediocre quality of the soils, more than 70 per cent of the total area of the Amazon Valley permits agriculture.[16] Furthermore, not all soils of the Amazon are mediocre. Lateritic soils are limited to the so-called *terra firme*, the land which lies above the level of the seasonal rise of the river. There are extensive areas of fertile soils, specially in the alluvial lowlands, although despite the travelers' impressions that the Amazon is a gigantic swamp most of the Valley is terra firme. With the advent of air travel in the Amazon, it has become quite clear that there are numerous interruptions in the tropical forest and that a great part of the area is solid earth. The eastern half of Marajó Island at the mouth of the river, the region of the upper Rio Branco along the Brazilian frontier with Venezuela and British Guiana, and a large area of the Valley north of Óbidos and Monte Alegre are grassy savanna lands. This savanna, which covers more

[15] See Josué de Castro, *op. cit.*, p. 73.
[16] *Ibid.*, p. 106.

than 20,000 square miles, has been described as "eminently suitable for cattle raising and perhaps also for general agriculture." [17] Furthermore, bluffs rise 100 to 150 feet from the river in many spots, and near Monte Alegre and Santarém the remnants of mountains and plateaus appear over 1,000 feet above the river. As the tropical geographer Pierre Gourou wrote, "Far from being a lake or a swamp, the Amazon is a low non-flooded plateau which rises sharply above the valleys of alluvial deposits." [18]

Like the flood plain of most great river systems, that of the Amazon River network is wide. Below Manaus the area annually flooded by the river is 25 to 30 miles on each side. As on the Mississippi, the river towns and villages are situated on bluffs and outcrops of terra firme. It is unfortunate that these lowlands are not more extensive, for the extensions of floodlands are notably rich, as is true of most deltas. The scientific exploitation of these alluvial lands, which are seldom used by the Amazonian farmer, would multiply Amazonian food production many times over.[19] Furthermore, the mediocre soils of terra firme can be made to produce more. Gourou points out that one limited area of the Valley, the land along the railroad between Belém and Bragança, which is mainly terra firme, supports a population many times as dense as the average for the Valley as a whole without any essential modification of the traditional methods of cultivation. The Amazonian soil is not in any way comparable to such fertile and productive areas as the Midwestern United States, yet it can be made to produce food not only for the present population of the Amazon but for several times as many people.

It also must be emphasized that the quality of the soil is only one of several factors which determine its productivity. As one geographer wrote, "Fertility is not a quality inherent in the soil alone; it can only be measured in terms of specific soil uses." [20] The Great

[17] Earl Parker Hanson, *The Amazon: A New Frontier* (Foreign Policy Association Pamphlet No. 45, 1944), pp. 22–23.
[18] "L'Amazonie," in *Cahiers d'Outre Mer,* Vol. II, No. 5 (1949), pp. 1–13.
[19] Gourou, *Les Pays tropicaux,* p. 6.
[20] Preston James, *Latin America* (New York, 1942), p. 543.

Plains of the United States, which are today the locale of our great wheat farms with their phenomenal production, were inaccessible to the American Indian without the European plow to break the tough sod. Without the necessary knowledge and technological equipment, the simple aboriginal Tasmanians eked out a miserable hand-to-mouth existence in a land which was potentially rich agriculturally.[21] Land is useful to man only in terms of the cultural equipment he has at his command at a particular time or place and in terms of the use he makes of it. With man's present knowledge of chemical feeding of weak soils, of adapting crops to specific soils, and other techniques of modern agronomy, it should not be difficult to improve the productivity of Amazonian soils. Even the most elementary technical innovations would be far superior to the primitive agricultural system used throughout the Valley at present.

While the Amazon Valley is not an especially propitious setting for man, it must be concluded that the physical environment is not the most serious obstacle to its eventual development and to higher standards of living for its inhabitants. All peoples have an equal potentiality to improve their social conditions, and their physical environment is only one factor of several which determine man's final adjustment to his habitat. As one writer recently stated: "The land, the climate, the mineral wealth are not determinants of human progress. They are merely determinants of theoretical limits beyond which the native inhabitant cannot go. Science and technology are pushing the limits back but they are finite. To what extent a given nation approaches the finite limit of civilization depends upon human factors." [22] This "finite limit" is still a distant horizon for the Amazon Basin, where modern science and technology are all but unknown. The "human factors" on which so much depends are part of the culture and the social system of the people. It is their cultural

[21] C. Daryll Forde in *Habitat, Economy and Society*, 6th ed. (London, 1948), p. 100, points out that "the bracing climate of the stormy western zone [of Tasmania] to which the vigor of west European peoples has so often been attributed failed to stimulate any important development of their [the Tasmanian] culture."

[22] Howard A. Meyerhoff, "Natural Resources in Most of the World" in *Most of the World*, ed. Ralph Linton (New York, 1949), p. 92.

traditions which make available to them the tools, the knowledge, and the technology to cope with the environment. It is the culture which determines the ends toward which the men of a particular area make use of their technology, and it is the social system which determines the organization of work and the distribution of the products of their work.

The main reasons why the Amazon Valley is today a backward and under-developed area must be sought in Amazon culture and society, and in the relationship of this region with the centers of economic and political power and with the sources of cultural diffusion. What is the present technical equipment of the inhabitants of the Amazon for exploiting their environment? How did they come to possess their present technology? What is the "good life" to Amazon man? In other words, what are his system of values, his incentives, and his motivations? What is the local form of the fundamental and universal institutions—family, church, and government—by which men everywhere organize their lives? What has been the economic and political relationship of the Amazon with the outside world? The answer to why the region is "backward" lies in such questions.

This book is, then, the study of a culture, of the way of life which has been created by man in the Amazon Valley of Brazil. Since cultures are historically developed, and since they are formed from elements of widespread origin by culture borrowing, we must look into the past and beyond the Valley for the sources and events which have influenced the contemporary culture of the Amazon. A knowledge of the way of life of Amazon man will indicate where changes must be made if living standards are to be improved. Such knowledge should allow us to foresee some of the reactions to be expected from the introduction of new elements into Amazon culture. The ideal of "making the benefits of our scientific advances and industrial progress available for improvement and growth of undeveloped areas" involves cultural change. It is not a simple process of sending technical experts to these areas, of conducting surveys and studies which would make known the basic economic resources of the areas, or even of bringing workers, engineers, executives, and others to the United States to train and acquire our accumulated experience—although all of these endeavors would be helpful. The job involves modification of a culture—of the pattern of life—and a readjustment of a people's relationship to their total environment.

A new idea will be accepted only when a basis is present in the preexisting culture to make the element a useful one. A program of introducing modern agricultural practices must not only make available more efficient methods, as our United States Department of Agriculture long ago learned; these methods must also be presented in terms acceptable to the people. A culture often presents barriers which cause even more efficient methods to be rejected. The mere fact that the soil of a particular region would produce best if planted in potatoes or soy beans would not persuade a people whose staple food is rice. To introduce the planting of potatoes in such a situation one must modify food habits and tastes—or create a money market for the product. If agriculture is intimately interwoven with religion, as among the Indians of Guatemala, the new methods of cultivation and new crops affect the religion; and unless the methods and crops are integrated into the religious system their introduction will run counter to it. Man is not a rational being in the sense that his behavior is always motivated by his own absolute advantage—for his concept of what constitutes an "advantage" is colored by the values of his particular culture.

Furthermore, culture is not transmitted mechanically, as a cargo of goods might be shipped from one group to another. Once innovations are accepted by a people, they become a part of their culture and are modified by that culture. The new elements acquire new form and a new meaning different from their form and meaning in the culture of origin. The introduction of new elements, in turn, causes readjustments in the borrowing culture. One has only to think of any of the numerous innovations in our own culture during the last generation. The cinema was molded by American culture in innumerable ways; and in turn, the cinema has modified American social life and to some extent family life. We are now experiencing similar secondary effects in television. Industrial development in non-industrial areas will call for new settlement patterns, realignment of socio-economic classes, modifications in family structure, and even changes in the motor habits of the people who must learn to manipulate machines. Projects for reclamation or the division of land will involve new patterns of land tenure and land use, new methods of cultivation, and many other direct and indirect changes in the society and the culture of the people concerned. Though culture is not a machine or an organism—both analogies have been used by theorists—it is an inter-related system, and the introduction of new elements calls for readjustment in the system. Any program which would introduce modern technology and industry among a "backward" people must realize the far-reaching social and cultural changes implied.

2. AN AMAZON COMMUNITY

No one community is ever typical of a region or of a nation. Each has its own traditions, its own history, its own variation of the regional or the national way of life. The culture of a modern region or nation has an organization which is greater than simply the sum total of the local communities which form it. There are institutions and social forces of regional, national, and even international scope which determine the trend of life in each small community. The church, the political institutions, the system of formal education, the commercial system, and many other aspects of a culture are more widespread and more complex in their organization than in any local community manifestation. Nor does any one community ever contain the total range of a regional culture; it may not contain all of the social classes, all occupations, or all of the political parties which are found in the region as a whole. A study of a small agricultural village of the United States, for instance, would probably tell us little of the complexities of American organized labor, of the elaborate commercial and financial system, or of the ostentation of the rich in our big cities. Yet studies of the banking system of a region, of the formal organization and the ideology of its religion, of its imports and exports, or of the dynamics of its population in the impersonal and objective terms of the economists or the sociologists seem lifeless, to say the least. They tell us little or nothing of life situations, of the working of widespread patterns and institutions as they are lived by people.

Everywhere people live in communities—in bands, in villages, in towns, in rural neighborhoods, and in cities. In communities face-to-face human relations take place, and each day people are subjected to the dicta of their culture. In their communities the people of a region make a living, educate their children, live as families, form themselves into associations, worship their supernaturals, have superstitious fears and taboos, and are motivated by the values and incentives of their particular culture. In the community economics, religion, politics, and other aspects of a culture appear inter-related and part of a total culture system, as they are in life. All of the communities of an area partake of the cultural heritage of the region, and each is a local manifestation of the possible interpretations of regional patterns and institutions.

Any community in the Brazilian Amazon would serve our purpose as a laboratory for the study of regional culture as it is lived out by one group of Amazon people. This study will focus upon a small Amazon community which will be called Itá, a fictitious name for an actual town on the Lower Amazon in which the author and his co-workers lived and studied. It is not an average Amazon town. Monte Alegre, Óbidos, Faro, Abaetetuba, and many others are larger, more prosperous, and more progressive. There are differences in Amazon culture patterns characteristic of the Upper Amazon, the Salgado, or the Islands which do not appear in Itá culture. Yet Itá serves admirably as a "case history." It has a long history in which most of the trends of regional history have been reflected. The present way of life in Itá and in its surrounding rural neighborhoods might seem old-fashioned and backward to the urbanite of Belém, Manaus, or even Santarém, but it is shared in its broad outlines by the majority of the rural population of the Amazon Basin and by the inhabitants of the working-class districts of the cities, which are filled with recent rural migrants. Because Itá is a poor community without any special industry or natural gifts and without any special distinction, a study of Itá focuses a spotlight on the basic problems of the region.

II

Itá is situated in the sub-region known as the Lower Amazon, below the juncture of the Negro and Solimões rivers. In addition, it lies close to the Islands of the delta, and thus two ecological sub-regions of the valley affect the life of the community. It is a small town with about five hundred inhabitants, yet it is the seat of a municipality, a county-like political subdivision of the state, which covers an area of 6,094 square kilometers—almost the size of the State of Rhode Island. The town lies on a low bluff formed by an outcrop of laterite which rises only three or four meters above the river but which affords a view extending for many miles up and down the southern Amazon channel. From the river the sight of the town is a welcome break in the monotonous forest-lined banks of the Amazon. It stands out neat and colorful against the dark green vegetation. The gleaming white church with its orange tile roof is the first building to be distinguished, then the two-story town hall, which has recently been completed, and a row of low houses, washed in bright colors and facing upon the river, appear. There is a dark red municipal wharf (*trapiche*) set on piles in the river channel and connected to the shore by a long board walk. A little downriver is a smaller *trapiche* owned by a local merchant where a sailboat with rust-colored sails is tied up. River steamers which stop at Itá always use the municipal wharf, which has a small covered warehouse. From the river the town appears framed by the dark green foliage of the enormous mango trees and the stately palms which line the waterfront. It seems an inviting place.

As one leaves the river boat and crosses the board walk, the romantic setting fades into realism. The street facing the river is unpaved, as are all Itá thoroughfares. If the time is that of the rainy season, the street oozes with mud. A sidewalk graces the front of some of the houses on the riverfront street, but others open directly upon the street. Many of the buildings are in bad repair, and one or two are ready to fall in from neglect. Back from the riverfront, the houses are less colorful and more rundown, and there are numerous palm-thatched dwellings where the poorer inhabitants live. Itá offers its best profile to the river, but close inspection shows even the riverfront to be somewhat worn by age.

A map on display in the town hall shows Itá to have a gridiron plan. Three main streets (*ruas*) run lengthwise parallel to the river and are intersected by side streets (*travessas*) that wind back from the river. Three public squares (*praças*) are shown on the map, and there is a riverfront garden. All the squares and thoroughfares have names. Each *rua* has the name of a patriotic hero of the state of Pará; each *travessa* is named after a saint; and two of the *praças* carry the names of famous men. It is soon apparent, however, that such city planning is an idea imposed from outside. The names shown on the map are seldom, if ever, used. Instead, the three *ruas* are referred to as "First Street," "Second Street," and "Third Street" (beginning at the riverfront), and no one can remember any of the names of the side streets at all. While the *ruas* are fairly straight, and the two *praças* well marked out, the *travessas* wind somewhat dizzily in and around the houses. Some of them are no more than narrow paths.

The town hall, which is situated in the middle of the largest *praça*, may be considered the central point of the city. Occupying an entire side of the square is the public-health post with its land-scaped yard and vegetable garden. The other *praça* is empty except for a small monument to a state hero. The other two important public buildings, the school and the church, are situated beyond the end of the long First Street, somewhat apart from the town. The school, a new building built by the federal government for adult education classes, is an adobe structure with a tile roof. It has one classroom and several rooms intended as living quarters for the teacher and family. The church lies several hundred meters beyond the school-house, still farther out of town, which is contrary to the general practice in the Amazon of making the church the central edifice. Between the church and the school is a soccer field where the two rather haphazard teams of Itá play on Sunday afternoons during the "summer" months.

The square blocks formed by the intersecting streets and side streets indicated on the town plan are in reality hard to discern. A block here and there is solidly occupied, but there are so many vacant lots in others that the form of the plan is lost. Paths cut through empty spaces and get lost in the wilderness of Third Street. Yet with so much space, the better dwellings of Itá are built flush on the street and connected with each other, presenting a solid front to the passerby. The back yard (*quintal*), surrounded by walls, is the focus of these long houses, which are larger than they seem from the street. Today only two full blocks of Itá are solidly built in the traditional manner. Because of the rapid decline in population after the Amazon rubber boom, many houses tumbled in, and a recent tendency to build homes surrounded by gardens has changed the town's appearance. On First Street is a series of two-family bungalows built as a housing project by the municipal government. They are set back two or three meters from the street with a narrow space between each. These are occupied by the mayor, the police chief, the federal tax collector, the postmistress (who uses her parlor as the post office), and the agent of the Federal Statistical Bureau. While these new houses have some space for circulation of air, they have miserably low ceilings and small rooms and are exposed on all sides to the sun. Though they are modern, they are hardly designed for the Amazon tropics, and are far inferior in comfort to the traditional houses with their high ceilings and protected veranda facing upon a shaded back yard.

All but one of the commercial houses of Itá are situated on First Street. This exception, behind the town hall on Second Street, is a small shop with little stock. Of the three stores on First Street, the Casa Gato, which has survived since the days of the rubber boom, has by far the largest stock. It also has a choice location near the board walk leading to the municipal wharf. The other two stores are farther down the street and are more recently established. All of these stores are also dwellings. A large front room opening onto the street is the shop. This contains the *balcão* (counter) and the current stock. Behind the shop is a large storeroom where the rubber and other products which the shopkeeper accepts in exchange for goods, as well as bulky stock such as sacks of salt, are kept. Customers lounge about in the shop, and *cachaça* (sugar-cane rum) is served over the counter. The living quarters of the shopkeeper and his family take up one side of the house, and the shopkeeper withdraws frequently during the day for a bit of conversation with his family. Important customers are invited into the parlor or, if they are intimates of the family, into the dining room for the inevitable *cafèzinho* (demitasse of black coffee).

All of the buildings on First Street are built of *taipa* [1] or of wood, all have wooden or cement floors, all have ceramic tile roofs, and all are painted either with a white or with a bright-colored wash. This type of dwelling is classified in Itá as a *casa* (house) to distinguish it from the less permanent palm-thatched structures of the town which are called *barracas* (huts). All the dwellings on Third Street, except two, are huts. They are two- or three-room structures, with woven palm walls and roof, set on stilts above the damp earth. The floors, which are generally made of narrow slats from the trunk of the paxiuba palm, provide an uncertain footing, but a few huts

---

[1] A type of wall construction traditional of Brazil. It is wattle work filled with clay and with a sand and lime plaster finish.

have floors of wooden planks. The homes on Second Street are a mixture of the two types. There are buildings which are classified by local people as "houses" but which are in exceedingly bad condition, and there are "houses" of whitewashed *taipa* walls which have palm-thatched roofs. A few dwellings on Second Street are clearly huts. One "house" on Second Street is also a bakery where a man and his wife make wheat bread whenever wheat flour is available. The electric powerhouse where the machinery of the defunct wood-burning generator is kept is also on Second Street, which in addition boasts two barbers, one of whom has one room of his dwelling arranged as a shop. In 1948 a shoemaker who had recently arrived and who was not expected to stay for long was established in a hut on Second Street. Thus in Itá the more permanent and better dwellings are near the riverfront, while the poorer huts lie back from the river and are hidden from view. On Second Street is found the confusion of the middle ground. The equivalent of the "wrong side of the tracks" in Itá is "back from the river."

First Street and even Second Street are generally relatively clean and free of weeds, for the municipal government pays day workers during the dry season to weed the thoroughfares. Especially before a holiday or the visit of a politician from Belém, street cleaning becomes energetic. Third Street, however, is overgrown with vegetation which is much too high to be called weeds. Only here and there on Third Street has some neat householder cleared the area in front of his house. Most of Third Street and the side streets which lead into it have the appearance of winding paths. Since those who live there complain of the unfair neglect of their street, the mayor from time to time arranges to have Third Street cleared.

The most imposing buildings in Itá are, as we have seen, the church, the town hall, and the Health Post. The church, a tall simple structure, has recently been renovated, completely reroofed, and whitewashed both inside and out by a German missionary-priest aided by local labor. As a result it is somewhat austere and entirely lacking in the elaborately decorated interior of the average small-town church in Brazil. The Health Post is a low building designed by a Swiss-American architect and built by North American engineers who worked with the Amazon health service during the war. It has a long veranda-porch, large screened windows, long narrow windows near the roof for ventilation, and other features designed for the climate. It stands apart in Itá as a modern building which is not merely a copy of Temperate Zone construction and which at least attempts to conform to its setting. The two-story town hall, however, is the most famous building along the lower Amazon. It would do credit to a North American or European town several times larger than Itá. Its architecture would be more fitting to the Temperate Zone. A portion of the upper floor houses all the public offices, leaving the entire lower floor empty. Standing in the middle of one of the public squares, it is exposed on all sides to the sun, and it has poor ventilation. The second-floor offices boil during the afternoon. The town hall, as we shall see, figures in Itá history as a "white elephant," and the cost of constructing it has drained the public coffers several times.

III

The county-like municipality of which Itá is the seat extends south of the Amazon and downstream, taking in numerous islands of the delta region. The area is so large that most of the approximately eight thousand people who live within the municipality seldom, if ever, visit the town. Deputy tax collectors, who are generally also rural commercial men or traders, are stationed at several points over the area. From time to time, the mayor, the state tax collector, the federal tax collector, and even the police chief make inspection trips of two to three weeks' duration. Trading posts (*barracões*) are situated at intervals along the waterways of the municipality. Most of them renew their stock and send away the products which they buy via regular river steamers owned by Belém commercial houses. Each trading post is the regular customer of a particular firm whose boat visits them each month or so. Since the exports and imports of most of the trading posts do not pass through Itá, the town is not the commercial center of the political unit it controls. Nor is it the social center for the municipality. People from distant localities in the municipality do sometimes visit Itá for the annual festival of St. Benedict, but this event draws people from the entire lower Amazon, and the distant inhabitants come as visitors just as do people from outside. The municipality of Itá is not a social or even a geographical unit easily controlled from the municipal seat. In a few Amazon municipalities, such as Altamira on the Xingú River, the seat is strategically located where political control may be exerted over its territory and its inhabitants, but in the municipality of Itá even political unity is weak.

A more restricted area, immediately surrounding the town and comprising about one-fifth of the total territory of the municipality, looks to the town as the center both of its economic and of its social life. Most of this area which we will call the "community of Itá," lies, as does the town, on the south bank of the Amazon, but it includes also a few small islands in the channel immediately in front of the town.[2] This community area includes approximately two thousand people, of whom only about five hundred live in the town. In front of Itá town the Amazon channel is more than five kilometers wide, and to cross it in canoes and small sailboats is often dangerous. For that reason, while many people from the south bank regularly work at rubber collecting on the Great Island, as the north bank is called, social relations with its inhabitants are normally infrequent. The land south of the river is for the most part terra firme. The area included in the community of Itá extends upriver as far as the Rio Jocojó and downstream as far as the Rio Pucuruí, both of which are small tributaries (*igarapés*) of the Amazon. Between these two tributaries are ten others, and the rural inhabitants of the community live in isolated homesteads scattered along the banks of these small streams. In fact, throughout the Amazon the main pattern of settlement is one of scattered households, situated close to the waterways, the principal transportation routes. There

---

[2] The name Itá will be used henceforth to refer to the community—the town and its immediate rural area—and not to the larger political unit of that name.

are two overland footpaths, however, which run east and west from the town, providing communication with the rural zones by land during the summer. Even in the dry season, however, heavy cargoes and burdens can best be transported by canoe.

The people who live on the tributaries nearest to the town, such as Itapereira and Jacupí, visit town each day or two to buy food, to loaf in the shops, or even to work for the municipal government. The people who live on the more distant tributaries such as Bacá and Jocojó come to town only once each ten days for their *quinzena*,[3] the day selected for trading. They may also appear now and again on Sunday for Church services and on almost any other day to visit friends and relatives. In the summer months there are numerous saints' festivals in the rural zone, and people from the different small tributaries travel about to attend them and to visit. Within the community area all families bury their dead in the town cemetery; those who live outside have their own cemeteries. Within the community there is an in-group feeling of belonging, and the public ceremonies on Independence Day and the festivals of St. Benedict and St. Anthony celebrated in town are spoken of as "our festivals." People living outside the community area are strangers. A brass band of the community which often plays for local dances refused, for example, to play at a saint's festival being held on a stream near their homes but outside the community area. The people were *bravo* (rude or tough) and their festivals were hardly more than *farras* (orgies) was the explanation of the bandleader. He did not feel at home among these strangers. People on a tributary which flows into the Amazon channel across from the town, and therefore outside the special limits of the community, told us, "We some-times attend their festivals," or, "We haven't been to Itá for over two years."

The people living along the banks of each small stream form a "neighborhood," or a subunit, as it were, of the larger social unit which is the community. Along the banks of a typical tributary,

[3] Literally "fifteenth"; traditionally, on the Lower Amazon, the trading day was set at fifteen-day intervals.

some fifteen to twenty houses are situated at intervals of two to three hundred or even five hundred meters apart. There are sometimes clusters of houses inhabited by different members of the same family. In one place three houses only about one hundred meters apart held the families of a man and his two married sons; in another, six houses stretched over more than three kilometers of one tributary were inhabited by cousins. The homes of a patriarch and his sons-in-law and of a widow and her three daughters and their husbands formed two other neighborhood clusters. While kinship ties are often important in determining the residence of people within a neighborhood, and in assuring mutual assistance among the inhabitants, such neighborhoods are not kinship units, nor are they clan-like social groups. Common residence, friendship, and the ceremonial tie of the godparent relationships are as strong as family ties between these neighbors.

Devotion to a particular saint forms another bond between the people of a particular neighborhood. On each tributary there is a religious brotherhood (*irmandade*) dedicated to a saint—to Our Lady of Nazareth, to St. Peter, or to St. John. Each year the saint's day is celebrated in the locality, and the organization of the festival is an important function of the brotherhood. It is within the neighborhood that men exchange labor with each other and form co-operative work parties for agriculture. Beyond the immediate family group the neighborhood is the setting for daily life in the rural zone of Itá. In fact, for the rural inhabitant neighborhood ties overshadow those of the community; yet the neighborhoods are integral sub-divisions of the community. Events taking place in any of the rural neighborhoods are soon known on the streets of the town.

Two neighborhoods in the Itá community differ from the dispersed type described above. The people who live on the Jocojó and Maria Ribeiro tributaries form small villages. The *vila* of Jocojó contains nineteen houses built along one fairly straight street. It is a small village with a white wooden chapel and a *ramada*, a large open structure used for dancing during festivals. An overly large hut without walls is used as a school, and in 1948 it functioned with about the same regularity and efficiency as the one in Itá. Jocojó parents were exceedingly anxious that their children take advantage of the school, for it was the only rural neighborhood which boasted one. The village on the Maria Ribeiro Tributary consisted of a small cluster of houses without a chapel for its saint and without a school, but both these village neighborhoods were characterized by unity of organization and the progressivism of their inhabitants. As long as the populations of rural Amazonas live scattered and distant from one another, it will be difficult to provide accessible educational facilities and adequate health protection for them. Concentrated villages such as these two atypical neighborhood groups of Itá would make it possible for the government to provide schools. A concentrated population allows the physician from Itá to give mass treatment. The health service would be able to provide controls for group protection which would be impossible for the scattered households. Such villages, therefore, provide a possible solution for the problems of the countryside of the Amazon.

IV

The people of the community of Itá are Brazilians. They participate within the limits of their available knowledge and potentialities in regional and national life. The *caboclos*, as city people in the Amazon refer to the inhabitants of small towns and to the rural population, speak Portuguese. They discuss state and national politics, and if they are at least semi-literate they vote. In Itá and in other similar Amazon communities September 7th (Brazil's Independence Day) is celebrated. The caboclo plays soccer, Brazil's national sport, and he may gamble at *jôgo do bicho*, a popular and widespread drawing, similar to a "numbers" game, to which Brazilians are especially addicted. In 1945 festivals in out-of-the-way trading posts in the municipality of Itá celebrated VE Day. The farmers and rubber gatherers who attended were not, of course, aware of the full significance of World War II, but they knew that their country was making war on the Allied side. The legal and political institutions, the educational system, the formal religion, and many other aspects of Itá society are those of the nation of which Itá is but a small and insignificant part.

Three cultural traditions have fused to form contemporary Brazilian culture. The traditions, the speech, and the governmental and religious institutions of Europe brought to the New World by the Portuguese are the dominant culture patterns throughout the country. Itá, like most Brazilian communities, derives most of its culture from Portugal. In addition, however, Brazilian national culture has been influenced strongly by the traditions both of Negro Africa and by those of the native Indians who inhabited the area before the Portuguese arrived. At least 3,000,000 African slaves were imported into the country during the colonial period, and it is probable that the total number was much greater. Numerous customs and traditions of African origin have been incorporated into Brazilian life. Brazilian popular music (the samba), Brazilian cuisine, Brazilian folklore, and other aspects of modern life clearly show African influence. Yet American-Indian culture patterns persist throughout the country. Slash-and-burn agriculture and the major food crops (manioc, maize, beans, and so on) are of Indian origin. Most of the names of flora and fauna, and numerous place names in modern Brazilian Portuguese derive from Tupí, a widespread Indian language. Both the European newcomer and his African slave learned to live in the New World from the aboriginal peoples.

These three cultural heritages are not, however, felt with the same force throughout Brazil. Brazil is a nation of striking regional differences produced by very different environmental circumstances and by poor communications. Along the northeastern coast of Brazil, where the majority of the Negro slaves were on sugar plantations, African influences were important in forming the present regional culture. In the extreme south of Brazil, European traditions have taken hold almost to the exclusion of American-Indian and African traditions. In the Amazon Valley, with its distinctive rain-forest environment and its magnificent interlaced system of waterways, the Indian heritage of Brazil persisted with greater force than elsewhere. In Itá, as in other Amazon communities, Indian influences are readily apparent in the way people make a living, in their foods, in their folk beliefs, and in their religion. Furthermore, a large portion of the people of Itá have Indian ancestors. The high cheekbones, the straight black hair, the bronze skin, and the almond-shaped eyes (caused by the epicanthic fold so characteristic of the Amerind) of many inhabitants of the Itá community indicate the strength of American-Indian genetic strain.

The strength of the Indian tradition in rural Amazon society and culture is not due, however, to the numerical strength of the Indian population which existed in the region prior to 1500. In fact, the aboriginal population in the Amazon Valley seems to have been relatively sparse, never exceeding half a million people spread over the immense area. Their culture was simple as compared to the complex native civilizations of highland Mexico and Peru. The tropical forest tribes were hand agriculturalists planting a series of native American crops such as manioc, maize, beans, peanuts, yams, peppers, squashes, and cotton. They depended also upon fishing, hunting, and the collection of forest fruits and nuts to augment their diet. Their subsistence methods, although well adapted to the Amazon environment, limited the size of their communities, which seldom exceeded more than three hundred to four hundred people. Each five or six years they were forced to move their villages despite the enormous expanse of uninhabited forest land, and each year they cleared new garden sites out of the tropical forest. Thus great areas of land were necessary to support a relatively small number of people.

Furthermore, the native peoples of the Valley were divided into innumerable tribes speaking a variety of native languages. A "tribe" was generally merely a series of villages speaking a common language and feeling that they formed "a people" against all outsiders. Rarely did even a "tribe" have any formal political organization; only in a few cases did the authority of a chieftain extend over more than one village. Even in their own village the powers of such native leaders were never great. In the Upper Amazon the segmentation of aboriginal society was so extreme that each village, composed of only one or two long houses, considered itself a separate people. Throughout the area there was constant warfare between tribes, and suspicion of the outsider kept inter-tribal relations at a minimum.

The lack of linguistic and socio-political unity among the Indian groups of Amazonia made the process of conquest difficult for the Europeans and disastrous for the Indians themselves. Both Portuguese civil officials and religious missionaries established early treaties with the Indian chiefs to ensure peaceful relations, but they soon found that such treaties were not recognized by the people of other villages. Unlike the conquest of Mexico and Peru by a handful of Spaniards, where the capture or the capitulation of a handful of leaders led to the subjugation of large populations, the conquest of the Amazon native peoples was necessarily a piecemeal affair. Each "tribe," almost each village, had to be won or attracted peacefully into the orbit of Portuguese colonial life. The result of such piecemeal conquest was a rapid disintegration of native "tribes," especially along the main streams of the Amazon River system, within about a century after the arrival of the Portuguese in the early seventeenth century.[4]

As in Mexico and in Peru, the Portuguese did not come to the New World to work: they came seeking a fortune. But in Amazonia they found neither the riches of the Potosí silver mines nor, as in

[4] Today a few tribal Indian groups still live in out-of-the-way localities of the Amazon Valley, mainly in the headwaters of the non-navigable tributaries. In numbers these tribal Indians are an insignificant percentage of the total population of the Valley. They certainly do not exceed 50,000 people at most, less than one-half of one per cent of the total population of the Brazilian Amazon. A few tribes, such as the Urubú Indians, inhabiting the forest between the Gurupí and Pindaré rivers, less than 200 miles from Belém at the mouth of the Amazon, and the Hawks (Gaviões) on the lower Tocantins River, are just now feeling the influence of Luso-Brazilian society. The process of detribalization and of incorporation into Amazon regional society which began in the early seventeenth century continues into the present. History in the Amazon is in many respects not a question of an absolute time sequence but one of space. Processes which were completed long ago in the main arteries of the Amazon River system are now occurring in their principal outlines off the beaten track in the Valley.

Mexico and Peru, millions of Indians to provide labor for them. Nor was the Amazon soil as suitable for sugar cane as the rich northeastern coast of Brazil, where a wealthy plantation society was formed in colonial times. The best the Portuguese were able to do in the Amazon was to extract the native products of the tropical forest, such as hardwoods, cacao, and cinnamon, for sale on the European market. It was not very lucrative in comparison with the trade carried on by the Portuguese with the Orient. The few colonists attracted to the Amazon region could not afford to purchase slaves from Africa, and few Negroes were imported into the region. Instead, the colonist sought the Indians as household servants, as collectors of forest products, and as agricultural workers to provide food for their settlements. In colonial times the Indians were the people "who paddled the canoes, who hunted and fished, who worked in the domestic and public services, who raised cattle, who served in the armed forces, who labored in the shipyards," according to Artur Cezar Ferreira Reis, the leading student of Amazon colonial history.[5] And the observations of a Portuguese writer in the sixteenth century apply aptly to the Amazon in the seventeenth century. "As soon as persons who intend to live in Brazil," wrote Pedro de Magalhães, "become inhabitants of the country, however poor they may be, if one obtains two pair or a half dozen slaves, which might cost somewhere in the neighborhood of ten cruzados, he then has the means of sustenance and crops; so little by little, men become rich and live honourably in the land with more ease than in the Kingdom [Portugal] because these same Indian slaves hunt food for themselves and in this way the men have no expense for the maintenance of their slaves, nor of their own persons." [6] Numerous slave raids called *resgates* were organized in Amazonia, penetrating deep into the interior and returning with captured Indian slaves and leaving behind them men, women, and children massacred in the process. Entire tribes were soon exterminated, and thousands of

[5] *Síntese da História do Pará* (Belém, 1942), p. 48.
[6] *The Histories of Brazil*, transl. John B. Stetson, Jr. (New York, Cortes Society, 1922) (1st ed., 1576), p. 41.

Indians were brought into the orbit of Luso-Brazilian colonial life.[7]

The appetite of the colonists for slaves soon clashed, however, with the interests of the religious missionaries who came to the Amazon with the first military expeditions. The missionaries, especially the Jesuits, soon established *aldeiamentos* (mission villages) at strategic points along the Amazon River and its main tributaries into which they attracted Indians from various tribes. Under the close paternalistic régime of the Jesuits, the mission Indians were taught catechism and Catholic ritual, new handicrafts, and Old World custom. In a relatively short time thousands of tribal Indians were transformed into "Jesuit Indians" living by rules laid down by the Jesuit priests rather than by their aboriginal culture patterns. Christian dogma and Catholic ceremonial were quickly substituted for their native religion, although native concepts and practices survived alongside the new religion. Even their marriages were supervised by the padres so as not to run counter to Catholic rules of incest and propriety. For a time the missions served to protect numerous Indian groups from slave raids. The Portuguese Crown issued numerous edicts prohibiting Indian slavery and granting the missionaries full powers over the Indian population.

But the scene of battle was far from Europe, and slave-hunting parties even attacked Jesuit missions, carrying off the newly converted Christians as slaves. The colonists found numerous legal loopholes to allow them to enslave Indians. They prevailed upon the Crown to allow them to make slaves of "prisoners of just wars" and of those who were "ransomed from the cord" (that is, those who were snatched from the hands of cannibalistic tribes). Just wars and "cannibalism" increased rapidly as soon as these rights were granted. Faced with the necessity of producing foodstuffs for soldiers and for European colonists, who were not inclined toward manual labor themselves, the Portuguese colonial officials condoned

[7] One Portuguese captain, the infamous Bento Maciel Parente, was accused of killing 500,000 Indians during his various expeditions. This is certainly an exaggeration, but that he and his men massacred many Indians and made many slaves is not to be doubted. See Serafim Leite, *História da Companhia de Jesus no Brasil* (Lisbon, 1938), IV, 137.

or ignored evasions of the law, and resorted time and time again to forced labor, sending soldiers to bring back Indian males for work in Portuguese settlements. Padre Antonio Vieira, whose letters and sermons are classics of Brazilian literature, complained bitterly in letters to the Crown that when missionaries visited Indian villages they often found them inhabited by a few half starved women, children, and old people. The men had been taken off for forced labor during the very months when they should have been planting their own gardens. The men were often away, he wrote, "eight to nine months of the year—without the Mass, without celebrating even a Saint's Day, without [keeping] Lent, without [receiving] the Sacraments, and without being able to make their own gardens." [8] The Jesuits worked hard to protect the Indians, but, as Roy Nash puts it, "the pocket book emotions of the colonists had been touched deeply." It was a battle "between the Brazilian slave hunters who wanted the Indian's body and the Jesuits (and other missionaries) who wanted his soul in which the aboriginal American was destined to lose both." [9]

The battle was decided, however, in the middle of the eighteenth century when the Marquis of Pombal, who governed with almost absolute powers in Portugal for more than twenty-five years, stripped the missionaries of all temporal power over the Indians and ordered the Jesuits expelled from Brazil. Pombal issued a series of laws aimed at incorporation of the Indians, those still living in tribal groups and those of the missions, into colonial life. He ordered that mission stations be transformed into towns and villages. Many important Amazon towns, such as Óbidos, Faro, and Macapá, became civil settlements at this time. Pombal issued decrees that the Portuguese language should be taught instead of the *língua geral*, a modified form of the indigenous Tupí language, which the missionaries had used in teaching their Indian converts. There was a conscious policy of stimulating miscegenation between the European and the native. Portuguese male colonists were offered special

[8] Leite, *op. cit.*, IV, 52.
[9] *The Conquest of Brazil* (New York, 1926), p. 106.

inducements in the form of land grants, free tools, tax exemptions, and even political posts to marry native women.

Pombal's reforms were aimed at the assimilation of the Indian into colonial society and at least theoretically at granting the assimilated Indian equal rights with the colonials. But freedom for the Indian was impossible without modification of the Amazonian economic and social system. Someone had to do the work, and the European colonist looked down upon manual labor as the work of a slave. Thus the extractive industries and the agriculture which provided food for the colony depended upon Indian servitude in one form or another. It was necessary to continue compulsory labor during the Pombal régime. It was decreed that all able-bodied Indian males between the ages of thirteen and sixty were required to register with the government-appointed director of the settlement in which they lived; one half of the men in each settlement were subjected for some part of the year to forced labor for the Europeans and creoles. The other half were allowed to remain at home to make gardens for themselves. This controlled system soon disintegrated into a form of peonage and debt servitude, and outright slavery persisted in the Amazon region despite laws to the contrary until late in the nineteenth century.[10]

Whereas the protection of the missions had in a sense restrained the process, Pombal's reforms and the continued demands on the Amazon Indian for labor had the result of stimulating the rate of assimilation of the native into colonial life. By 1821, when Brazil achieved its independence from Portugal, the population of the Amazon Valley was mainly mestizo, and the way of life of the majority of the population was essentially Portuguese, although strongly influenced by the unique Amazonian environment and by the Indian cultures which had existed there. A regional culture basically European in its main institutions but strongly influenced by the unique Amazonian environment and by the native cultures of the region had been formed.

The accounts written by nineteenth century travelers give a

[10] *Ibid.*, p. 120.

picture of the degree to which this process of assimilation and ac-
culturation of the Amazon native had progressed. It is estimated
that in 1852 as many as 57 per cent of the inhabitants of the Valley
were Indians and that 26 per cent more were mamelucos or Indian-
European mixtures; the rest were Europeans and Negroes. It is
evident, however, that these "Indians" and mamelucos were not
Indians in a social and cultural sense. Their way of life was more
Iberian than native Indian. Although the nineteenth century visitors
speak of "Indian custom" and "native life," they actually describe
Portuguese customs. Mrs. Agassiz, the wife of the famous Swiss
naturalist Louis Agassiz, who led an expedition into the Amazon,
speaks of "a hideous old Indian woman who performed the strange
rites of *crossing herself* and throwing kisses into a trunk which contained *a print of 'Our Lady of Nazareth.'*" [11] H. W. Bates, the
English naturalist whose account of the Amazon has become a
classic, describes the festivals for the patron saint, St. Thereza, of
Egá, the small village in which he resided for many months. He
tells us of the enactment of a folk drama on St. John's eve in which
Caypor, a kind of sylvan deity, appeared together with Christian
figures—a custom obviously introduced by missionaries to replace
aboriginal ceremonies.[12] Herbert Smith's short but excellent description of the "semi-civilized Amazonian Indians" near Monte Alegre
in the lower Amazon also indicates the strength of Iberian custom.[13]
He describes adobe houses rather than the palm-thatched long house
of aboriginal times. The music, dancing, and feasting on a saint's
day which he mentions is the same as in Itá today. The Amazonians
gave a "blessing" in good European style, offering their hand and
saying, "God bless you my child" (*Deus te abençoe*). Biologically
they were "Indians," but they were by culture Brazilians with more
in common with the Luso-Brazilian world than with the autoch-
thonous Indians still living in the isolated forests of the Amazon.
Since the nineteenth century the Amazon caboclo has increasingly

[11] *A Journey in Brazil* (New York, 1896), p. 181. Italics are my own.
[12] *The Naturalist on the River Amazon* (London, Everyman's Library, 1930
ed.), pp. 284 ff.
[13] *The Amazons and the Coast* (New York, 1879), pp. 371–397.

been brought into closer touch with regional and national life. He is today a citizen of a national state, and his way of life is but a regional variety of a national culture.

The regional culture of Itá and of other Amazon communities, as stated earlier, retains many patterns from native Indian heritage. Despite the efforts of the missionaries to make Catholics out of them, many rural Brazilians of the Amazon retain folk beliefs of aboriginal origin. Nowadays in rural neighborhoods, and even in lower-class districts in Amazon cities, medicine men (*pagés*) cure by old native Indian methods. A large number of Tupí terms have been integrated into the Portuguese language as it is spoken in the Brazilian Amazon. The techniques and skills used in hunting and fishing and the folk belief that centers on these pursuits are of Indian origin. Indian traditions are felt in these and in other spheres of contemporary Amazonian life

The Indian traits which survive as a part of Amazon regional culture are mainly derived from Tupí-speaking Indian tribes. These peoples, who inhabited practically the entire coast of Brazil, and who seemed to be moving inland up the Amazon mainstream at the time of the arrival of the Europeans, were the first Indian tribes with whom the Portuguese had any prolonged contact. It was mainly with Tupí-speaking natives that the Portuguese traded for brazilwood, against whom they made war, and whom they enslaved during the first century of the colonial period. The Tupíans taught the newcomers how to plant "new" crops, and they taught them the names and the utility of the New World flora and fauna. Furthermore, as Gilberto Freyre so picturesquely put it, "No sooner had the European leaped ashore than he found his feet slipping among native women." [14] Portuguese men took native wives and concubines who must have been women from Tupían tribes. The offspring from these unions, the first Brazilians, raised by their mothers and dominated by their fathers, were carriers of a mixed

[14] *The Masters and the Slaves,* trans. Samuel Putnam (New York, 1946), p. 15.

culture—Tupí and Portuguese—and they were often bilingual. The mamelucos had an important role in the extension of Portuguese control over the Amazon region, and they carried with them customs, knowledge, and beliefs learned from their Indian mothers.

Furthermore, during the first century after the arrival of the Europeans in Brazil, Tupí-speaking people were the primary concern of the Catholic missionaries. Most of the earlier descriptions of Brazilian natives were written by missionaries, and they describe the Tupinambá, as the Tupí-speaking coastal tribes were called. Because the missionaries were first faced with Tupí languages, and Tupí speakers must have seemed more numerous to them than the so-called Tapuya (generally Ge-speaking tribes of the interior), the missionaries adopted Tupí as an intermediary language for teaching Christian doctrine, just as Quechua was adopted in Peru and Nahuatl in Mexico. The missionaries learned to speak a Tupí language, and it was reduced to a European script. A generalized and modified form of this language came to be known as the língua geral (the general language) and was used for teaching and for preaching Christianity throughout Brazil. Native peoples of other tongues were taught língua geral, and it became the language of the Indian-European mestizos and of the Indians living in mission stations and in European settlements.

As late as the mid-nineteenth century, perhaps more people spoke língua geral than Portuguese in the Amazon. Bates writes that "Tupí is spoken with little corruption along the main Amazon for a distance of 2,500 miles." [15] Alfred Russel Wallace remarks that in a small settlement near Manaus, "only one of them here could speak Portuguese, all the rest using the Indian language" (that is, língua geral). Wallace states that near the larger towns and cities, língua geral was "used indiscriminately with Portuguese," and that in the Lower Amazon most people were bilingual, but that above Santarém on the Upper Amazon it was the only language known. It was used by tribal groups who also retained their own language

[15] *Op. cit.*, p. 282.

as a means of communicating with traders and with tribes speaking distinct native languages.[16] Not until the late nineteenth century did Portuguese replace língua geral as the language of Amazonia, and even today it is spoken in some isolated areas by partially assimilated Indians and mestizos.

With this language, many traditions of Tupí origin spread throughout Amazonia even in areas not inhabited in aboriginal times by Tupían peoples. European concepts transmitted through língua geral were subjected to modification and accretion of aboriginal details in the process. The Christian God and the Devil were given the names (in língua geral) of Tupan and Jurupari. Both took on characteristics of the aboriginal supernaturals of these same names. Witches and werewolves of European medieval belief were easily identified with Tupí forest demons and were also given aboriginal names. Thus, along with the Iberian patterns imposed upon and taught to the Amazonian peasant population by their European conquerors, a body of aboriginal culture patterns has persisted in rural culture throughout the Brazilian Amazon. These aboriginal patterns have fused within the fabric of the predominantly Iberian culture to form a way of life, a culture distinctive of the region and well adapted to the particular Amazon environment.

V

Although Itá is not an important Amazon town, it has a not unimposing history which reflects practically every major trend in the history of the Amazon Valley. Itá is almost as old as Jamestown, Virginia. As early as 1616 a fort was established on the present site of the town by the Dutch. Although the area of the New World in which Itá is situated was granted them by the Treaty of Tordesillas in 1494, the Portuguese did not in the sixteenth century have a very firm hold upon their New World possessions. Portugal, with a population of a mere one million people in the sixteenth century, had a vast empire and a lucrative trade with the Orient.

[16] *A Narrative of Travels on the Amazon and Rio Negro*, p. 168.

Brazil was necessarily neglected; it had a sparse native population and its native products, with the exception of brazilwood and a few spices, were not much sought after in Europe. Furthermore, from 1580 to 1640, during the period of "Captivity," when the Portuguese crown passed to the Spanish royal family, Portugal was for all purposes a part of Spain. For these reasons Brazil became fair game for the enemies of Spain. Because the Portuguese lacked the man power and because Spain was occupied on more lucrative fronts, the English, the French, and the Dutch encroached upon Brazil. Not only did these countries establish forts and colonies in South Brazil, but by the end of the sixteenth century the Dutch and the English had set up trading posts and forts near the delta on the Amazon River and the French were entrenched at São Luis just south of the mouth of the great river system.

In the late sixteenth century, however, Portugal took a new interest in its New World possessions, especially since sugar cane planted in the rich red earth of the northeastern coast of Brazil began to produce wealth equal to that obtained from the Orient. The Portuguese dispatched an armed force to "drive out the foreigners." In 1616 the French were expelled from São Luis and the Portuguese established a fort at Belém in the mouth of the Amazon delta. In the next few years they drove out the English intruders established on the north shores of the great river near its mouth and in 1623 they captured the Dutch fort at Itá, making it a Portuguese stronghold for the control of the lower Amazon. The Dutch attempted to recapture Itá in 1639 but failed, and by 1640 the Portuguese had reestablished full control over the lower Amazon region.

The population grew in the shadow of the Portuguese fort at Itá, and by 1639 the settlement was given the status of a "town" or *vila*. Numerous Indians were attracted to the growing settlement, and the Portuguese soldiers at the fort took Indian wives. These Portuguese-Indian families were the basis of the new town's population. It is reported that Carmelite missionaries were established there by 1654. In the next year the Jesuits arrived. Both of these missionary groups brought Indians to the settlement, and the Jesuits soon formed "mission villages" in the near vicinity. They also used the town as a base of operation for the founding of other mission villages upriver.

The small town continued to grow by attracting Indians from the nearby missions into its orbit, but not always by peaceful means. In 1667 the *capitão-mor* at Itá is said to have treated a group of Taconhapé Indians, who had been "persuaded" to travel downriver to Belém to work on the construction of the Santa Casa de Misericórdia (a hospital), so brutally that they fled into the forest never to reappear. On another occasion the *capitão-mor* at Itá ordered the missionized Indians in the vicinity dispersed by force, a reflection of the battle between the Jesuits and the colonists who were backed by the government. As early as 1692 the Jesuits were forced out of Itá, and the religious life of the town was handed over to the monks of Piedade, a less aggressive and less powerful religious order.

The situation of Itá on a bluff commanding a wide view of the Amazon main channel gave it considerable strategic importance. Boats moving up and down the river were required to stop at Itá to pay taxes, and the little fort was an effective point of control against the possible encroachments of foreigners. Because Itá was a control station, most travelers on the Amazon had to stop there and many writers mention the town briefly. The French scientist Charles de la Condamine visited Itá for three days in 1743 and was given the hospitality due an honored guest by the commander of the fort and other local authorities. In 1758 Governor Francisco Xavier de Mendoça visited the town. He reported that Itá was a center of Portuguese influence in the lower Amazon. Many former mission Indians had been attracted to Itá.

At the beginning of the nineteenth century, the town of Itá contained "86 fires" (individual families) or 564 souls. According to the famous German scientist Karl von Martius, who visited Itá in 1819, these people were either a mixture of the "indigenous race" with Portuguese or "pure Indians." Their houses were for the most part palm-thatched structures. The place seemed isolated and abandoned. One of the townspeople remarked to von Martius that things had been better in the time of Pai-Tucura (Father Grasshopper), as the Indians called the Capuchin monk who had lived there. The garrison had been reduced and the activities of the religious orders had been curtailed by the laws issued by Pombal. Although there is mention of plantations of cacao and coffee near Itá, the people seemed to devote themselves mainly to the collection of sarsaparilla and native cacao, which was found in abundance in the delta islands near the town.

In 1842 Itá had but two streets with two squares. As in other Amazon settlements, one section of the town was inhabited by the Indians and their descendants and was known as the "village" (*aldeia*). The other section was called the "city" (*cidade*) and there the Europeans and mestizos, who were merchants, government officials, landowners, and artisans, lived.[17] The city evidently grew at the expense of the village, for as people took on Iberian language and custom they lost their identity as Indians and as "slaves." A visitor to Itá in 1850 estimated its population as 715 people, of which 482 were classified as "white or mestizo" and only 233 as "slaves" (that is, Indians). The travelers who paused at Itá during the last decades of the nineteenth century mention it only in passing; the town had evidently lost its importance as a customs post; it is said that the fort was entirely abandoned.

But at the end of the century, with the advent of wild rubber as an important export product, Itá seems to have regained some of its past prominence. From 1900 to 1912, the Amazon Valley held a virtual monopoly on rubber production. During this period the Valley was fabulously prosperous. There was a dramatic headlong rush for the "liquid gold"; there was a stampede to purchase rubber forests. A large number of people from northeastern Brazil, where droughts occurring each ten to twelve years caused thousands of people to die of thirst, starvation, or pestilence or to migrate,

---

[17] "Nearly every Amazonian town is divided into *cidade* and *aldeia*, the 'city' and the 'village'; the former the modern town; the latter, the original Indian settlement from which it sprang." Smith, *op. cit.*, p. 118.

were attracted to the Amazon as rubber gatherers. The influx into the Amazon was so great in the last part of the nineteenth century that the population of Manaus, which was 5,000 in 1879, was 50,000 in 1890; and Belém, which was only 15,000 in 1848, was over 100,000 in 1890.[18] The population of the Valley is thought to have doubled from 1850 to 1900. Money was plentiful. A splendid opera house was built in Manaus, halfway up the Amazon River, and opera companies from Europe braved the dangers of yellow fever and malaria to play there. Imitations of European town houses and villas, totally unsuited to the tropical climate, were built in Belém and Manaus with rubber wealth. People imported their clothes from abroad, and many persons are said to have sent their fancy dresses and dress shirts to Lisbon to have them laundered. There was gambling, exploitation of newcomers, prostitution, and lawlessness of all kinds.

The delta islands in front of Itá contained rich stands of rubber trees second in their yield only to the headwaters of the Amazon tributaries and the territory of Acre. Itá therefore became the center of an active commerce stimulated by the high prices of rubber. The population grew to more than two thousand. Twenty general stores were opened. At the height of the boom, from 1909 to 1910, a weekly newspaper was printed and published. Advertisements in the *Correio de Itá*, as it was called, indicate the prosperity, the active social life, and the preoccupation of the townspeople with the outside world during this period. Such stores as the Bola de Oiro (the Golden Ball), the Bazaar, and the Casa Gato advertised merchandise recently arrived from Belém and abroad. A barber shop called the "15th of November" announced "hair tonics of the finest quality" and advised its clients that no calls for services outside the shop were accepted but that "subscriptions might be paid monthly in advance" for shaves and haircuts. Each week Professor Antenor Madeira offered in a sedate announcement private lessons in Portuguese, French, Latin, arithmetic, algebra, geography, and history. There were editorials on the dangers of the growing independence

[18] Pierre Denis, *Brazil* (London, 1914), p. 358.

of women in the United States and upon the position of Brazil in the international scene. A local poet writing under the name of Tula published a piece each week or so. It is evident from the news stories that Itá people were intensely interested in local and state politics. One editorial accused the women of a local religious brotherhood of praying to the saints to punish the leaders of the political opposition. The editorial asked that the saints be kept out of politics and demanded also that the local priest refrain from political topics in his sermons.

The social notices in the *Correio de Itá* tell of birthday parties, the coming and going of important men and their families, and of receptions for important visitors. In December of 1909, for example, the *intendente* (equivalent to the mayor) offered a banquet of fifty places at which two wines and champagne were served in honor of the birthday of Senator Antônio Lemos, the most prominent politician of the state of Pará. In January of 1910, the owner of the Casa Gato, Coronel Filomeno Cesar de Andrade, offered a birthday party for his two daughters at which there were "dances and games for prizes until late into the night." Old people who remember these days in Itá tell of balls held in the two-story *palacetes* of the local rubber barons of the day. At these balls an orchestra played in a large entrance hall for two rooms of dancers, one containing the "first-class" invitees and the other the "second class" or the "people." In the first-class room champagne, wines, beer, imported liquors, fine cakes, and many varieties of Brazilian sweets were served. In the other room *cachaça* (strong sugar rum) and occasionally beer were the drinks, and *beijús* (manioc cakes) and *brôa de povilho* (muffins of tapioca flour) were served instead of cakes. Often, however, *beijú chica* (a fine manioc cake), a soft drink of *guaraná*, and other regional dishes were served to all, transgressing class difference. Despite the desire to be cosmopolitan, the upper class of Itá was regional in formation.

Old people also tell of a demimonde in Itá during this epoch. There were several gambling houses where the *seringueiro* (the rubber collector) from the Islands might spend his pay. And, in common with most Amazon towns during the rubber boom, Itá boasted at least one house of prostitution. Old men today speak of a gay night life when they were young. There were long evenings of conversation and drinking in the common room of the bawdy house—for Brazilian houses of prostitution have always been a place for social gathering of young men. They tell of serenades which lasted far into the morning hours. Everyone agrees that the difference between the tempo of social life in Itá in those days and now is that between night and day. Today people enjoy the simple occasions of festivals and dances, but they complain that the town is dead and that all the gay young men have moved away to Belém.

Among the varied foreign groups who came to the Amazon in the early part of this century, attracted by the rubber commerce, were a number of Jews from North Africa. Just how many came to the Amazon is not known, but a synagogue was formed in Belém and they opened commercial houses in many Amazon towns. Itá became a well known center for these Jewish immigrants. The *Almanac do Pará,* an official publication, states that as early as 1889 six of the fourteen commercial houses in Itá were owned by Hebrews. Such names as Aben Athar, Levi, Bensabeth, and Azulay were important in community affairs in the early days of this century. The Jews had an important role in Itá life. They were "strong" commercial men, and two *Hebraicos* were mayor of the town. Today one of Itá's most successful native sons, of whom all are proud, is a descendant of one of the Jewish families. Yet the remaining Jewish family in Itá tells of occasional hostility against the Jews in former times. It was a sport of youthful drinking companions "to give the Hebrews a beating," and one elderly man recounted with some gaiety the story of the sacking of the Jewish-owned Bazaar by a group of young drunks. Such hostility, however, seems to have been related to the intense political feelings of the times, for our storyteller also remembered that the young men were instigated by a politician whom the Jewish store owner had opposed in an election. Today the Jewish cemetery, which is well kept and clear of weeds, attests to the strong Jewish families who once lived there.

Dona Deborah, the widow of the last Jewish merchant, sees to it that it is cared for. She is the only orthodox Hebrew in town; her sons and daughters have all married into the Catholic faith.

It was during the last years of the rubber boom that the fabulous Itá town hall was initiated. It was planned as the largest building on the lower Amazon. An Italian engineer arrived to draw the plans for the building and to supervise its construction. It was to be two stories high and there was to be a majestic staircase from the second story to the public square which faced upon the Amazon. By 1912 the basic framework of the structure was completed. According to local legend, the building was not finished then because the mayor expropriated for the town hall the stone building materials which had been accumulated to build a church for St. Benedict, the saint to whom the people of Itá had become intensely devoted. "The saint put a *maldição* [curse] on the building," the town's people still say. Quite obviously, the saint was aided by the rubber crash in 1912, which put an end to such public extravagance and which caused the demise of most of the local commercial establishments.

VI

The collapse of the Amazon rubber industry came as a shock to the people of the Amazon Valley. During the boom years, people were optimistic. The Almighty, it seemed to everyone, had especially blessed the region with "black gold." Even the tropical climate was described as one especially favorable to man and superior to the cold Temperate Zone. As late as 1909, men in the Amazon were able to say: "We need not concern ourselves about the Indian-rubber plantations which have sprung up in Asia. The special climatic conditions of the Amazon Valley, the new system of treating our product, now being applied with such success to our crops of hevea, the vast expanse of our Indian-rubber districts, some of which have not yet been exploited, and finally the manifold needs of modern industry, enable us to pay little heed to what others are doing in the same line of business. Indeed, were it not our duty to keep our eyes on the scientific discoveries relating to Indian rubber, we could well afford to disregard foreign plantations altogether." [19]

In 1912, as the world knows, the bubble broke. Some years earlier, Henry Wickham Steed had smuggled rubber seeds out of Brazil to Kew Gardens in London. From these tender plants, the rubber plantations of Ceylon and Malaya were formed. At first the Eastern plantations were not too successful; there were difficulties in adapting the Brazilian seedlings to the Asiatic environment. But by 1910 the Oriental rubber plantations began to be rewarding. Under plantation conditions a variety of rubber tree was developed which produces more latex than the native *Hevea brasiliensis*. Labor is cheaper and more plentiful in the Orient. In 1910 the East produced only 9 per cent of the world's supply of rubber; by 1913 its production equaled that of the Amazon Valley. In the years that followed, the Oriental plantations gradually surpassed the Amazon both in production and in price.

After 1912 the Amazon economic structure fell apart, and the optimism and ostentation of the boom years disappeared. Most of the commercial houses of Belém and Manaus collapsed in the 1912 crash, and a chain reaction of economic disaster extended down to the rural traders and to their collectors. The entire commercial system, which was over-extended and depended upon credit advances from top to bottom, was highly vulnerable. Trading posts were abandoned or continued to do business on a small scale with little stock. Collectors were allowed to leave the rubber fields. Many returned to Ceará, others settled on the traders' land as subsistence farmers, and a few eked out an existence by continuing to collect rubber or other products, such as Brazil nuts, which brought a higher price. Communications with Europe, North America, and southern Brazil became less frequent. The opera house at Manaus was closed and the public facilities of both Belém and Manaus slowly deteriorated. The population of many small towns suddenly dwindled, for people left to look for work elsewhere or returned

[19] *Album do Estado do Pará*, compiled at the behest of Dr. Augusto Montenegro, governor (1901–1908) (Paris, 1910), p. 182.

to the northeast. In many small towns houses were emptied and abandoned. Soon their streets were dotted with structures caving in from neglect, and the rural population outside the cities and towns lived again in isolation.

The Amazon Valley, so prosperous and seemingly with such a brilliant future during the first decade of this century, became in a short time isolated and backward. A profound pessimism settled over the region, which was reflected in the attitudes of the inhabitants. Their pessimism influenced in turn the opinions of outsiders who visited the Valley. "The Amazon," wrote one highly gifted local essayist, "has been until now the main victim of its own greatness." [20] Backwardness was explained as "not the fault of man but the fault of the [physical] environment." [21] Health conditions, which of course became worse owing to lack of medical supplies in the interior, seemed to everyone an insoluble problem. Economic abandon and isolation were charged to the many difficulties which God had created as part of the Amazon environment.

The years 1912 to 1942 were bitter ones for Itá, as for most of the Amazon Valley. The political administration which took over just after the rubber crash sold the building materials which had been accumulated to finish the town hall. Even parts of the unfinished structure were demolished to be sold for cash. Numerous families moved away shortly after 1912. Commercial men closed their stores and left town either bankrupt or discouraged. The rural population of the community turned from rubber collection back to subsistence agriculture. The population of the town declined abruptly, and by 1920 there were only three hundred people living there. The ox-cart road leading from the town to the headwaters of the nearby streams was abandoned and soon became over-run with weeds. The gas (carbide) lighting system which had illuminated the streets during the good years fell into disrepair. Homes and public buildings were empty and soon began to tumble in from lack of protection against the steady work of termites.

[20] Alfredo Ladislau, *Terra Immatura* (Rio de Janeiro, 1933), p. 29.
[21] Vianna Moog, *O Ciclo do Ouro Negro* (Pôrto Alegre, 1936), p. 81.

In 1929, when two journalists from Belém visited Itá, the town had reached the depths of decadence and abandon. At that time it almost might have been described as a ghost town. The writers' stories which were published in the *Folha do Norte*, the foremost newspaper of Belém, mention the dangers of traversing the board walk leading to the municipal dock. A few planks were missing, others were rotten, and the whole structure wobbled dangerously. One of these observers, a well known writer who signed himself "João da Selva" (John of the Forest), called Itá an "ex-city on whose streets are grouped the ruins of houses and a few others which are gradually crumbling." He mentions the unfinished town hall and writes that the building serving as a "town hall" at the time "is not worth even classification as a 'decaying house,' for it is literally falling to pieces." The other journalist objects; he found the same building no better than a "stable for goats." The building which once held the gas plant, wrote João da Selva, was but "four walls which the wind has no wish to uncover so that the sky might be testimony to what has happened inside."

In the salon of the ruins of a once fine residence, João da Selva noticed a harp with a few strings and the remains of a grand piano, now half destroyed by termites; the room containing these "memories of civilization" was being used at the time as a stable for a cow. He describes his walk ("Whatever else was there to do?") along a tortuous path to "what they called the Third Street." There he was shown the decaying remains of a hearse, "a first-class hearse as good as those of the Santa Casa in Belém which some mayor purchased out of pity for the poor corpses carried to the cemetery in a hand-barrow or in a hammock." Evidently the hearse had been too wide to pass along the trail leading to the cemetery, and after the rubber crash the trail was not widened. Again a hammock strung between two poles served to carry the people of Itá to their graves. João da Selva was anxious to leave Itá, but it was not so easy to escape. In the old days all river steamers paid a call at Itá, but now the *Moacyr*, the riverboat on which he had intended to leave, passed majestically down the center of the Amazon without bothering to stop.

Not all Amazon towns reached so low an ebb, but most communities of the region felt the effects of the economic abandonment of the Valley in one form or another. Almost all towns declined in population. The system of transportation, which was mainly by riverboat, slowly began to suffer from the lack of replacement of equipment, and communication between the various centers was less frequent. Steamships from Europe and from southern Brazil to Belém and to Manaus became more and more infrequent, and contact with the outside world diminished. The municipal and state coffers were empty, for the principal source of income had been rubber. The municipal facilities of many towns fell into disrepair. Rural schools often closed for lack of teachers. Even the cities of Belém and Manaus deteriorated during this period. When World War II brought travelers from all the world through Belém, the British-owned electric-light system of the city was in such bad condition that there was insufficient energy to drive the streetcars; and electric power was lacking for hours almost every evening. The streets of Belém were full of holes, and a sewer system which had never been completed was more effective as a breeding place for mosquitoes than as a mechanism for waste disposal. Belém was still using an antiquated telephone system with the old farm-type crank signal system. In the Brazilian Amazon there were short intervals of temporary relief during the period from 1912 to 1942, because of the occasional activities of an energetic politician, a bit of federal aid, or a slight rise in the prices of forest products, but as a whole it was a time of isolation, of slow disintegration, and of increasing poverty.

World War II brought a new epoch to the Amazon Valley. When the rubber plantations of the East fell into Japanese hands, the Allies turned frantically to the Amazon region for natural rubber. Large sums of money and tremendous efforts were expended in a campaign to increase the production of rubber. The Rubber Development Corporation, a wartime agency of the United States Government, cooperated with the Brazilian Government in improving communications and transportation, in importing trade materials necessary for rubber gathering, in extending credit to producers, and in other enterprises designed to increase production. Taking advantage of a drought in the arid northeast, a large number of refugees were transported into the Amazon Valley to provide labor for rubber production. Wild rubber was shipped by air from Manaus to the United States. Technicians, many of whom had considerable experience in the Orient, flooded into Belém and Manaus and spread out over the Valley. This wartime rubber campaign, however, was not a success. The rubber production of the Brazilian Amazon, which was about 19,000 tons in 1940, increased to only some 25,000 tons in 1944.

The failure of the rubber-development program was due to several causes. First, the very nature of the wild-rubber industry makes for limitations in its development. The trees are spaced wide apart in the forest and the collection of the latex is therefore an arduous and time-consuming occupation. Secondly, the opening of new (or the reopening of old) rubber trails in the Amazon calls for an intimate knowledge of the terrain and of the process of wild-rubber collection. The inexperienced laborers brought in from the Brazilian northeast and from elsewhere in the country lacked the experience of the Amazon caboclo and they were unable to clear trails which were productive. The time was too short and the experienced rubber collectors too few seriously to increase total production. Finally, the campaign was unsuccessful because the experts and administrators from southern Brazil and from abroad did not understand Amazon society. They were unaware of the incentives which would have stimulated the Amazon rural population to greater efforts, and they misunderstood the traditional force of the Amazon commercial system, which they saw as too inefficient and exploitative, and thus as a barrier to a greater rubber output.

But the rubber campaign brought numerous benefits to the Brazilian Amazon. Rubber prices were relatively high, and people were able to buy a few manufactured items which were imported into the region. The Brazilian Government took a new interest in the Valley. As early as 1940, President Getulio Vargas had promised a renewed national interest in the area in a speech given at Manaus, and beginning with the war serious steps were taken to implement his promises. In 1942 the SESP was formed by international agreement between Brazil and the United States as part of their joint war effort. One of the major programs of the SESP was a gigantic public-health program in the Amazon states of Brazil. By 1949 the SESP had established health posts in thirty Amazon towns and hospitals in Breves and Santarém, two important centers of the Lower Amazon. In addition to giving medical assistance to a large portion of the Amazon population, the SESP had installed water-supply systems in several small Amazon communities, constructed over 8,000 sanitary privies throughout the Valley, and built a system of dikes and drainage canals in and near Belém which both reclaimed land and protected the city against malaria. The SESP set up a system of regular spraying of domiciles with DDT which as early as 1948 protected some 40,000 homes and public buildings in 146 communities.

This great public-health program, financed at first by the United States and Brazil, is now almost exclusively supported by Brazil. A group of North American technicians still remains on the SESP staff in the Amazon Valley as consultants, but in several Amazon towns one may meet Brazilian public-health officers with the pennants of Michigan, Columbia, or Johns Hopkins University on their living-room walls and Master of Public Health diplomas hung in their offices. These are the men who were sent by the SESP to study in the United States. Everywhere one finds public-health officers trained in the new faculties in São Paulo and Rio de Janeiro. The SESP and the other programs maintained by the Institute of Inter-American Affairs of the United States Department of State throughout Latin America are today considered models of the method of carrying out the Point Four program.

Itá felt the effects of reawakening federal and world-wide interest in the Amazon Valley as early as 1943. Although not an important population center, Itá's strategic location on the Amazon mainstream again served it well. Because it was an excellent center from which a large rural population might be reached along the Lower Amazon and in the delta, the SESP established a health post at Itá in late 1943. A laboratory technician was first stationed there to collect mosquitoes and to distribute Atabrine, the most efficient anti-malaria drug known at the time. Shortly, a physician, a male nurse, and a public-health inspector arrived and a post was established in one of the few houses of sufficient size which still remained standing. In 1944 a modern building was constructed to house the health post, and a Diesel launch was stationed at Itá for the use of the physician in visiting nearby towns and villages. The selection of Itá as a site for a health post increased its importance as a town, and its population began slowly to grow.

The SESP brought important innovations. It constructed hygienic privies for more than 90 per cent of the dwellings of the town. A sanitary inspector has stimulated the townspeople to clean up their back yards and to clear out the weeds. Each three months the SESP sends a team of men to spray all homes and public buildings with DDT, and the major foci of mosquito breeding near the town have been eradicated. New cases of malaria are now rare among the townspeople. While 16 per cent of 354 individuals examined in Itá in 1942 showed positive blood smears for malaria, by June of 1944 less than one per cent of 337 examined were positive. Itá, which was once famous along the Amazon for its serious and almost annual epidemics, is now relatively free of malaria.

In a two-year period (1944–1945), 6,329 people were attended in the Itá health clinic of SESP; it administered 1,069 anti-smallpox vaccinations (100 per cent of the townspeople and many in the rural districts and in nearby towns) and 469 anti-typhoid immunizations. A health club was formed among the school children in order to stimulate interest in modern health habits. Pamphlets, posters, talks by the physician, slide projections, and home visits by the *visitadora* (a young nurse's-aide trained by the SESP) are being used to educate the people of Itá in better health habits and in the advantages of the public-health program. The *curiosas* (midwives) were invited to the health post for instruction in the simple hygienic principles to be followed while attending a childbirth. These mid-wives have been provided with sterile gauze, sterilized instruments, and simple equipment to make their services safer to their patients. Most people of Itá still get their water, both for drinking and for general household uses, from the river or from a few wells, all of which the health service has classified as dangerous; but the people of Itá hope to be able to construct a water-supply system in the near future, as other Amazon towns have already done, through a cooperative plan with SESP. By 1948 the SESP was an integral part of community life. It had already become a necessity for the Itá people. Rumors that the federal government might bring the service to an end because the United States Government might not renew its contract with Brazil to continue the joint health service caused considerable stir. The people of Itá were indignant that they might lose their physician and the benefits of the health post. They criti-cized both their own federal government and the policy of the United States, which was only that, they claimed, of "a wartime friend."

Higher prices for rubber and concomitant high prices for other products during World War II also stimulated Itá on fronts other than public health. Taxes levied on rubber and palm-nut exports raised the municipal income. As a consequence, the construction of the town hall was finally completed in 1947, except for the installa-tion of the tile floors. After thirty years of delay, the town of Itá repeated its ostentatious folly. The cost of finishing the town hall left the municipality so heavily in debt that the municipal income from taxes was mortgaged for years. Still, the municipal government had somehow been able to find funds to repair the public dock, to build the two-family bungalows mentioned earlier, and to pay work-ers to weed the streets from time to time. The federal government had built a new schoolhouse which was designed for use as a night school for adults but which was being used as a primary school. With gifts accumulated by the devotees of St. Benedict, the church had been repaired. There were high hopes of converting to Diesel fuel the wood-burning electric generator which had been installed

many years ago and no longer functioned. Better conditions had by
1948 attracted a few people back to the town; from a low of less
than 300 people in the 1930's, Itá had almost 500 people in 1948
and more than 600 in 1950.

Despite a few improvements, however, Itá is still a backward,
decadent, and isolated community. There was no telegraph or wire-
less station in 1948; the Amazon Cable Company, which once maintained a station there, had ceased to function. A PBY seaplane of
the Panair do Brasil (a Pan-American World Airways affiliate)
stopped once a week going upriver from Belém and once a week on
its downriver run from Manaus to bring mail and a rare passenger.
Most of the boats of SNAPP, a riverboat company owned by the
federal government, stopped at Itá, and occasionally a privately
owned river steamer made a call. During a three-month period
twelve river steamers stopped at Itá to leave and to pick up mail,
to deliver merchandise, and to load rubber and a few other exports.
Considering its meager commerce and the trickle of mail which
flows in and out of Itá, these communication facilities would seem
to be more than adequate. During a normal month only about forty
letters are received in the post office, and about the same number
are dispatched. The bulk of any incoming mail is directed to the
various government officials or to commercial houses, and most of
the outgoing mail consists of government reports. There is little
movement of merchandise in and out of the town itself because most
of the exports from the municipality are shipped from downriver
trading posts directly to Belém.

A mirror of the backwardness of Itá is the size of its reading public
and its facilities for formal education. In 1948 only two people in
town regularly received newspapers or magazines, although this
reading matter was borrowed by about ten others. More than 40
per cent of the townspeople and almost 80 per cent of the rural
population of the community were completely illiterate: those who
read with ease were a small handful. There was little knowledge of
the outside world and little interest; the mayor had a battery-run
radio and each evening five or six people gathered outside his house

to hear the news broadcast from Rio de Janeiro. Furthermore, the school system offered little hope for a more enlightened and literate public. In the entire municipality of over seven thousand inhabitants, there were seven one-room primary schools, each with one teacher. Two of these schools were in the Itá community—one in the town and another in the small settlement of Jocojó. The teachers, who were women, were not graduates of the state normal school; both had as their major qualification for teaching, the ability to read and write. These two primary schools in the Itá community, like all primary schools in Brazil, are co-educational. In Brazil primary schools have five grades, but the Itá schools offer only the first three years. The two teachers are not equipped to teach the fourth and fifth year. In 1948, 61 students (26 boys and 35 girls) matriculated in the town school, but there was an average attendance of only 40 to 45 students. The school in Jocojó had 36 students enrolled but only 20 or 25 came to school on any one day. Most of the children of school age (7 to 12 years) of the two settlements were enrolled, but few ever finished the three-year course, or for that matter ever learned to do more than write their own names and painfully spell out the meaning of a simple sentence. Only one child received the "certificate" for finishing the course in 1946 and only two in 1947.[22]

The school system of Itá is theoretically regulated by the Department of Education of the state of Pará. Actually, the schools are seldom, if ever, inspected, and they are run more or less according to the ideas and whims of the two teachers. The town school is held five days a week from about 8:00 A.M. until noon; the hours are a little vague because the teacher's clock often stops and it is seldom synchronized with the other clocks of Itá. There is a midyear vacation in July and the long vacations last from December until mid-February. The town school was almost totally without teaching materials in June of 1948, but in August a long-awaited

---

[22] No schooling whatsoever was provided for the rural families of the community except for Jocojó. More than half of the two thousand people in the community lacked educational facilities entirely.

shipment of supplies, sent by the Department of Education, arrived from Belém. It contained 26 ABC books, 27 multiplication tables, 12 pencils, 11 penholders, 20 pen points, 7 envelopes, 1 eraser, 1 blotter, 1 package of chalk, 1 small bottle of red ink, 60 short educational pamphlets, 72 sheets of writing paper, and an attendance book for the teacher. This was to supply more than sixty students for the entire year, and it had to be divided with the Jocojó school. Furthermore, in 1948 neither teacher had received her pay for five months and the town teacher threatened continually to leave. Theoretically, reading, writing, arithmetic, Portuguese grammar, and "general notions of geography" are taught, but since the town teacher was in 1948 also the town *beata* (religious devotee) who cared for the church, stories of saints and prayers were taught whenever possible.

This situation is more or less representative of the entire Brazilian Amazon. The state of Pará, with a population of more than 900,000 people, had only 81,592 children enrolled in primary schools in 1936—about one-third of the children of school age (7 to 11). In 1936 only 3,000 children were graduated from the primary schools. In the entire state there were only six secondary schools, all of which were in Belém, and all but one were maintained either by religious groups or as private enterprises. As stated earlier, over 60 per cent of the total population of the Valley is illiterate and it is obvious to anyone who knows the rural districts intimately that many of those classed as literate are "semi-literate," reading only with great difficulty and able only to sign their names. Unless educational facilities are made available to Itá and to other Amazon communities, it must be expected that the region will continue to be backward. Permanent success cannot be expected for a public-health program such as that being carried forward by the SESP, or for any other development program, unless the educational level of the people of the Valley is raised.

Itá is backward in other ways. The traditional predatory economic pattern of the Amazon Valley continues in Itá as it does in most rural zones throughout the Valley. People still live by collecting rubber and other natural products of the forest or by the old Indian slash-and-burn methods of agriculture. In fact, agriculture in the community is so weakly developed that most of the basic foodstuffs must be imported. Itá not only imports beans, rice, sugar, coffee, and canned goods but also large quantities of manioc flour, which is the staple of the people's diet. When the price paid for rubber or another extractive product is high, agriculture is often almost totally neglected. The collectors live on canned goods and dried foods such as dried fish, meat, beans, and rice imported at tremendous cost from southern Brazil. Practically all manufactured articles, from matches and needles to machinery of any kind, come from southern Brazil or from abroad. Transportation is slow, inefficient, and costly. It takes a month to six weeks for a shipment to reach Belém at the mouth of the Amazon River from Rio de Janeiro or Santos, and much longer to reach Itá. Manufactured articles and imported foods are thus exceedingly expensive when they arrive. The exaggerated idea of a "normal profit" held by local merchants and the relatively low prices paid for products of the forest make such prices even higher to the collector or farmer of Itá. The economic structure of Itá, and of most of the Amazon Valley, is still oriented toward export for the foreign market as it was in the past. As in most colonial areas of the world, such orientation actually deprives people of the basic necessities of life by directing their efforts toward the production of raw materials for export rather than toward production for their own consumption. The result, especially during periods of low prices for these exported raw materials, is a low standard of living—even poverty.

Out of the historical background of Itá and of the entire region emerge the basic reasons for its relative backwardness. A culture is above all a product of history—of the man-made sequence of events and influences which combine through time to create the present way of life in any area. The aboriginal cultures of the Amazon forest were well adapted to the tropical environment, but their technological adaptation was of such simple form that it offered only survival or bare subsistence to the European newcomer. In the first two centuries of the colonial rule, during which a new way of life took form in the Amazon Valley, the European contributed little in the way of new technical equipment or practices that added to man's ability to wrestle a living from the Amazon environment. From the beginning the Valley offered little to lure the European, who came looking for quick wealth, as did the Spanish conquistadors. The few Portuguese attracted to the region soon established a slave system using the native people to collect the native products of the forest for export. Neither the most efficient European technology nor the most advanced Western social organization and ideology was brought to the Amazon. After 1500 the region remained as marginal to the newly developing colonial societies of the New World as it had been marginal to the centers of complex civilization in aboriginal times.

Both the slave system and the extractive economy established early by the European colonists have left an indelible mark on Amazon society. The slave system has resulted in a highly crystallized class system. There is an attitude of dispraisal of all physical labor on the part of those who are not descendants of slaves, and an attitude of contentment with cheap human labor rather than a desire to adopt labor-saving devices. The dominant class has been content, too, with the continuation of the native system of agriculture, which allows the people of the Valley to eke out an existence from the land. Instead of improving the techniques and methods of agriculture, their efforts have been directed toward the increase of the production of extractive products. One cannot change what has gone before; but out of a study of the past it becomes clear that the most serious barrier to a better standard of living for the inhabitants of the Amazon Valley is man's inability to direct his efforts for his own benefit. With different technological equipment and with a different orientation of Amazon society, a different social and cultural adjustment might have been created.

If the present reasons for the backwardness of the Amazon Valley are mainly social and cultural in nature, and are thus man-made, then there are no immutable barriers to man's ability to plan and to control the direction of its future development. Obviously, there are numerous limitations imposed by the physical environment and climate, and, what is equally obvious, economic and social problems cannot be solved locally because the Amazon region is intimately tied to Brazil as a nation and to the world beyond. Still, social change, whether it comes as a reflection of changes in the nation and the international scene, or as the result of purely local developments, ultimately involves changes in the society and the culture of the local community. It is on this level, within the framework of the small community, that the social anthropologist is best equipped to offer help to the social planner and to the administrator charged with health programs, agricultural reform, educational campaigns, and other efforts toward improving economic and social conditions.

3. MAKING A LIVING IN THE TROPICS

The majority of the people of the Brazilian Amazon region earn their living by antiquated methods and techniques which have long been superseded in other parts of Brazil and in most parts of the Western World. The contemporary resident of rural Amazonia purchases manufactured articles from modern factories, travels on steam or Diesel-driven river steamers, sees modern ocean-going transports and airplanes, and depends upon the vagaries of distant markets and of government policies; yet most of these people make a living by primitive hand agriculture (technically it is horticulture), by hunting and fishing, by collecting the natural products of the forest, or by some combination of these activities. Although people have iron tools, a few new crops, and numerous imported foods and articles, the basic crops and methods of agriculture have been little changed since aboriginal times. The actual products collected from the forest are nowadays dictated by distant markets, but they are still mainly those known to the Indian.

As it was for the aboriginal people before them, the staple in the diet of the people of the Brazilian Amazon is manioc, or cassava, as it is sometimes called. This root crop, which is by now diffused throughout the tropical world into Africa and Asia, is native to America. Manioc is a hearty plant, well adapted to the tropics and to the leached tropical soils. It grows in a variety of soils. It resists insects, especially the saúva ant, better than most crops. It prospers either in heavy or in light rainfall. In the Amazon, terra firme is considered the best land for manioc plantations. A site cleared out of virgin forest is, of course, to be preferred, but in the vicinity of most Amazon towns and villages most of the original forest on terra firme has at one time or another been cleared away. *Capoeira alta* (high second growth) is generally the best available land for manioc gardens. People living near the towns are forced to plant on *capoeira baixa* (low second growth). In the floodlands some maize, rice, and beans, which are quick-growing crops, are raised between the annual rise and fall of the river. Sometimes squash, beans, yams, peppers, peanuts, pineapples, and bananas are planted on the same plot with manioc on terra firme. In general, however, the Amazon farmer is a producer of manioc.

It is commonly said in Itá that every particle of the manioc tuber is used. Even the peelings are fed to the chickens. From the poisonous juice of the bitter variety of manioc, a famous Amazon sauce called *tucupí* is prepared by exposing it to the sun in a bottle for fifteen to twenty days. From the fine powder, rich in sugar, which is sifted out in making manioc flour, the people of Itá prepare *mingau de tapioca* (a sweet pudding). From this same powder and from a heavy dough prepared from the tuber, *beiju*, a sort of biscuit, is made. By far the most common form of preparing manioc is as *farinha* or manioc flour. This flour, with a consistency like that of coarse corn meal, is present at all Itá meals. It is eaten dry, mixed with gravy or grease as *farofa*, or simply mixed with a little water as *chibé*. A family of five people normally consumes two kilos or more of *farinha* each day.

The preparation of manioc flour is a time-consuming task. In Itá both varieties of manioc, the sweet or non-venomous variety and the larger tubers of bitter variety (*mandioca braba*), which contain a high percentage of prussic acid, are used in making flour. Because bitter manioc is larger and more productive, however, most of the flour is of that variety. Essentially, the methods of making manioc flour are those used by the tribal Amazon Indians. The main task is that of removing the poisonous liquid. Two methods are used. First, after the tuber has been peeled, it is grated either on a toothed grater by hand or with a *caitetu*, a cylindrical grater revolved by a set of bicycle-type gears turned by hand. Then the venomous juice is squeezed out of the grated pulp. A tubular basket, called a *tipití*, is used for this purpose as it was in aboriginal times. The pulp is stuffed into this long, flexible tube, and as the *tipití* is stretched the liquid is squeezed out. Or the juice is removed with a box-like press, the top of which is forced downward with a cantilever device. Once the juice has been removed, the dough is forced through a sieve to take out the fiber and coarse grains. Finally, it is toasted on a large copper griddle.

A second way of making manioc flour differs in the method used for preparing the tuber. Instead of being grated, the tuber is placed in a stream or in a trough of water for about four days until it is *puba*, that is, softened to the point of semi-decay. The skin can then be easily removed, the juice squeezed out, the soft dough passed through a sieve, and then toasted. In Itá the best *farinha* is made by a combination of the two methods. Half of the tubers are grated and half are allowed to soften in the water. The dough of both is mixed before toasting. It takes a man and his wife a full day's work to prepare one alqueire (30 kilos, or about 66 pounds) of *farinha* after the tuber has been harvested.

Each year in the summer, from June through August, the Itá farmer works at clearing a site for his manioc gardens. His first job is to clear away the underbrush with a bush knife; then the large trees are felled with an ax. For a month or six weeks the brush and fallen trees are allowed to dry, and in September or October, depending upon when the clearing was done, the site is burned off. The farmer then begins the dirty job called *coivara*, which consists of gathering together the partially burned trunks into piles and digging out the worst of the unburned root systems. The more thoroughly the site is burned off, the less difficult is the job of *coivara*. The garden is now ready for planting, although to the unpracticed eye it seems to be but a tangled half-cleared area burned out of the forest. Planting takes place from late October through December, during the early rains of the winter months. "Shoots" or "cuts" taken from the stalk of the bush are planted in the earth, where they soon take root. Sometimes secondary crops such as *jerimú* (a squash), maize, watermelon, and peppers are planted in the same area; they are fast-growing plants and may be harvested before the bush-like vegetation of the manioc takes over.

Manioc is a slow-growing plant. It is usually mature only after one full year of growth; but it may be harvested after six months, while it is green, before the tubers have reached full size. Even after it is ripe, however, harvesting may be done at intervals, as the tubers are needed for a period of almost a year. In harvesting, the manioc bush is cut away and the tubers are dug from the ground with a hoe. Most Itá farmers immediately replant manioc on the same spot, and as they harvest they progressively replant the same garden site. Because the second planting is about half as productive as the first, a garden site is generally replanted only once. After the second harvest the site is allowed to return to bush. This in general is the agricultural cycle of Itá manioc cultivation.

The farm work involved in manioc cultivation, however, varies in accordance with the type of land selected. Virgin forest and high second growth are more difficult to clear than low brush, but the fresh soils guarantee a higher production. The clearing of low second growth or brush is an easier task and the job of *coivara* is generally not necessary, but weeds grow fast in such an area and the harvest is less productive. Itá farmers estimate that one man working alone in a garden site of one *tarefa* [1] of high second-growth forest would spend five days clearing the underbrush, five days felling the large trees, one day burning off the area, five days piling up the brush and digging up the roots (*coivara*), and twenty days planting the garden. While the manioc was growing he would spend an additional sixteen days clearing away the worst of the weeds. Thus the Itá farmer has invested some forty-two work days for one tarefa of manioc. The time involved on one tarefa of virgin forest would be somewhat more and on a tarefa of low brush considerably less.

The work on a garden, however, is never carried out by one man alone, nor is it done as systematically as this estimate might make it appear. First, a work day for the Amazon farmer is rarely from dawn to dusk. Generally, the farmer leaves his house early in the morning after taking a small demitasse of black coffee and a handful of manioc flour. He works until midday, or slightly after, returning to his house for a heavy midday meal. After his meal he rests and spends the afternoon at other tasks.

A full day is spent in the field only when the farmer is a participant or the host of a *puxirão* or *convite*, as the cooperative work parties are called. These work parties may be organized for any of the various tasks of manioc cultivation, but they are most commonly held for the heavy work of clearing the garden site. The host on such an occasion issues an invitation to several men—to close relatives, to *compadres*,[2] or to friends. Sometimes neighbors, knowing that a work party is planned, will appear without special invitation. The size of such work parties varies considerably. Juca, a farmer

---

[1] A *tarefa* is 25 *braças* by 25 *braças*; in Itá a *braça* is 2.5 meters, and a *tarefa* is thus 3906.25 square meters.

[2] See p. 151.

who lives in Itá and plants just outside of town, always invites only four or five old friends, individuals with whom he has worked for many years. In Jocojó a cooperative work party will generally be attended by the fifteen or twenty men living in the neighborhood. On such occasions the host takes care of all expenses. He serves coffee at his house before leaving for the field; he buys cigarettes or tobacco for the participants; and he supplies *cachaça* (a crude sugar-cane rum) for an occasional nip during the work and for a *mata-bicho* (literally "kill the animal") before the midday meal. The host's wife, assisted by the wives of the guests, prepares a large meal. A pig or several chickens are killed for a large work party. A host remembers who has participated in his work party when an occasion arises, for the workers are never paid in money and it may be several seasons before the host has a chance to repay his guests with a similar amount of work. "We work twice as fast when we work together," explained one farmer, and people prefer to do the heavy agricultural work in cooperative work parties.

In addition, families work together in some of the tasks in the field. The clearing of the field, the burning, and the *coivara* are male endeavors; but wives work alongside their husbands at planting and during the infrequent weedings of the garden, as well as in harvesting the tubers and in manufacturing flour. Thus a man and his wife will be able to plant a tarefa in ten days, which if he worked alone would require twenty days' labor. Together a man and his wife can weed a field in eight days' time as well as he could do it alone in sixteen days. Together they should be able to prepare one alqueire of *farinha* in one day.

Itá farmers estimated that a family must have at least four tarefas (15,625 square meters) of garden with ripe manioc in order to be able to supply the needs of a family of five and to have a surplus for sale if they wish to live from farming alone. To do so, a man must plant a new site of four tarefas each year. Thus, in September of 1948 a farmer should have, for example, four tarefas of manioc which was first planted in 1946 and replanted during 1947 from which he can still harvest a few tubers. He should also have four tarefas of manioc planted in 1947 which is just fully mature. And during the previous months he should have cleared four tarefas to be planted in October or November. He therefore would be using twelve tarefas of land, or approximately 46,875 square meters at one time. This estimate is based on his own needs, the prices paid for his surplus product, and the average productivity of the land. It will be seen, however, that it is about the maximum amount of land which a family might be able to work without extra help.

One tarefa of relatively good land (that is, forest or high second growth) will produce enough tubers to make approximately 900 kilos of manioc flour, and the same plot when replanted progressively as the first crop is harvested will produce about half that amount. A man who plants four tarefas of land each year should be able to manufacture some 5,400 kilos of *farinha*—3,600 from his new gardens and 1,800 from his replanted gardens—during the year. His family, if he has a wife and three children, will consume about 720 kilos of manioc flour in a year, leaving him 4,680 kilos, or in local terms some 156 alqueires (30 kilos to the alqueire) for sale. At the prices paid in 1948, this would bring him the sum of about $351 (in cruzeiros, cr. $7,020.),[3] which is an income higher than the average income either of the low-class townsfolk or of the farmers. It is not a good income, however, in view of the cost of medicines, of clothes, of household equipment, of patronizing a festival, and of other necessary expenditures for his family. Under the best circumstances manioc farming with the tools and methods now employed in Itá provides only a bare subsistence.

Furthermore, if an Itá farmer were to carry out the ideal program, as described above, he would have little time for anything else—for fishing, for repairing his house, for building or repairing a canoe. Theoretically, the agricultural work for four tarefas each year would add up to 168 days of work, and theoretically it would take another 360 days for him alone to prepare 5,400 kilos of manioc flour. If his

---

[3] The rate of exchange is calculated at 20 Brazilian cruzeiros to the dollar, the approximate official rate in 1948. The "open market" rate of exchange, at the time, was about 24 to 25 cruzeiros to the dollar.

wife aided him in planting, in weeding, and in manufacturing flour, the time would still amount to 330 work days, certainly a full-time employment. Actually, of course, few Itá farmers have four tarefas of manioc garden in production, and the few who did in 1948 had growing sons or other dependent relatives to help them. According to estimates which 39 town dwellers made of their gardens, planted the year before, they had on the average only 2.7 tarefas in manioc. The estimates given by 29 rural farmers averaged only 2.9 tarefas per man. Only 11 town dwellers and only 10 rural farmers of a total of 68 farmers who gave us estimates had as much as four tarefas of mature manioc.[4]

Very few people, therefore, earn a living from agriculture alone. Almost without exception, Itá farmers must augment their incomes from other activities, and many people plant only for their own consumption. Townspeople work as day laborers, for which they are paid 15 cruzeiros (about $0.75) per day, and the farmers who live in the rural neighborhoods work at extractive industries— collecting palm nuts, timbo vine, and rubber, or cutting firewood for the river steamers. Each year the younger men of the small village of Jocojó leave after the festivals of St. John and St. Apollonio in July to work in the rubber trails in the Island region. They return only in October in time to finish clearing garden sites and to plant their gardens before the heavy winter rains begin. Even those farmers, such as Jorge Porto, who own land and who are among the few "full-time" farmers must work rubber trails or spend some time during the year working at another activity which brings in cash. Itá is a farming community where it is very difficult to derive even a minimum living from farming alone.

The community of Itá, and in fact the whole Amazon Valley, does not produce enough basic foodstuffs to feed even its present sparse population. According to the records kept by the local statistical agent in Itá, more than 350,000 kilos of manioc flour, 5,000

[4] In 1948 we were able to measure the gardens which twenty Itá farmers had prepared for planting in manioc. These gardens, which would be harvested in 1949, averaged only 2.6 tarefas; only 5 men had four tarefas.

kilos of beans, 47,000 kilos of sugar, and 34,000 kilos of coffee—all of which might have been grown locally—were imported into the municipality. The age-old Indian system of cultivation is inefficient and unproductive in comparison with more modern methods used in Europe and in North America. The land which is exploited in Itá, the terra firme, is mediocre compared to the low-lying islands and lowland banks of the Amazon, the floodlands. These low areas of the municipality offer a great potentiality for the cultivation of wet rice, sugar cane, Indian jute, and of such quick-growing food crops as beans and maize which may be planted and harvested during the summer when the river is low.[5] Even a minimal use of modern agricultural knowledge and techniques would increase the production in the region several times over. Better transportation and a few innovations, such as centralized flour factories, simple machinery, and traction animals, might increase agricultural production in Itá as they have in the Belém-Bragança region near the mouth of the Amazon. But as long as the present predatory agricultural methods persist, food will remain a basic problem.

II

The tropical forest Indians who inhabited the Amazon region before the arrival of the European depended, in addition to their gardens, upon hunting and fishing for their sustenance. In the early days of the European era, hunting and fishing were of great importance in feeding the colonists and their slaves. It was the Indian who taught the European newcomer to live in the strange Amazon environment. The Indian was the hunter and fisherman, and the methods of hunting and fishing of contemporary Amazon regional culture are therefore mainly of aboriginal origin. Although the modern inhabitant of the Valley hunts with a shotgun or a .44 caliber rifle or fishes with a metal fishhook or a European-type net, he does so with knowledge of the local fauna derived from his Indian cul-

[5] Pierre Gourou, "L'Amazonie," *Cahiers d'Outre Mer*, Vol. II, No. 5 (1949), pp. 1–13.

tural heritage. In addition, numerous aboriginal techniques are still used, and many folk beliefs of Indian origin persist in regard to hunting and fishing. Nowadays, however, neither hunting nor fishing is important in the regional economy. Along the main arteries of the Amazon River system, hunting is no longer a lucrative occupation. After centuries of human occupation, the country has been hunted out.[6]

In such Amazon communities as Itá, hunting has become almost a pastime; no one would depend upon the results of the hunt for food. Fishing is still relatively important, however, as a subsistence activity. Although fish are less numerous than formerly in the main rivers, most Amazon families fish for their own consumption and a few often have a surplus for sale. In some localities, such as in Santarém at the mouth of the Tapajoz River, there are professional fishermen. In the backwater lakes, or *igapós*, of the upper Amazon, the giant *pirarucu*, a fish which sometimes weighs four hundred pounds, is harpooned to be dried and salted and sold up and down the river as "Brazilian codfish."

The most favorable months for fishing in the vicinity of Itá are those of the summer, from June to December. During these months the small streams, swollen during the rainy season, return to their banks or dry up, and the fish return to the main streams. In August and September several species of fish start their annual migration up the Amazon to the headwaters to deposit their eggs. In June and July fresh-water shrimp move up river. During the summer months fish are plentiful in Itá and are a major item in the diet of most families. During the winter months (the rainy season), on the contrary, there are times when the only fish to be had is dried *pirarucu*, imported codfish, or tinned sardines and tuna. From January to May the Amazon and its tributaries are swollen; the tributary streams overflow into the forest and, as people say, "the fish go to the forest." During these months fishing by hook and line, by

[6] Excellent hunting areas are still found, however, in the headwaters of the Amazon tributaries—in the state of Mato Grosso to the south and along the Guiana frontier to the north.

trap, by net, and other methods used during the summer is impossible, and only a few fish may be speared in the flooded lowlands.

Several methods of fishing are used during the summer months. The most common, of course, is by hook and line. Every evening in Itá people may be seen moving out into the river in their canoes for a few hours' fishing, and some men fish late into the night with fish lines. The most productive methods, however, are the use of poison, traps, or nets. In Itá only one type of net, the *tarafa*, a circular net, thrown by one man, is used. Traps are of several varieties. The largest is a permanent fish trap, the *cacurí*, which projects out into the river some thirty to fifty meters. In 1948 there were five traps in Itá. They were owned by Abilio Costa, a storekeeper, by Dona Dora Cesar Andrade, by Benedicto Marajó and his brother, and by Juca in partnership with the barber, Ernesto Morais. The trap owned by Dona Dora was first built by her husband some twenty years ago, and it has been repaired or rebuilt each year since. Its location is considered especially good, and each year her catch in fish is superior to the others. The trap owned by Juca and the barber is new, having been built in 1948 at the cost of almost $50 (cr. $1000). It is estimated that it must be rebuilt again after two years at almost the same cost; thus few people can afford this type of permanent fish trap.

The trap takes the form of a wall of stakes made of the trunk of the assai palm, which protrudes out into the river and forms a barrier to the fish moving upstream or being carried downstream by the current. At the end of the barrier there is a circular trap into which the fish move, and beyond this trap is a smaller inner chamber which may be closed when the fish are to be removed. During the early part of the summer, trap owners expect to catch only a few kilos of fish each day, but as the fish migrate upriver later in the season they sometimes remove a hundred kilos daily, selling most of the catch to the townspeople. In 1946, considered an excellent year for fish, Dona Dora Cesar Andrade took some 2,000 kilos of fish from her trap. She sold about 300 kilos locally at 4 cruzeiros (20 cents) a kilo, and exported the rest salted to Belém.

In 1948, though Juca and his partner expected to catch less than half that amount of fish, they nevertheless hoped to catch enough to supply their families and to be able to sell the rest on the local market to pay for their trap.

People without the money and the time to build a trap, and especially those who live along the banks of the small streams, often fish by blocking off the stream with *tapagems* (barrier traps). Itá is far enough downstream on the Amazon to feel some effect of the ocean tides. A very small difference in the water level in the main channels causes many small tributaries to fill up and to drain empty twice each day during the dry season. The Amazon fisherman builds a barrier across such small streams, with a gate which can be opened to allow fish to enter upstream with the incoming tide and which can be closed to trap them as the tide flows out. For several months each year such traps provide a welcome addition to the tables of many rural families. In addition, in shallow pools or in small streams, many people fish with timbo roots or the *tingui* vine. The shredded root or the crushed vine produces a poison which, when placed in a half-dry pool or shallow stream, stupefies the fish so that they rise to the surface and are easily caught. Fish are also speared or shot with the bow and arrow; in many rural homes one still sees the *espeque*, a multi-pointed lance or a bow and arrow of the type once used by the Amazon Indian.

Though hunting is not an important activity in Itá, there are an interest and preoccupation with it that are inconsistent with its contribution to people's livelihood. Many rubber gatherers carry a shotgun with them on their daily round on the rubber trail; sometimes an agouti, a paca, a wild forest fowl such as the jacu, or even a wild pig crosses their path and they may make a kill. A few rural farmers who own rifles or shotguns spend a day or so now and again hunting. Sometimes they set a *tocaia*, a trap formed by arming a gun so that it will go off when an animal attempts to make off with the bait or when the animal breaks a string stretched across the trail. With a *tocaia* a farmer may sometimes kill a small forest deer or a paca which comes to graze in his garden. Hunting, therefore, sometimes provides a welcome addition to the relatively meatless diet of the rural population.

Yet the intense interest in hunting in Itá and the numerous folk beliefs which cluster around the sport are a reminder of a time when hunting had a basic importance in the town's economy. In the rural neighborhoods of Itá several men are famed as hunters. Such men are Eneas Ramos and Domingos Alves. Both earn their living from other pursuits—agriculture or rubber collecting. Domingos is a farmer living near his gardens only two or three kilometers from the town. He hunts two or three nights a week. He owns two dogs trained for hunting the paca and he owns both a rifle and a muzzle-loading shotgun. Domingos almost died in 1947 from a broken leg resulting from a fall when running through the thick underbrush after a tapir he had wounded. There is generally game (*embiara*) in his house. The almost inevitable subject of conversation either with Domingos or with old Eneas Ramos is hunting. Like most devotees, they tell graphically of successful hunts—of the time they killed a jaguar or of the night they killed two deer. They discuss the habits of animals and the techniques of stalking particular game.

In telling of their hunting experiences, Domingos and other local hunters do not distinguish between the tangible natural world and the supernatural. A class of plants, called by the generic term of *tajá*, of which there are several species, is thought to be of tremendous help to the hunter. There is the *tajá de veado* (for deer), the *tajá de anta* (for tapir), and many others. Hunters plant them near their homes. Each type "calls" or attracts the animal after which it is named, if used correctly by the hunter. Blood from three deer which have been killed by the hunter, for example, must be poured over the leaf of the deer *tajá;* the leaf should then be crushed in the palm of the hand and rubbed over the hunter's forehead, back, and arms. If this is repeated several times, he will have the power to attract deer as he wanders in the forest. Hunters also tell of the dangers, both supernatural and natural (but equally real to them), of hunting. The giant constrictor, the Giboia, sometimes attacks a hunter. A hunter may pass by the Giboia in the forest without seeing it, but the snake has a mysterious force which causes the hunter to wander in circles, always drawing nearer until the Giboia is able to attack him. One should not kill or eat the tree sloth during the month of August, hunters say, because they are with fever and will transmit it to man. In June the large lizards called *jacuruaru* should not be eaten, for they are believed to fight during this time with venomous snakes and thus to be filled with poison.

Other dangers to the hunter are *Anhangá*, a dangerous spirit which takes the form of an animal, and *Curupira*, a small supernatural who lives in the forest and who calls to the hunter, attracting him deeper and deeper into the forest until he is lost.[7] Furthermore, if a hunter "persecutes" a particular species, that is, if he kills too many of the same animal, the animal may steal or rot his shadow, causing him to become insane, to "talk nonsense," to have body aches, and to fall ill with fevers. To protect themselves, hunters like Domingos and Eneas take care not to offend the animals. After killing two or three pacas in a short period, they hunt other game, "a tapir, a deer, and another animal, before again killing a paca." A hunter may wear a cross made of *cera benta* (holy wax from the candles in the church) as protection against *assombração de bicho*, as the spell of the animal is called. Once when Eneas Ramos was hunting, a large howler monkey began to advance upon him. He remembered that he had killed several recently. Eneas turned and ran. The next evening he had fever and headache. Because he knew that the howler monkey had tried to steal his shadow, he resorted at once to a cure. As Eneas related it, he fumigated his body with smoke produced by burning a mixture of a nest of *cunauaru* frog,[8] a bit of holy wax, one dried pepper, and the shavings of a deer horn. This mixture is burned in a ceramic vessel or in a gourd container. It should be passed three times under a hammock in which the patient is stretched, so that the smoke will cover his body. Sometimes the spell of the animal is

---

[7] The belief in these two supernaturals is discussed in more detail in Chapter VII. Both are of Indian origin.

[8] The *cunauaru* is a small frog which nests in hollow trunks. The nest has the consistency of a rosin which produces an aromatic smoke when burned. Throughout the Amazon Valley the nest is burned for medicinal purposes.

so strong that a medicine man, or *pagé*, must be called to bring back the hunter to health.

The difficulty that plagues hunters and fishermen most often, however, is *panema*. A hunter or a fisherman who has had repeated failures which cannot be explained by natural causes attributes them to panema, a negative power which infects a person, his gun, his fish line, or trap. The term has become widely used in rural Amazonia and in the city in the sense of "bad luck." For example, a gambler catches panema and loses steadily. In Itá, however, panema means an "impotence in hunting or fishing" resulting from a supernatural cause. It can be transmitted from one person to another, almost like an infectious disease. By eating game or fish a pregnant woman is believed to be able to transmit panema to the hunter or fisherman who killed or caught it. A man may catch panema from his friends who have ill feeling toward him caused by a disagreement over food. If a hunter's wife carelessly throws the bones of the game into the yard, and a dog or pig eats them, the hunter may suffer from panema. Evil magic made by one's enemies can also cause the condition.

Eneas Ramos related a typical case of a hunter suffering from panema. Many years ago, when he was an active hunter, Eneas killed many deer. During a two-month period, however, he did not see a deer in the forest, although he hunted almost every day. One day a friend mentioned that his wife was several months pregnant. Eneas remembered that he had given his friend portions of deer which he had killed. Eneas knew, then, that the woman was "poisonous" and that she had communicated panema to him. "Not all women are poisonous and cause panema, but Catita was," he said. "When she was pregnant a flower that she picked would wilt at once." Eneas went at once to inform his friend of his predicament; it is considered dangerous for the hunter to seek a cure for panema transmitted by a pregnant woman, for the treatment might well cause her to abort. But Catita knew a way to cure Eneas without bringing on an abortion or stillbirth.[9]

---

[9] See Chapter V for other cases where treatment of panema by hunters brings on abortion and stillbirths in women.

Panema from other sources—from the ill feeling (*desconfiança*) of one's friends, from evil magic, or from dogs or pigs eating the bones of game or fish—is more difficult to diagnose. The hunter or fisherman has no way of knowing of such events; but through his suspicions or through the reconstruction of past events he is generally able to lay his finger upon the cause. Raimundo Profeta, after he was panema, remembered that he had refused a neighbor a piece of venison and attributed his panema to *desconfiança*. Eneas Ramos believes that he once got panema because two children left his house crying when they were refused a piece of tapir meat. In another case, when envious neighbors collected the fishbones from a fisherman's yard and gave them to the pigs to eat, his fish lines and his net became panema and his catches were negligible during the best months of the fishing season. An enemy may also, by throwing the bones of the animal or fish into a privy, cause the hunter or fisherman to suffer from panema. So great is the danger of catching panema that many hunters and fishermen hesitate to sell meat or fish. They will make presents only to relatives or close friends in whom they have confidence and whose womenfolk they know not to be pregnant.[10] This is especially true when a fisherman has a new fish line. Under no circumstances should the fish be eaten by anyone other than the immediate family, for the line and the fisherman are especially vulnerable to panema. Gustavo Ramos, the son of Eneas, threw the bones from fish caught with his new lines high on the roof of his house, so that they could not be reached by dogs or pigs or picked up by a stranger.

There are numerous prescriptions for curing panema. Most of them are concoctions in which garlic and pepper are the main ingredients, and they are used in the form of baths or fumigations. The composition, the dosage, and the number of treatments vary widely with the individual's preference and with the seriousness of the case. Old Eneas Ramos, as a famous hunter, also knows many cures for panema. People come from the rural districts of Itá asking him to treat them, and he gladly dispenses his knowledge without

---

[10] Domingos Alves avoids this danger by giving or selling only the meat removed from the bone.

charge. One of Eneas's strongest prescriptions for a hunter suffering
from panema is this: Mash into a gourd of water a bit of the nest
of the *cauré* hawk, a bit of the nest of the *cunauaru* frog, a bit of the
leaves of the vanilla plant, a few leaves of the *aninga* (a water plant),
two red peppers, and a bit of garlic. Allow the mixture to soak in the
sun and in the "dew of the night" for several days. It should be
applied lightly in a bath on three successive Fridays beginning on a
Friday of a new moon so that the treatment ends before the full
moon. A full moon, he explained, would void the treatment.

Another prescription recommended by Eneas is applied as a fumigation and is somewhat less complex. A bit of the nest of the
cauré hawk, a few peppers, a spider web (specifically, the web of
the *aranha rica*), and a bit of garlic are placed in an open ceramic
bowl over a few burning coals from the fire. The hunter allows the
smoke to pour over his arms, his legs, and over his back. Eneas
recommends that the hunter end the treatment by holding the
ceramic bowl close under his chin, allowing the smoke to curl up
over his face; he should keep his mouth open, allowing saliva to
drop into the bowl until the burning coals are extinguished.

A hunting dog with panema may be treated either with baths
or by fumigations in the same way with the same concoctions. A
contaminated rifle should be treated by blowing smoke from a
fumigation up the barrel. A fish line is washed in a bath prepared
according to the fisherman's favorite prescription or it may be
fumigated with a mixture, preferably in the street or where two
paths cross "where many people pass." It is the practice of Domingos
Alves and several others, during the fishing season, to cure themselves with a fumigation each week, as a preventive.

The Amazon folk beliefs which cluster around hunting and fishing are for the most part aboriginal in origin. Anhangá was considered to be a ghost or a spirit by the Tupí-speaking Indians of
Brazil, and they also believed that it took the form of animals and
birds. Curupira for these Tupían peoples was also a forest demon
much feared by the hunter. Fevers and temporary insanity, which
in Itá are thought to result from the theft of the soul by animals,
is similar to the punishments meted out to the Tenetehara Indian

hunters by the supernatural "Owners of the Forest." Panema, as a loss of power in hunting and fishing, is a belief also shared by these tropical forest Indians in a form almost identical with that of Itá.[11] The strength of the Indian tradition in modern Itá culture seems to concentrate on those aspects of life having to do with man's adaptation to the Amazon environment. The Portuguese and the Negro had to learn how to fish and to hunt the paca, the tapir, and the other New World animals from the native American. As they learned, they also acquired his supernatural beliefs.

These folk beliefs explained, as adequately to the European newcomer lacking modern science as to the Indians themselves, the unpredictability of hunting and fishing. Why is it that a hunter, famed for his knowledge of the habits of deer, skilled at stalking, entirely at home in the forest and generally very successful, will suddenly be unable to find a single deer—or if he does, miss his shots? In Amazon agriculture, however, which also follows Indian methods, supernaturalism does not seem to play much of a part. If a garden grows poorly, people explain that the ants attacked it or that the land selected was not appropriate. They do not charge the lack of a good harvest to the spirits of the forest or even to evil magic. The reason for this difference between hunting and fishing and agriculture, in regard to supernatural explanations, lies in the nature of the agricultural pursuit. In the Amazon, agriculture centers upon manioc, a plant which is exceedingly hardy. A failure of a manioc crop is almost unheard of. Unlike the situation in semi-arid regions, rainfall is not a variable factor. Although Amazonian agriculture is primitive and relatively unproductive, it is not uncertain and unpredictable; for this reason supernatural explanations are less called upon.

III

From the beginning, one of the products which Europeans sought in the Amazon Valley was rubber from the tree *Hevea brasiliensis;*

---

[11] Cf. Charles Wagley and Eduardo Galvão, *The Tenetehara Indians of Brazil* (New York, 1949), pp. 58 ff. and 102 ff.

but for over two centuries, rubber was only one of many useful products to be gathered in the Amazon forest. It was exported in small quantities to be used for shoes, for rubber balls, for bottles, for waterproofing fabrics, and other similar purposes. Not until the process of vulcanization was developed in the middle of the last century was Amazon rubber sought after in any great quantity. Since then the collection of latex from the wild rubber tree has been one of the major economic activities of the Valley, and it continues to be so, despite the competition of Eastern-plantation rubber.

Within the municipality of Itá, the low islands and the lowland margins of the rivers and tributaries contain rubber forests which produce a latex known as "delta type," which is second in quality only to the *Acre fino* produced in the upper tributaries of the Amazon Valley. Rubber still represents over 50 per cent of the total value of the municipal exports. In 1946, 58,479 kilos of "fine rubber" were sent downriver to Belém, and 30,881 kilos were exported in 1947. Most of this rubber comes from the distant areas of the municipality, but some rubber is collected near the town and rubber collection is an important aspect of Itá's economic life. Most Itá men have at one time or another worked as rubber collectors. Many go each year to work for a few months in the nearby islands of the delta, and a few have signed up to work in the rich rubber forests of the upper Xingú River or upper Tapajoz River. In years when rubber prices are high, Itá families move across the Amazon mainstream to the island lowlands, abandoning their farms to collect rubber. When rubber prices drop, there is a steady migration to terra firme and to farming. But even with low prices, there are always many families who continue to work at collecting rubber, as they have all their lives, and many others who work at rubber collecting during part of the year to supplement their incomes. Wild rubber is the principal "money crop" of Itá.

The methods of exploiting the native rubber forest determine, to a great extent, the settlement patterns and the spacial distribution of population in rubber-collecting areas, and these methods are approximately the same throughout the Valley. Thus, a knowledge of the traditional system of rubber collection is important for the understanding of rural Amazon society. Rubber-producing Hevea trees are not found in homogeneous groves; in general rubber trees are spaced through the forest fifty to one hundred meters apart. A collector must clear a path from one tree to another. Such a path, connecting approximately 100 trees (or 150 to 200 in the upper tributaries where trees are closer together), forms an *estrada* (road). These roads generally begin near the dwelling of the seringueiro and form a large circle ending somewhere near its start. In the Island Region of the Amazon delta, rubber roads average four to seven kilometers in length, depending upon the spacing of the trees in the forest. It is customary for each seringueiro to work two roads; he collects from only one road each day, allowing the trees on the other to rest. To take latex from a tree in successive days is said to tire the tree, lowering its production of latex. The huts of the rubber gatherers are, therefore, generally situated at a considerable distance apart; they are found about one to two kilometers from each other along the bank of the mainstream or of a small tributary. The rubber roads run inland and back from their houses, and the river is always their means of communication with the trading post or with the town.

The working day of the rubber collector begins before sunup, as early as three or four o'clock in the morning in the high tributaries, and somewhat later in the island region. An early start is thought to be necessary because the tree is said to produce more *leite* (milk) when it is cool and before the morning winds rise. The collector's first job is the cutting (*corte*) of the bark, or the bleeding (*sangra*) to allow the latex to flow. Among collectors and among the *seringalistas* (the owners of rubber forests) there is much discussion as to the best method of cutting the tree. Most agree nowadays that the type of *corte* called the *bandeira* (flag) causes less harm to the tree. The type of cut called the *espinha* (fishbone) produces more latex but slowly kills the tree. The *espinha* is formed by cutting one deep vertical incision in the bark and additional incisions each day at an angle to this central cut so that they will drain into it.[12] The *bandeira* is a spiral circular incision around the trunk; at each visit to a tree the seringueiro cuts a new spiral directly under that made two days before. Each season the *bandeira* incision begins high on the trunk and is worked downward as the season wears on. Such incisions should not be deep enough to scar the tree permanently; for that reason most owners of rubber forests oblige collectors to use a special knife rather than the small hatchet (*machadinho*) used during the early days of rubber collecting. Under each incision, at the end of the circular spiral cut of the *bandeira*, the collector inserts a small tin cup (*tijela*), about two inches deep, which catches the milky white latex as it slowly oozes forth.

It takes a rubber collector about three to four hours to make the trip over a road, cutting each tree and placing the cups to catch the latex. If he begins at 5:00 A.M., he will be back at his hut by 8:00 or 9:00 A.M. In the upper tributaries of the Amazon Valley, many rubber workers, leaving home earlier and in the dark, wear a headlamp. Much has been written about the great dangers to which the collector is subjected, especially on his early morning round—of poisonous snakes which drop out of the trees, of savage Indians who waylay him, and of the narrow log bridges over which he must pass in swamps. In a few out-of-the-way areas of the Amazon, Indians still attack collectors—generally in reprisal for attacks upon their own villages—and poisonous snakes are known throughout the Valley, but none of the many rubber collectors of Itá with whom we talked had experienced such exotic dangers, even when they worked in the Upper Amazon. Their stories were more concerned with the length of the road and with malaria than with savage Indians or snakes.

Most Itá collectors take only a small demitasse of black coffee, or no nourishment at all, before setting out on their initial round of the rubber trail; but when they return from bleeding the tree they generally have their *almôço* (midday lunch), the major meal of the

---

[12] The *espinha* thus forms a pattern like the vertebra and ribs of a fish.

day. Often, however, the collector must find his lunch before he eats. He must take time out after his first trip around the rubber road to fish, unless he has been lucky enough to kill a forest fowl, an agouti, a paca, or even a wild peccary which he has encountered on the rubber trail. After his meal the collector must make a second round of the trail. This time he collects the liquid from the cups, depositing the latex in a gourd container. In the vicinity of Itá, a rubber road produces only about two or three kilos of liquid latex a day in June and July, the early part of the season. As the season wears on, however, and as the incisions are made lower and on the thicker portions of the trunk, a day's production may rise to four to six kilos. This is still less than the production of the roads in the Upper Amazon tributaries, which give as much as ten kilos per day.

A collector's day is not over, however, when he returns with the day's collection of latex. After having walked some eight to twelve kilometers, he still must *defumar* (coagulate the latex with smoke). After a short rest in a hammock, this job occupies most of his afternoon. It is done in a small palm-thatched hut over a clay fireplace (*buião*). The fireplace is built so that smoke is channeled out through a narrow opening. The best fire for the purpose is kindled with *urucuri* palm nuts, which have a high oil content and provide a great deal of smoke. Green wood placed on a hot fire may also be used. Itá collectors estimate that it takes about an hour to smoke four kilos of liquid latex. The latex is poured gradually over a paddle-like instrument which is slowly turned in the smoke which streams out of the mouth of the fireplace. As the rubber hardens on the paddle, more liquid latex is poured over it until an oval ball is formed of coagulated rubber. Generally, after a layer about a half inch thick has been formed on the paddle, the hardened rubber is removed and wrapped around a pole forming the core for a larger *bolão* (ball). This is added to day by day until it sometimes weighs 75 to 100 kilos. The job of smoking is considered a distasteful one. The fire toasts the legs of the worker and smoke fills the air in the low hut. It is hot inside, and the collector chokes and perspires. Many rubber collectors impute the frequency of pneumonia, and even tuberculosis, to the many hours they spend in smoke huts preparing rubber for the market.

In the Itá region the rubber collector is able to work at his occupation only about five months out of the year, although the collecting season is not much longer in the Upper Amazon. During the winter, from December through May, rain drips into the cups which are attached to the trees to catch the liquid latex. The water mixes with the latex, causing the cup to overflow on to the ground. Furthermore, the trees in the Lower Amazon do not produce well in the winter, and the flooded rivers and constant rain make the rubber roads all but impassable. The rubber-collecting season is therefore limited generally to the summer, from June to early December. Yet even in the summer there are a few rainy days, and many days are otherwise lost for work. Because most of the low islands are especially swampy, the collectors must build footpaths of logs above the water level in order to traverse portions of their rubber trails. During the month of August, the peak of the dry season, the rubber tree flowers. Few people work their rubber roads during this period because the blossoms from the trees fall into the collecting cups, causing the latex to coagulate. Furthermore, it is believed that cutting during this period harms the tree and permanently lowers its production.

The collecting season is relatively short, but if a collector works at least five days a week throughout the full season he may produce as much as 500 kilos of coagulated rubber—at the rate of about 50 to 60 kilos each 15-day period. It is customary in the Amazon to deduct 20 to 30 per cent of the weight of the rubber at the trading station to account for the loss through dehydration between the time the collector delivers it and the riverboat collects it from the trader. After this deduction, known throughout the Valley as the *tara*, the collector will be paid for only 300 to 400 kilos of his season's work, depending upon how dry the rubber balls are when he presents them at the trading post. In 1948 traders paid approximately 50 cents per kilo (cr. $10) for rubber. A collector thus might expect to earn $150 to $200 (cr. $1,500 to cr. $4,000) during a season.

The minimum expenditures for foods and other necessities for a collector and his wife were estimated at approximately $10 (cr. $200) per month; yet the average expenditures of the collector families included in our household studies showed an average monthly expenditure of $24.25 (cr. $485.20). In any case, a collector who is fortunate enough not to have to purchase cups, knives, a gun, and other instruments for his work might well finish a season with a small profit. In 1948 some collectors in the Itá region earned only from $50 to $150 (cr. $1,000 to $3,000) above their basic expenses. The cost of tools for rubber collecting, enforced idleness, sickness, together with the high prices which the collector pays the trader for his basic supplies, usually eat up most of these meager profits. In most cases the collector must replace cups, knives, and other tools; he must buy fishhooks, a gun, or other necessities; he often pays the owner of the rubber forests 10 to 20 per cent of his production for the right to collect on the land.

Under the present circumstances, and with the techniques of exploiting wild rubber which are widespread throughout the Amazon Valley, rubber collecting does not furnish a minimum living wage. Like agriculture, it must be combined with other economic activities if a man is to eke out a living for himself and his family. Often several members of a family must work at collecting in order to secure their basic necessities. In one case a man and his twenty-year-old son worked four rubber trails while his wife and their eighteen-year-old daughter took over the job of smoking the latex. The help of the women allowed the men time to plant a small garden and to fish. In spite of their activities, however, the family was in debt.

Many collectors in the Itá region work at other extractive industries during the season of the year when they are unable to collect rubber, for several other native products of the tropical forest, which have a market value, may be collected during the off season. In January and February the nut of the *ucuuba* palm, which grows along the small tributaries, falls into the flooded streams. People in the lowland areas collect them from canoes to sell at the trading posts. They are used for palm oil. Over a hundred tons of these palm nuts were exported downriver by Itá merchants during 1947 and 1948. Another forest seed, the *paracaxi*, is also collected in February. The seeds from this plant are allowed to soak in water for about eight days and are then cooked over a slow fire. The oil which is thus extracted brings about $2.50 (cr. $50) for a can of twenty liters; it is used both as a lubricant and for the manufacture of soap. Other vegetable oils, such as those derived from *patúa*, *andiroba*, and *copaíba* trees, are also exported. Wild cacao is found in the Amazon forest, and collector families spend time harvesting the seeds. Collectors may fell hardwood trees, such as *andiroba* and *macaúba*, in certain limited areas to be sold for lumber. Timbó vine, used for insecticides, brought a good price to the collector until recently, when synthetic products such as DDT replaced it on the market. *Buçu* palm leaf may be cut and sold for thatch. Common firewood is always salable along the Amazon mainstream to the numerous wood-burning steamers. Animal pelts, such as that of the deer, of the jaguar, and of wild pigs, bring in small sums to the collector families. In addition to these supplementary extractive products, many collectors plant small gardens during the dry season with quick-growing crops such as beans, corn, melons, and pumpkins. Without these additional sources of income and of food, a collector could not maintain himself. In fact, the rubber industry of the Amazon Valley seems destined to a slow death. It is a strange phenomenon that, in the native home of rubber, industry cannot compete with the rubber plantations of the Orient nor with the synthetic rubber industry of the industrial West.

Even plantation rubber has not, to date, proven to be commercially successful in the Amazon. Long ago rubber trees were planted in small quantities in various localities of the Valley. In Itá more than two hundred trees were planted near the edge of the town some forty years ago. Today the trees are rented out by the municipality to individuals to be exploited. Although it is a comparatively easy and comfortable job to collect the latex, the production is not particulariy lucrative, for the trees do not produce so well as the wild hevea. The Ford Motor Company attempted to exploit Amazon rubber on a plantation basis on a large scale. In 1924 Ford was granted extensive concessions on the Tapajoz River at Fordlandia and at Belterra. Several million rubber trees were planted on the two plantations. After World War II, however, the Ford Company resold the plantations to the Brazilian Government for a relatively small sum after spending millions of dollars on equipment and on rubber cultivation. The failure of this great private corporation after more than fifteen years indicates some of the difficulties inherent in the plantation rubber industry in the region.

The major difficulties of the Ford concessions were not tropical disease nor climate. In both Fordlandia and in Belterra, modern hospitals provided up-to-date medical care. In both concessions modern sanitation provided health conditions superior to those in the average Brazilian city. Housing conditions, both for the plantation workers and for company officials, were excellent. The major difficulties seem to have been the problem of adapting the native rubber tree to plantation conditions, and the problem of securing a stable supply of labor. When the rubber trees were planted in close proximity, they proved to be much more vulnerable to their natural insect and disease enemies. To secure a disease-resistant rubber tree on their plantations, the Ford Company hired specialists who had previous experience in Eastern plantations. They found it necessary to graft the native tree with a plantation variety imported from the Eastern rubber groves. Most of the rubber-producing trees on the Belterra concession in 1945 had a native Brazilian root system, an Oriental trunk, and a native leaf system. Rubber planting was thus a complex and a costly process. Second, the Ford concessions suffered from a lack of labor. Despite favorable living conditions on the plantations—the schools, the hospitals, modern housing, availability of foods, and other facilities not generally found in the Amazon Valley—rubber workers would not remain in sufficient numbers to work the large plantations efficiently.

The Amazon rubber collector is known for his nomadic way of

life. In general, he is attracted into, or forced into, rubber collecting
with the hope of making a quick profit after a season or two. Few
consider rubber collecting as a life-long occupation. Consequently,
the rubber gatherer goes to little trouble to build permanent improvements or adjuncts for his physical comfort. Since the collector
generally occupies land for which the trader for whom he works
has some sort of title, he hardly bothers to build a permanent house,
and since his income is low he accumulates few material possessions. Only his debts keep him from moving on, seeking always
for a more favorable situation after a season in one locality. The
rubber gatherers whom we knew had a feeling of instability, a desire to flee, and a vague hope of striking it rich. Their semi-nomadic
habits and their "strike-it-rich" attitudes, generated by the social
and economic system of the rubber industry of the Valley, are not
conducive to long-term employment on commercial plantations. Re-
cruits to the Ford concessions, paid at the low normal rate for day
labor in the Amazon, soon moved on to look for a rich rubber field
where they might build up a reserve in a year or two. Amazon
plantations, dependent upon an uncertain labor supply, cannot
compete with those in Africa nor with those in the Orient which
may call upon enormous populations for labor. Only if Brazilian
Government agronomists are able to produce a Brazilian tree better
adapted to plantation conditions, and if a stable labor supply becomes
available in the region, can the Amazon Valley look forward to
developing rubber as a lucrative industry.

IV

The rubber industry, however, has influenced Amazon society in
many ways. The social system of large areas of the Valley, especially where rubber collecting is still (or has been) the basic economic pursuit, results directly from the commercial system related
to the rubber industry. Throughout a large part of the Valley, the
structure of the rural neighborhoods is determined, to a large
extent, by the credit system, the economic dependence upon the

trader, and the vague landholding system which has developed out of the rubber-collecting industry. Furthermore, relationship of the rubber-collector neighborhoods to the wider community and to the city is, in turn, determined by the credit and the trading system of the wild-rubber industry.

The commercial system by which rubber collecting is organized is controlled at the top by the exporter-importer companies of Belém and Manaus (*aviadores*). These large companies send out merchandise on credit to local traders (*seringalistas*), and they purchase rubber and other products in return. These supply houses and exporters are owners of the riverboats which regularly ply the mainstream and tributaries, providing, in many cases, the only means of communication between trading stations and the towns and cities of the region. In turn, the local trader supplies necessities to his customers, the rubber collectors, and he purchases from them the results of their collecting. Each is in debt to the other—the collector to the trader, and the trader to the import-export firm. Each advances merchandise to the other on credit. And, needless to say, in such an uncertain business the large exporters of Manaus and Belém are in debt to banks and rubber importers in Rio de Janeiro, London, and New York. In rubber-collecting zones a rural neighborhood is formed by a trader and his collector-customers who live scattered near the rubber trails and who come periodically to the trading post which is the center of the neighborhood. Such a neighborhood has contact with the outside periodically through the visits of the steamer owned by the company of which the trader is a customer-debtor.

In addition to debt, land tenure reinforces the exporter-trader-collector dependency relationship. Legal titles for land are often confused and precarious in the Amazon region. Titles have been issued for land at various periods by the state governments; some of them are legally valid, some of them give the "owners" rights only to the exploitation of rubber or to Brazil nuts on the land, and some of them, although indicating full ownership, are worth only the paper upon which they are written. In any case, it is control over the land, and not legal documents, which in practice generally determines "ownership" of the land. A trader generally establishes his *barracão* (trading post) at the mouth of a small river or tributary. The banks of the river and the rubber forest inland from the stream are thereby "owned" by the trader or by an absentee "owner" from whom the trader rents. His collector-customers inhabit and exploit the lands back from the river controlled by his trading post. Enormous areas in whole river valleys were thus controlled by single individuals and by export companies during the rubber boom. In these areas the "owner" had absolute control over the lives of the people within his domains.

Just upriver from Itá, for example, the family Pereira Silva "owned," until less than a decade ago, all the land between the two great rivers extending north of the Amazon mainstream to the Guiana borders. This area covered two county-like municipalities. With this domain there were two towns, both municipal seats, and there are several smaller settlements which grew up around the company trading posts. The Pereira Silva company owned its own steamboats and exported its products directly to southern Brazil and abroad. State and federal police powers hardly reached into their domain, for armed company employees "kept the peace." It was a common legend in Belém that during the early decades of the twentieth century most of the prisoners from the jail were sent upriver to end their days in semi-slavery for the Pereira Silvas. On one occasion, some years back, the workers on the Pereira Silva domains revolted. They overpowered the armed guards, took control of a large riverboat, and sailed for Belém. In the Belém harbor, however, they were met by state police and, according to several reports, returned upriver to work out the rest of their lives in the most distant rubber trails in the Pereira Silva territory. Nowadays, the Pereira Silva lands have been divided into several large properties, as have most enormous rubber territories throughout the Valley; but old "Colonel" Pereira Silva still controls enormous tracts of land, and he is much feared by people in the Itá community, who tell of how his men controlled the rubber collectors on his property with the lash and with the rifle.

The relationship between the trader-owner and the collector as it existed during the heyday of the rubber boom has been described by many writers. The contemporary Portuguese novelist Ferreira de Castro, in *A Selva*,[13] has described the brutality and the absolute life-and-death control of the trader over his collectors. Euclides da Cunha, whose precise and colorful observations of the rebellion of a handful of Brazilian religious fanatics against the Brazilian federal forces in northeastern Brazil has become a national classic,[14] also visited the Amazon during the early days of the rubber boom. In a brief essay he gives a detailed picture of the recruiting of labor in the drought-stricken northeast region of Brazil and the debt-slavery system in the Amazon. According to Euclides da Cunha, the proprietors of rubber forests sent agents to the northeastern states who enlisted men for rubber gathering in the Amazon Valley. As soon as the new collector left his native community, he began to owe his *patrão* (employer). "He owed the steerage passage as far as Pará, and the money he received to prepare for the trip." Then his debt began to mount steadily. He was charged the cost of his passage up the Amazon into one of its tributaries to the trading post. There he was supplied with utensils for collecting latex, a gun and some ammunition, food to carry him through the collecting season, and some quinine to cure his almost certain malaria. All these things were charged to him at high prices. Euclides da Cunha calculates that at best the new rubber worker would owe the trader-owner some 2,090 milreis [15] before beginning work. He also estimates that under the most favorable conditions the new collector might realize 2,000 milreis during the first year. Under ideal conditions the recruit might double his production the second year and thus pay off his debt and have a profit; but, inevitably, idleness caused by fevers,

[13] Translated into English, by Charles Duff, as *The Jungle* (New York, 1935).
[14] *Os Sertões*, translated into English, by Samuel Putnam, as *Rebellion in the Backlands* (Chicago, 1944).
[15] The milreis was the old monetary unit equivalent to the cruzeiro.

the cost of replacing tools, inactivity during the heavy rains, occasional splurges at festivals, and inexperience made necessary additional credit advances and added to the collector's debt. "It is evident," Euclides da Cunha wrote, "that the collector able to free himself by luck is rare." [16]

The trader-owner of the trading post was protected by "law" in the days which both Euclides da Cunha and Ferreira de Castro described for the Amazon Valley. These "laws," which guaranteed to the trader the payment of the advances which he made to his collectors, were embodied in the "Rules of the Rubber Fields," a systematized agreement among the owners of rubber lands as to their relations with their debtor-collectors. The "Rules" were formulated to prevent collectors from escaping and to keep them in debt. According to the "Rules," an owner might impose a fine upon a collector for cutting a tree too deeply when "milking" the tree or for using a hatchet more than "four palms" wide in the process. The "Rules" stated that a collector might not make purchases at any other trading post than the one which had made him credit advances. If he did, he might be fined 50 per cent of the cost of the objects purchased. The collector might not leave the employment of the trader to whom he was in debt without complete liquidation of his account. To prevent escape, traders established their principal trading stations at the mouths of tributaries, where guards, armed with .44 rifles, watched day and night for collectors who might try to escape downriver. Even if a collector was able to by-pass the guards by fleeing overland through the tropical forest or by slipping downriver in the dark, the agreement among the traders prohibited their giving refuge to the fugitive. Each trader was obligated by the "Rules" to capture escaped debtors and to return them to their creditor traders. If by considerable luck a collector fleeing from his debts reached Belém or Manaus, he might be arrested by the police to be returned upriver to his employer-creditor. The "Rules" were not government decrees, but the owners of rubber fields and the traders put constant political pressure on

[16] *À Margem da História* (Pôrto, 1941), pp. 23–24.

the government to help them enforce the "Rules of the Rubber Fields" as if they were formal law.

After 1912, with the end of the fabulously high rubber prices, both the commercial system and debt-slavery related to the rubber industry began to disintegrate. The rubber "barons" lost their absolute political power along with their wealth. International scandals called attention to the "slavery" of the Amazon rubber collector. Traders without credit from the exporter were often glad to allow their collectors to leave. Yet even today essentially the same system of debtor-creditor relations persists, although in a somewhat milder form, throughout a great portion of the valley.

Even in the farming area of the community of Itá, a similar pattern exists between the agriculturalists and the local traders and storekeepers. Most of the inhabitants of the farming neighborhoods are the *fregueses* (customers) of a specific trader or of a town storekeeper. The farmers who live along the Igarapé Jocojó and along the Igarapé Ribeira, for example, are traditionally the customers of the Casa Gato in Itá. Most of them are in debt to Dona Dora Cesar Andrade, who advances them food and merchandise, and she buys their surplus farm produce, if any, from them. Dona Dora has titles which give her "ownership" to most of the land bordering these small streams. Both Dona Dora and her brother-in-law, Rui, who is manager of the Casa Gato, complain bitterly that "our customers trade elsewhere." They consider it unfair, almost illegal, for other traders to purchase manioc flour or forest products from their customers and for their customers to make purchases elsewhere. Still, their "customers" come to Itá after dark to sell their manioc flour to another store or they go upriver to another trading post, situated on the Amazon bank, to sell and buy. "I tell them of their debts and of the (rights to use) land and they are ashamed," said the manager of the Casa Gato. He also threatens to remove them from the land and he limits their credit. But Dona Dora also knows that her "titles" to the land are of doubtful legal validity, and she would not attempt to evict farmers, many of whom have occupied the land for twenty years or more. Furthermore, because farmers have less to sell to the trader than the rubber collector, they depend less upon purchases from the trader, and it is more difficult for the trader to maintain control over his farmer customers than it is to maintain it over the collectors.

In the rubber-collecting area of the municipality of Itá, the traditional trader-customer relationship still functions as a very strong social and economic bond. The trading post is the center of a rural neighborhood in which the inhabitants are all customers of the trader. These collectors are socially and economically tied to the trading post which serves them both as a market and as a social center. An example of a typical collector neighborhood is that surrounding the trading post of Francisco Firmo, lying directly across the Amazon channel from the town of Itá. His trading post is situated at the point where the small Rio Urutaí flows into the Amazon. Francisco Firmo has twenty-one customers, that is, the people from twenty-one scattered households who trade only at his store. A list of the names of the family heads of these households is posted on the door of his store. The rubber trails which these customers work are "owned" by Senhor Firmo. He does not have a valid title to the land, but he does have documents showing that he purchased the *seringais* (rubber fields) from a former owner who had received a concession from the state government to exploit rubber in the area. More important than documents, however, is the fact that people of the community recognize Senhor Firmo's "ownership" of the land. Each of the twenty-one families has received credit advances from Francisco Firmo, and a study of his books indicated that he advanced an average of about $100 (cr. $2,000) to each family for the collecting season. Several of these customer families have debts of several years' standing.

Francisco Firmo's customers live at various distances from his trading post. Six houses are situated on the Amazon mainstream and the others are up the Rio Urutaí. Each house is spaced some three hundred to eight hundred meters from the other and is built at a point on the river which gives access to two, three, or more rubber trails. As compared to the larger rubber trading posts on the upper

Xingú, Tapajoz, and Madeira rivers and those in the District of Acre, Francisco Firmo's has a small number of customers. In the more productive districts fifty to sixty or more families are often thus attached to a trader.

It is traditional through the Amazon Valley for the customers of a trader to come to the post on an appointed day (*quinzena*) to deliver the rubber they have collected and to stock up on supplies. The *quinzena* at Francisco Firmo's post, and generally in the Lower Amazon region, takes place on the average of once each month rather than at regular fifteen-day intervals. The *quinzena* usually takes place just before the arrival of the *Union*, the wood-burning riverboat of J. Fontes Company of Belém, which supplies Francisco Firmo with trade goods and which purchases his rubber and other produce. The *Union* ties up for a few hours at the wharf in front of Senhor Firmo's post around the twentieth of each month. For a few hours there is fevered activity while the sailors unload supplies and while the rubber and other products are weighed and loaded aboard. But the busiest day of the month at the post is the day before the arrival of the steamer, when most of the customers and their families come to trade. Francisco Firmo sends out a message to his customers setting the date for this trading day in accordance with the schedule of the *Union*, which is anything but regular in its sailings. But people do not limit their trading to the one day, and each Sunday a few customers gather at the post to trade, to drink, and to visit. But the *quinzena* each month is an occasion when all wish to be present. It is a day both of trading transactions and of recreation for the family, comparable to Saturday afternoons in a small American town.

In June of each year on the day of St. John, Francisco Firmo invites all of his customers and their families to the trading post to hear prayers for the saint, to eat at his expense, and to dance out the night. For Senhor Firmo is especially devoted to St. John, who, he feels, protects his trading post. His customers look forward to the annual festival, and Senhor Firmo's friends from other trading posts also attend. On his birthday, the trader offers a party with drinking and dancing for his *freguêsia* (customer group). The trading post has a large veranda opening up on the dock. There is a storeroom where the merchandise is displayed and other storerooms where the produce is kept for shipment. In addition, there are the living quarters of Senhor Firmo's family, including a large salon used for visiting and for dancing on festive occasions. The structural form of a typical *barracão* indicates that it functions both as a market center and as a social center for the rural collector neighborhood. And Senhor Firmo is, at the same time, the creditor-employer of his customers and the social leader of the neighborhood.

In turn, commercial relations also determined Senhor Firmo's social relations with the big city. He is a customer of the large wholesale import-export company, J. Fontes of Belém. The supplies and merchandise, such as kerosene, canned goods, kitchen utensils, candles, lamps, knives, hoes, manioc farina, dried fish, cloth, machine-made clothes, and other items which he carries in stock, are furnished on credit by J. Fontes Company. Against his debt, the company discounts the rubber and other products which he ships on the *Union*. Like his own collector customers, Senhor Firmo seldom sees actual cash. Sometimes he sells some rubber secretly for cash to a *regatão*, one of the itinerant boats which poach upon the regular company customers, just as his customers may trade secretly elsewhere. Sometimes he earns cash by selling to collector customers of other traders who pass by his post. But generally Senhor Firmo deals only with his own customers and his own creditors. When he needs funds for a trip to Belém or for some other occasion, he draws cash against his credit with J. Fontes. The company often pays his bills for him with other city firms. Two years ago, when Senhor Firmo's wife needed glasses, she traveled to Belém on the *Union*. J. Fontes Company sent her to an oculist, charging the doctor's bill and her passage to Senhor Firmo's account. Once, many years ago, he tried to settle his account with J. Fontes Company, and asked to be allowed to deal with them on a monthly cash basis. He soon found that they were not interested in short-term accounts. Even in years when rubber brings high prices and when Senhor Firmo has a surplus to his account, he does not withdraw his profits, but allows them to remain on deposit with the company. "J. Fontes does not care if my account is paid up," he explained; "they want the rubber I send them." In the Amazon the trader makes more profit on the resale of the products purchased from his customers than from what is sold to them despite the high prices charged. Similarly, J. Fontes Company realizes more from the export of rubber than from the merchandise they sell to the traders.

The commercial system of the Amazon is no longer maintained by the old "Rules of the Rubber Fields," nor by the police and the .44 rifle as it was during the first decade of this century. Yet the obligations of the collector to the trader and the trader to the import-export firm have remained essentially unchanged as the basic relationships which channel commercial and social relationships within the region. The strength of the traditional system is an important element to contend with in any attempt to modify economic and social conditions in the Valley. Attempts during the last war to sell supplies directly to the trader, short-cutting the import-export firm, and to collect rubber directly were doomed to failure by the pressure of the long-standing credit and social relationships between the trader and the big city company. To break away from his only source of credit and regular supplies—often his only source of communication with the outside—did not seem rational to the trader. Attempts to form cooperatives and to extend government credit to rural Amazonian populations often clash with this system of relationships, for cooperatives would do away with the trader. And yet even this Amazon commercial system can be helpful in introducing new innovations. New ideas, new forms of technology, and new instruments may be introduced through the city firms, to their traders, and finally to the collectors and farmers in distant areas of the Valley.[17]

[17] Early in 1943, when it looked as if wild rubber might be crucial to the Allied war effort, administrators were told that malaria was seriously impeding the collection of rubber and that there were no specifics available in the distant parts of the Valley to treat malaria. Several million tablets of Atabrine (an anti-malaria drug) were quickly sent by air freight to Manaus. Then there was the

V

Many of the basic problems of man's adjustment to the tropical environment of the Amazon community may be seen in the ways in which the people of Itá earn a living. The two principal occupations of the community, subsistence farming and the collecting of native products of the forest, are those characteristic of large areas of the Amazon Valley. It is apparent that neither of these occupations will alone furnish any more than a bare subsistence for a family in Itá. Even by combining collecting and farming it is possible to maintain only a low standard of living. The primitive system of agriculture adapted to the weak upland soils of the Amazon, and carried out without the aid of any modern instruments, except a few iron hand tools, does not produce enough food for the relatively sparse population of the community, for it requires a great expanse of land. Therefore in regions such as Itá, where men have farmed by this same system of cultivation for several centuries, there is, in a sense, a land problem. In aboriginal times Amazon Indian villages moved their locations each five or six years in order to have favorable garden sites near at hand, but under modern circumstances it is not possible to lead this semi-nomadic kind of existence. Furthermore, the present population of the Valley is several times greater than it was in aboriginal times. In the vicinity of most Amazon communities, there is, therefore, a shortage of land considered in terms of the methods used to exploit the area.

In addition, rubber collection actually seems to be a barrier to the production of an adequate food supply. Rubber and other forest products provide people with the necessary cash or credit without

---

problem of how to get the drug quickly and cheaply into the hands of the rubber gatherer. There were also the problems of transportation to the high tributaries and of the high prices which would certainly be charged for the precious drug if sold through the normal channels. It was decided to offer Atabrine gratuitous to the import-export firms with the understanding that it would be furnished free to the trader and, in turn, the collector. The drug was made quickly available, even in the distant high tributaries of the Valley, through the mechanism of the relationship of the city firm, local trader, and the collector.

which they would be unable to purchase the numerous necessities which must be imported from outside; but at the same time these collecting activities for export direct the efforts of a large part of the population away from food production. The return which they receive from collecting does not bring sufficient income to purchase the food and other material necessities which must be imported from outside the region. The emphasis upon an extractive economy and collecting raw materials for distant markets since the beginning of European settlement has impeded man's effectual adjustment to the Amazon environment more than the physical environment.

Improvement of social conditions in the Amazon depends, of course, upon the development of a more lucrative and more efficient economic basis for Amazon society. Agriculture must be modernized and adapted to local conditions so as to provide an adequate food supply for the present population; and this is even more urgent and crucial if immigration into the Valley is contemplated. The old collecting industries, such as those of Brazil nuts and wild rubber, must be so organized that they will provide an adequate livelihood for the Amazon producer—or they must be abandoned. In addition, new cash crops must be sought which may be produced on a commercial basis in the Amazon soil and for which there is a stable and lucrative market.[18]

Economic change in Itá depends upon improvement of transportation and communications, wider and more efficiently administered credit facilities, the removal of trade barriers, and the availability of modern technological equipment—all of which are determined beyond the frontiers of any single community. In other words, the improvement of the economic system of Itá will depend upon national and international trends and policies. Yet it is in the local community that national or international policies and trends deal with concrete human situations and affect the lives of the people.

[18] One possible cash crop is jute. Within recent years there has been a rapid commercial development of this product along the middle course of the Amazon mainstream.

4. SOCIAL RELATIONS IN AN AMAZON COMMUNITY

In the small Amazon community of Itá, as in all human societies, men are ranked in prestige. In Itá social rank depends upon a combination of criteria, some of which are fixed at birth, such as one's sex, race, and family membership, and others, such as occupation and education, which are left to individual choice and initiative and which depend, too, upon the available opportunities and the capacity of a person to make use of them.[1] Because Itá is a small and isolated community, the distance between the highest and lowest individual in the social scale of prestige is not so great as it is in a large city or in a society with a more elaborate social structure. The system of social rank is none the less an important aspect of Itá's social life.

There was a time, however, when the difference between the lowest and the highest in social rank in Itá was greater. In the first centuries of the town's history, those who were born of Indian or

[1] Cf. Ralph Linton, *The Study of Man* (New York, 1936), pp. 113 ff.

mixed-blood parentage in the "village" quarter of the town carried the stigma of their slave parents. Individuals were born as slaves or as freemen. Mobility upward was extremely infrequent. During the rubber boom the economic difference between the rich rubber merchants and the miserable rubber gatherers made social distances great. At that time there was an "aristocracy" in Itá. Families such as that of the baron of Itá were proud of their Portuguese ancestors. They educated their children in the large cities of Brazil and Europe. They were wealthy in land, and they participated in the political and social life of the wider Amazon region. Such people traveled frequently to Belém and to Manaus, and they received visitors from other communities. They formed the *alta sociedade*—the aristocracy. As landowning merchants, they controlled economic and political life, occupying all of the public positions of the municipality. Such people as Coronel Filemeno Cesar Andrade, a wealthy merchant who came to Itá from Maranhão; Flaviano Flavio de Batista, who was a landowner, the *intendente* (mayor) of Itá, and a political leader recognized and respected in Belém; and Dr. Joaquim Nobre, the judge, a graduate of the Law School in Belém who maintained his legitimate wife and children in Belém and a second family in Itá, were representative figures of this class. Class lines were more strictly maintained in the days of these aristocrats before the rubber crash. A member of the lower class would not sit down in the presence of one of these *brancos* (whites), as they were called. There were always two rooms of dancers at any party, one room for the lower class and the other for the aristocracy. In Itá, as in most Latin American communities, strong class distinctions between the colonial aristocracy and the people of aboriginal and slave origin persisted into the twentieth century.

Nowadays only a few descendants of these aristocratic families live in Itá. The few who do remain are relatively impoverished and have lost their high social rank. At the end of the rubber boom, most of the aristocratic families moved away one by one. Their successful sons left to study in Belém or in South Brazil. Such men as the Jewish physician, mentioned earlier, never returned after they had completed their education, even though their parents stayed for a time. Today, except for the public-health physician of the SESP, there is not a single individual with a complete secondary education in town. Only the Casa Gato of the strong commercial houses of the rubber times remains. Neither the traditional aristocratic families (who still control large landholdings in the Amazon), the professional class, the military, the Church officials, the industrial and commercial groups, nor the political leaders—who together form the contemporary upper class of the Amazon region—are present in Itá society today.

To the outsider, therefore, Itá may appear to be a homogeneous society of rural peasants, of people who differ little from one another in social rank. In Belém upper-class people are apt to classify the people of Itá, with the exception of a few government officials stationed there, as caboclos. Travelers from larger centers generally call on the SESP doctor, Dona Dora at the Casa Gato, or on the mayor, a young man who was once a sailor in the Brazilian navy. City people recognize these people as roughly equivalent to the urban middle class. Visitors from Belém sometimes comment upon the lack of upper class in Itá. They may remark that "the mayor is nothing more than a caboclo," or they may wonder at the high social position of Dona Dora, who is a dark mulatta and whose husband was a Negro. Yet, as one lives and participates in Itá social life, it soon becomes apparent that people, within the confines of the community itself, are quite sensitive to differences in social rank. In fact, people are quite explicit and overt as to the different social strata in their society.

Such present-day distinctions in social rank result from the class system of colonial Amazon society, from the former servitude of Indians and imported African slaves, and from the social ascendancy of the Portuguese colonials. They also reflect the economic and social position of the various groups who inhabit Itá today. In their simplest form the social strata of Itá are, in the words of the people themselves and in order of social prestige:

1. the First Class (*Gente de Primeira*), or the "whites" (*brancos*), who form the local upper class;
2. the Second Class (*Gente de Segunda*), who are the lower-class town dwellers;
3. the farmers (*Gente de Sítio*), who inhabit the agricultural lands of terra firme; and
4. the Island collectors (*caboclos da Beira*), the people who live in huts built on stilts over the low swamps and inundated islands, earning their living from a purely collecting economy.

It cannot be said that all Itá people are fully aware of all these categories. As the city folk tend to view Itá as a homogeneous society of small-town peasants, the First Class people of Itá are apt to view all the people below them in the social hierarchy as simply "the people," or as "caboclos." In turn, the town-dwelling Second Class indicate their superiority to all the rural population by speaking of them as "caboclos," and the farmers reserve this term for the Island collectors, to whom they feel superior. And finally, the Island collectors would be slightly offended if they were called "caboclos," for they make little distinction between themselves and the farmers.[2] The system of social stratification of Itá society differs, therefore, in accordance with the social position from which it is viewed. And, as will become apparent, socio-economic differences are greatest between the First Class and the three lower strata. Among the Second Class, the farmers and the Island collectors, the lines of social discrimination are not clearly drawn; social mobility takes place with great ease, and economic conditions differ less than between these three groups and the First Class. In a sense, therefore, it is perhaps proper to speak of Itá as a society with but two social classes—an upper and lower class; but a simple twofold division would not fully express the social distinctions made by the people themselves.

[2] The Island collectors use the term "caboclo" to refer to the tribal Indians who inhabit the headwaters of the Amazon tributaries. The Amazon "caboclo," therefore, exists only in the concept of the groups of higher status referring to those of lower status.

To the few people who claim some relationship with the old Itá aristocracy, such as Manuel Serra Freire, the state tax collector, and Dona Branquinha, the schoolteacher, few people truly belong to the "whites" or the First Class. Dona Branquinha would accept only one family, that of Dona Dora Cesar Andrade, as high society or First Class. She would not even count Dona Deborah, widow of an important Jewish merchant, as First Class because her son lives "in friendship" (that is, without benefit of Church or civil marriage) with a young girl whom Dona Branquinha herself raised. To Dona Branquinha dances today are not parties but "orgies where young ladies of family are mixed with everybody." Senhor Serra Freire said that "formerly political posts were held only by First Class," and he pointed out the lowly origins of the present mayor as a sign of the decadence of Itá society. He felt that it was not proper to bring his family to public functions, and during our residence in Itá Senhor Serra Freire did not attend any of the social affairs offered by the public officials. Even people of the lower classes recognize that there are few aristocrats of local origin left in Itá today. A woman of low status remarked, "The only real First Class in Itá today are people from outside." Except for two or three families of merchants, the group recognized as "whites" or First Class are composed of the mayor, the police chief, the federal and state tax collectors, employees of the SESP and their respective families—all salaried officials and government employees.

Yet the lines of social cleavage between the First Class and the lower groups, between the "whites" and the "people," are still relatively strongly felt in Itá. As late as 1942, the "line" between the two groups was rather strictly maintained. During the celebrations on the birthday of a well known political hero of the region, there was a parade and an afternoon of fireworks and public speeches which were attended by everyone, seemingly without distinction. But in the evening there were two dances. One, held in the public dance pavilion, was an open dance for the "people." There men danced in their shirt sleeves, and both men and women danced barefooted on the rough boards. In the home of the mayor, who was at that time Benedito Levi, a descendant of one of the Jewish families, there were dancing and refreshments for the "whites"—a group of some thirty people. A few young unmarried girls of good reputation but of Second Class families were invited to the festivities of the "whites." One young lady of the Second Class came with her mother to the First Class dance dressed in party dress and shoes, while her brother danced in the public pavilion. A man accepted as First Class attended without his common-law wife because she was not "of the First." It was explained that he had never legalized his marriage because his "companion" was not "of good family."

In similar festivals held in 1948, the "line" between the upper and the lower classes seemed less rigid. At a dance offered by the mayor in 1948 many people of the Second Class were invited and attended. There was some comment to the effect that the mayor would need their votes in the next election. The return of Brazil to a system of free elections aften ten years of dictatorship did give the voter, regardless of class, more importance. Many Second Class people, however, would not attend the mayor's party even though they were invited, because they "felt ashamed in front of so many important people." Others did not come simply because they could not afford shoes and the clothes for the party. And the Second Class people who did attend parties were made to feel their lower position. The First Class guests were offered seats, served coffee, and invited to drink beer in the back room with the host. Second Class people were not invited to sit and they were offered refreshments last. The expression *meu branco* (my white) is still heard with considerable frequency as a term of respect for rank in Itá, and lower-class people always stand up when addressing a "white" such as Dona Dora Cesar Andrade or Dona Branquinha. Between the upper and the lower strata the lines of social discrimination are still clearly drawn.

Social discrimination is not so great between the three lower class groups. In general the farmers live on the same side of the Amazon mainstream as the town, and they visit it frequently. Lower-class townspeople have good friends and many relatives among the rural farmers, and they participate in the many festivals offered by the rural religious brotherhoods. They realize that they are not much different from the farmers—for they, too, are apt to earn at least a part of their living from farming. Yet rural farmers lead an isolated life, and their standard of living is somewhat lower than that of the Second Class town dweller. Townspeople have a few advantages over the farmers: they can send their children to school and the health post is near at hand. Therefore Second Class town dwellers tend, on the whole, to feel superior to their rural friends and relatives.

Both the lower-class townspeople and the farmers, however, look with some disdain upon the caboclos, who earn a living from the collection of rubber and of palm nuts alone. Although in years when rubber prices are high, people from the town and from the farming zone move to the Islands to collect rubber, they are only temporary inhabitants of these isolated areas. They feel that they are different from those who permanently work at collecting. Such people are considered "hicks." When the collector comes to town to attend the festival of St. Benedict or St. Anthony, he wears his white suit, which has been starched to the point that it stands up alone. "He brings his shoes, which he may not have worn for two years. He endures the pain caused by his shoes for most of the first day but he takes off his shoes to dance," the townspeople say with considerable amusement. "He steps on his dancing partner's feet, and no one wants to dance with a caboclo." During the second day of the festival, "the caboclo's feet are swollen; he is not used to shoes and he is not used to walking on the hard ground" (in contrast to the soft mud of the swamps). As everywhere else, people find the "hick" ridiculous, and those from the town of Itá and from the farming area think of life on the Islands and on the floodlands as slightly barbaric. They point at the numerous "shotgun marriages" performed by the police chief among the Island caboclos and at the fights which occur at their dances as indications of their lower moral standards and general backwardness. The collectors participate so seldom in the social life of the town of Itá that our companions

from town were never able to tell us the names of dwellers of the
huts along the riverbank in the rubber-collecting areas of the community. Yet they knew by name each of the isolated dwellers in the
nearby farming area. But the Island caboclos do not treat the lower-
class townspeople and the farmers with the same excessive respect
and politeness which all the lower-class groups show in front of the
upper class. "They [the collectors and farmers] are less civilized,"
said Juca, a Second Class town dweller, "because they are isolated
and poor."

II

The people of Itá classified about one-third of the residents of
the town as "whites" or First Class and the remainder as Second
Class or lower-class townsfolk. In terms of the total number of inhabitants of the Itá community, including the rural zones, this means
that the First Class forms less than 10 per cent of the total population
and the lower-class townsfolk form approximately 20 per cent. Our
rough census of the community area indicated that about 60 per
cent of the population were farmers (Gente de Sítio). Only about
10 per cent of the inhabitants of the community were Island collectors, since the bulk of the latter live outside the community area, in
the Island region of the municipality. There was some difference
of opinion among our many Itá friends regarding the social position
of a few individuals in the lower rungs of the First Class. Manuel
Cesar Andrade, a young man of low-class origin, who had been
raised by Dona Dora Cesar Andrade, for example, was given First
Class status by several people only after some hesitation. And, as
stated earlier, a few of the people of the First Class, such as Senhor
Serra Freire and Dona Branquinha, considered the group of "real
First Class" to be very few in number today. On the whole, however, there was remarkable agreement among our Itá friends as to
which families were First Class and which by default belonged to
the lower-class groups of the town and rural areas. A series of
criteria, some of which were explicit in their minds and some of

which were implicitly understood, were used by the people of Itá in placing people in their proper social class.[3]

An explicit and important criterion was occupation. Several writers have called attention to a so-called "gentleman complex" in Brazil. Physical work in the last century was limited to the slave-peon caste and to those recently freed, and after emancipation manual labor continued as a symbol of low social status. As people moved up in the social scale, they adopted the attitudes of the former landed gentry and slaveowners, and an attitude of disparagement of any form of manual labor persists in contemporary Brazil. It is a social value which is shared not only by the descendants of the slaveowning families but also by the new middle and commercial upper class of the cities and by the people of innumerable small towns throughout the interior of the country. Even in Itá, a small and isolated town in the Amazon Valley, the work one does is an indication of one's social class. Since the people of Itá are not descendants of the slaveowning gentry (in fact, many of them are most certainly descendants of slaves), emancipation from manual labor is all the more important as a symbol of upper-class status. Of seventeen men who were classed as First Class in our household survey, none worked with his hands. All were public employees or earned their living from commerce. The group included such people as the state tax collector, the mayor, the vice mayor, and the owners of the three commercial houses. Although the wives of these men did some domestic work, most of their families also had servants. In contrast, of fifty-five Second Class men included in our survey, all but two (clerks in the town hall) earned their living from some form of manual labor. The few artisans in Itá, such as the shoemaker and

---

[3] Detailed schedules covering family composition, income, expenditures for food, occupation, property, etc., were collected for 113 households in the Itá community. They provide a sample of over 30% of the total population (estimated at 350 households); this sample was distributed as follows: 17 households in the First Class, 55 in the Second Class, 31 in the farmer group, and 10 in the Island collector group. Difficulties of transportation made it impossible to make our sample of both rural groups representative of their numerical strength in the total population, yet I believe that our rather inadequate sample of the two groups indicates valid differences in living standards.

the carpenters, were considered Second Class. Even agriculture is a lower-class occupation. Only one family among the seventeen First Class families had a manioc garden, and it had been planted by hired labor.

The size of one's income and the standard of living which one is able to maintain are also explicit criteria used by people in Itá to determine the social class of an individual. All of the families who were considered to be First Class had this in common: they dealt in money. All of them had a relatively steady income from salaries or from commerce, and therefore had either cash or credit in the local stores. As one Second Class man put it bluntly: "The 'whites' are those who have a little [money] saved in their trunks. The difference is that when I want a coconut I must climb a tree and pick it myself, but when they want a coconut they pay someone to pick it." Our survey of family incomes bore out the idea, which is widely held in Itá, that money is an important criterion of social position. The average cash income for seventeen First Class families was approximately $75 (cr. $1,597.10) per month as against an average of only $23 (cr. $452.30) per month for fifty-five Second Class families living in town.[4]

First Class families were better housed, better dressed, and better fed than Second Class. In all cases, those who were pointed out as members of the First Class lived in a dwelling, classed as a house (*casa*), which was situated on the First or Second Street rather than in the palm-thatched huts (*barracas*) in which 75 per cent of the Second Class families lived. In the houses of the First Class families there were 0.9 persons per room, while there were 1.2 persons per room in Second Class huts. In the Brazilian Amazon, footwear (both shoes and sandals) is an item of dress of special importance both socially and as a protection against hookworm. The men of the First Class families had an average of 3.3 pairs of shoes, while those of the Second Class had on the average only 1.8 pairs. First Class

---

[4] The monthly income for the First Class families ranged from $25 (cr. $500) to $250 (cr. $5,000); of the Second Class families from as low as $2.50 (cr. $50) to $85 (cr. $1,700).

women had an average of 3.6 pairs of shoes in contrast to an average of only 1.7 pairs for Second Class women. First Class homes were better furnished; they had more chairs, more linens, more kitchenware, more china, and more hammocks than the Second Class homes. The few beds found in Itá are found only in houses of upperclass families. As in many out-of-the-way parts of the world, the sewing machine is an extremely valued object both for its contribution to household economy and for the prestige which it brings to the owner. All but three of the women among the seventeen First Class families did own a sewing machine, while only eleven of the fifty-five Second Class housewives included in our survey owned one.

The average monthly expenditure for food and other household necessities for the First Class families was approximately $48 (cr. $962.20) per month in contrast to about $15 (cr. $207.20) for the Second Class families of the town included in our survey.[5] The difference in cash expenditures between the two groups is somewhat offset, however, by the fact that many of the Second Class families have gardens from which they harvest manioc for flour and sometimes a little maize,[6] and by the fact that many Second Class men fish during the dry season. Yet these added sources of food scarcely balance such a wide margin of difference in basic expenditures. Certain foods never entered into Second Class budgets. First Class families regularly ate bread, canned butter, and other imported foods, such as condensed milk, cheese, and guava paste—items which a Second Class family might purchase once a year for a birthday or another festival. First Class families purchased more beans, rice, dried meat, sugar, coffee, and other items which must be bought in one of Itá's three stores. Although even the average Itá upper-class standard of living is poor and inadequate, the differences both in

[5] First Class family expenditures ranged from approximately $23 (cr. $455) to approximately $130.50 (cr. $2,609.50); Second Class family expenditures ranged from as low as $2.50 (cr. $55) to $45 (cr. $900).

[6] Twenty-two out of fifty-two Second Class men were agriculturalists by profession, and sixteen of fifty-five Second Class families had gardens to supplement their income.

income and in normal expenditures between the upper and lower class of the town of Itá set the two groups apart.

The standard of living of the two rural groups of the farmers and of the Island collectors is more difficult to measure, since they depend so directly upon their gardens, upon fishing, and even upon hunting for their food supply. Yet an analysis of their cash incomes and of their cash expenditures indicates that their living standards differ little from those of the lower-class town dweller. The average farmer family had a cash income of approximately $15 (cr. $301.90) per month, while the average income of the few collector families included was about $33 (cr. $661.30) per month. The higher cash income of the collector results from the sale of forest products, but it is offset by higher cash expenditures for food and other household necessities. The farmer families spent an average of about $10 (cr. $203.30) per month, while the collector families spent, on the average, slightly more than $24 (cr. $485.20) for purchased food and other necessities. The Island collectors are dedicated almost entirely to harvesting the natural products of the forest, and most of them lack even small manioc gardens for subsistence. Of the ten families of collectors for whom we took detailed budgets, only two had gardens. Such families must buy their own manioc flour.

One hundred per cent of all rural families of the Itá community (both farmers and collectors) live in palm-thatched huts. They have slightly less room than the urban lower class: 1.7 people per room for the farmer group and 1.5 persons per room for the collector group. In addition, rural people have fewer shoes and sandals than the town lower class: the men of the farmer group had an average of 1.3 pairs each and the collector men had 1.5 pairs each. The women of the farmer families had 1.7 pairs of footwear and the women of the collector families 1.8. Only five women whose husbands were farmers had sewing machines, but five out of ten collector families (with larger cash incomes) owned them.

Such statistics indicate that the two rural groups have a slightly lower standard of living than the lower-class urban groups. But the greatest difference in living standards is between the lower class as a whole (the Second Class of the town and rural farmers and collectors) and the upper-class "whites" or First Class. The lower-class people both of the town and of the countryside live on a semi-starvation diet. Purchased foods and necessities such as sugar, coffee, salt, dried and fresh beef, kerosene, soap, and tobacco are used in small quantities and almost as luxuries. In 1948 day labor in Itá was paid only $0.75 (cr. $15) per day, and the price charged for any manufactured article was extremely expensive in relation to such wages or in relation to the prices paid for manioc flour, rubber, timbo roots, palm nuts, and other products which brought in cash or credit to the rural people. Thus lower-class people are generally in debt to the local commercial houses.

III

Although such statistical averages reflect closely the class cleavages of Itá society, the complex and interrelated factors which determine a standard of living and the human problems involved cannot be well described by statistics. Case histories of three families selected from our detailed studies of family budgets are, in the writer's opinion, more illustrative of the way the people of Itá live. These families were not the richest or the poorest of their respective socio-economic strata; they were selected because they seemed representative of the average of each group.

The first, which we may call Family A, are "whites" or First Class. They live, characteristically, on First Street, but in a rather dilapidated adobe house. The family consists of a man, his wife, and three small children—two daughters and an infant son. The father is the secretary at the Town Hall, earning a salary of $75 per month (cr. $1,500). Their house has five rooms: a "visiting room" or parlor, two bedrooms, a dining room, and a kitchen. Baths are taken in the nearby river, and there is an outdoor privy installed by the public-health service. The house faces directly on the street. Behind it is a long fenced-in back yard which contains twenty banana trees, fifteen pineapple plants, five coconut trees, and other fruit trees. The

family also keeps twenty chickens in the back yard, more for their
meat than for their eggs.

Family A's house is well furnished by local standards, although
to the outsider it would seem rather empty. There are six wooden
chairs, three tables, a china cabinet, four trunks for storing linens
and clothes, two kerosene lamps, and a bed which is seldom slept in.[7]
Like other families in Itá, Family A sleeps in hammocks which may
be seen rolled up against the wall during the daytime. Husband and
wife sleep in one of the windowless alcove bedrooms while the
children sleep in the adjoining room. The kitchen, in the rear of the
house, has a platform upon which an open oven-grill has been built
for cooking. Kitchenware consists of four cast-iron pots and various
locally manufactured ceramic utensils. The dining room, which has
the typical form of a partially open veranda, overlooks the back
yard. It is used not only for meals but also as a general room for
family living. Intimates of the family are received in the dining
room rather than in the formal visiting room in the front of the
house. In the china cabinet in the dining room are twelve plates,
ten demitasse coffee cups with saucers, six large coffee cups with
saucers for morning coffee, four water glasses, and ten knives, ten
forks, and ten spoons.

For Itá, Family A is also relatively well dressed. The father has
two cotton suits made for him by an itinerant tailor who comes to
town about twice a year. He has three other pairs of trousers for
everyday use. He has five shirts, four neckties, two pairs of shoes,
and two pairs of open sandals; these he always wears about the
house and sometimes even in the street. His wife has four "good"
dresses which she saves for festivals and for churchgoing. She has
four older dresses and four pairs of sandals for everyday use. Each
child has three "uniforms"—cotton dresses for the girls and one-piece
cotton suits for the small son—and each has a pair of shoes, worn
only on special occasions.

---

[7] Even the upper class in Itá prefers hammocks for sleeping. A bed is a
prestige item which, according to our informants, is used only for sexual
relations.

Except for the little food which they raise in their back yard, Family A buys all of its food. Like most Itá families, they have a charge account with one of the four commercial houses. They are customers of the Casa Gato, where they spend a monthly average of $50 (cr. $1,000) in food and other "necessities." Most of this sum goes for such staples as manioc flour, coffee, sugar, fresh meat, salted and fresh fish, beans, and rice. Family A (like other First Class families) also buys bread to eat for breakfast. They also often have canned butter, canned milk, and some sweets such as *goiabada* (guava paste) and *marmelada* (quince paste), the most common desserts throughout Brazil. The husband smokes ready-made cigarettes and now and again he drinks a bottle of beer or has a drink of *cachaça* at the Casa Gato. Their account is seldom paid up; despite the fact that the husband has a regular salary, the cost of clothes, medicines, donations for the Church, and of an occasional party keeps them slightly in debt to the Casa Gato. But it is considered good business in Itá to allow a customer with a regular income to remain in debt, for he will feel obligated to continue purchasing from his debtor. Clerks at the Casa Gato are rather liberal with Family A, urging husband and wife to make purchases beyond normal "necessities." Family A's way of life is not a comfortable one when compared to that of the more favored populations of the world, but for Itá it is considered almost rich.

Our second example, Family B, is classified locally as Second Class, or lower-class town dwellers. Like Family A, it is composed of a man, his wife, and three children (two girls and a boy). But the oldest child, a twelve-year-old boy, helps in the garden and is a real economic asset to the family. Family B lives on Third Street in a palm-thatched hut. The father is a day laborer earning only $12.50 to $15 (cr. $250 to cr. $300) per month in cash, but this income is augmented by the produce (mostly manioc) from his garden, which he plants on land belonging to the municipality and cultivates with the help of his son and his wife. In addition, during the summer months Senhor B fishes, both to add to the family larder and to sell. Some years, when rubber prices are high, he spends a month or so as a rubber collector in the Island region of the municipality. Family B also has a few chickens (ten hens), and their yard contains banana, papaya, and other fruit trees. Unlike Family A, who lives almost exclusively upon salary, Family B depends to a great extent upon farming, fishing, and collecting for a livelihood.

Family B's material standards are markedly lower than those of Family A. Their *barraca* has only three rooms: bedroom, dining room, and kitchen. There are a dining table and two wooden benches; they have two straight-backed chairs to be used by guests. A wooden box set on legs serves to store food and dishes. There are two trunks to hold the family clothes, and a single kerosene lamp provides illumination for the whole house. The family has only six plates, six demitasse cups and saucers, six spoons, two dinner knives, two water glasses, and a few odd pieces of china. Each member of the family has a hammock, but the children must sleep in the dining room. The husband has one full suit and two pairs of trousers. He owns two shirts, one for work and one for dress. His wife has one good dress for special occasions and two old dresses for everyday wear. The husband, the wife, and the older boy have shoes which are kept carefully in the trunks. On a normal working day all go barefooted. The younger children have only one change of clothes for everyday use, but the older boy has extra pants and a new shirt for dress-up occasions.

Family B also are customers of the Casa Gato, but the clerks do not urge them to make additional purchases. Though their gardens produce enough manioc to provide flour for their own use, in addition they spend, on the average, almost $10 (cr. $195) per month for other basic foods, such as fresh meat (2 to 4 kilos per month), coffee, sugar, rice (2 to 3 kilos per month), beans (1 to 2 kilos per month), and salt. They rarely consume such luxuries as canned milk, sweets, cottonseed oil, bread, and butter. Their diet is remarkably meager. They eat only one solid meal each day—midday dinner. The family goes to work or to school each morning after only a small demitasse of black coffee and a handful of *farinha* to last them until midday. Their diet is, as Josué de Castro writes regarding Amazon diets in general, "sparing, scanty, of startling sobriety. What a man eats during one whole day would not be enough for one meal in other climatic zones which form other habits." [8] Family B obviously suffers from malnutrition. The children have stomachs swollen from hookworm, and the entire family are frequent visitors to the health post. Three children born to the couple have either died at birth or before reaching one year of age.

Like most families in Itá, Family B is in debt. Although their small income exceeds normal monthly expenditures, they splurge from time to time. During a drunken spree the husband ran up a bill of $10 (cr. $200) for *cachaça;* on another occasion he and his wife accepted responsibility as one of the sponsors of the festival of Nossa Senhora das Dores. The food, liquor, and fireworks for the festival cost them over $20 (cr. $400). They were able to persuade the Casa Gato to give them credit for new clothes for the festival of St. Benedict in 1947. Because they are always in debt and because the husband enjoys going to the Casa Gato frequently for conversation, Family B tends to buy in quite small quantities: one small package of matches, a half-bottle of kerosene, or a half-kilo of beans. The standard of living of the Itá lower class is close to a bare minimum of existence.

Yet the rural groups discussed earlier, the farmers and the collectors, live in even greater poverty. The problems of these rural people vary somewhat according to their occupation. The collector, without a garden to supply his family in manioc flour, must buy almost all his food. Farmers, with little cash or credit at the commercial houses, must depend almost exclusively on their gardens and upon fishing and hunting to feed their families. The case of one farmer family will illustrate the very minimum existence of this rural lower class. This family, Family C, lives in a hut in Jocojó. There are four people in the family: a man, his wife, and two children, neither of whom is old enough as yet to be of help in the garden.

[8] *Geografia da fome*, p. 66.

Both the man and his wife work in the fields, but the heavier tasks are performed by the husband. During a part of the year, the husband earns some income from collecting rubber or timbó root in the nearby forest. In 1947 he had a surplus of almost one thousand kilos of manioc flour, bringing the family the sum of $80 (cr. $1,600). He earned another $20 (cr. $400) in rubber collecting. This was the total cash income of the family.

Their hut is almost bare of furnishings. The kitchen has a table and two wooden boxes that a trader gave them. A wooden bench takes the place of chairs. The man and his wife keep their few clothes in a painted tin trunk.[9] The house is lighted with three small kerosene containers (*lamparinas*) which produce considerable black smoke and have little effect upon the darkness. The wife has only one small metal pan and two cheap ceramic pots for cooking. Although they have three forks, the family generally eats only with spoons. There is a tin plate for each member of the family. They own five demitasse cups and saucers for coffee and two water glasses. Both the husband and the wife have individual hammocks, but the children share a hammock for sleeping.

Family C spends, on the average, $6.75 (cr. $135) for food and other necessities each month. They are the customers of a trading post at the mouth of the tributary on the Amazon mainstream. Prices at this trading post are even higher than in Itá stores, and Family C receives little for its money. Their purchases are normally limited to sugar (4 kilos per month), salt (1 kilo), a liter of kerosene, a small piece of tobacco, coffee (2 kilos), two boxes of matches, three kilos of sun-dried beef, and two bars of rough laundry soap. Fresh meat, except that which results from the hunt, is eaten only when they visit Itá or during a festival when a pig is butchered. Beans, rice, bread, *goiabada*, and other foods which are common in Brazilian homes are for them rare luxuries. The few clothes they have are exceedingly expensive; a piece of poor cloth for a woman's

[9] This type of tin trunk is used throughout rural Brazil both to carry belongings and as a coffin for children and infants.

dress costs as much as $5 (cr. $100), and the cloth for a man's trousers about $3.75 (cr. $75). Therefore Family C has a minimum of clothes. Neither the husband nor wife has shoes; he has only one suit for festivals, and she has a good dress which is carefully guarded for special occasions. Their everyday clothes are old and ragged. Their small son, who is eight years old, runs nude about the yard, and the daughter, who is ten, has two rather ragged dresses.

Family C, like Families A and B, is in debt. The trader from whom they buy lays claim to the land on which they plant, and he also owns the rubber trails from which the husband collects latex. The trader advances them food and merchandise against the manioc flour and the rubber which they turn over to him. Rarely do they have any cash at all. Sometimes they get cash by selling a pelt or an *alqueire* (30 kilos) of manioc flour to an itinerant trading boat. When they wish to contribute to the annual festival of St. Peter at Jocojó each year, they must give rubber or garden products. Although the rural worker in Itá provides a large part of the food for his family from his own gardens, or by hunting, fishing, and collecting edible fruits from the forest, the price of foods which must be bought, such as rice and beans, is beyond his purchasing power. Most rural families eat badly most of the time and face periods of semi-starvation. The low social status of the farmer and collector families of the rural neighborhoods of Itá results primarily from their low economic condition.

Despite these marked local differences in living standards between the upper and lower classes, Itá lacks the great contrast between the extremely rich, with their great ostentation and luxury, and the extremely poor, which is so characteristic of the large urban centers of Brazil. Compared to the rural farmers, collectors, and the town Second Class, the Itá "whites" seem wealthy indeed; but in larger perspective even the upper class, except for the owners of the Casa Gato, are poor. In short, the entire community of Itá has a remarkably low standard of living, especially when compared to a small town of equal size in the United States or in France.

IV

Although social rank in Itá is closely correlated to economic position, many other factors contribute to it. There are individuals classified as First Class who have lower incomes than others who are classed as Second Class. There are also people recognized as Second Class with sufficient income to be placed in First Class but lacking in the other qualifications necessary. Raimundo Gonçalves, for example, who has a salary from the federal government as foreman at the recently constructed airport at Itá and who employs men to plant large manioc gardens, is classed by everyone as Second Class. Dona Branquinha, the schoolteacher, although she lives in a rather large house on First Street, has an income only one-fifth as large as that of Raimundo Gonçalves. She earns hardly enough to eat even poorly; but in any list of the "whites" of Itá, Dona Branquinha's name is always one of the first three or four to be remembered. The reasons why Dona Branquinha is invariably assigned to the upper class and why Raimundo Gonçalves is always classed as Second Class are non-economic in nature. They are differences in family, in education, in achieved positions within the community, and in personal characteristics. In Itá, as in other human societies, the criteria of social rank tend to cluster; that is, a man of superior economic position is apt also to be a member of a superior family, with a better education, and with a position of leadership in his society. A poor man is more apt to come from a family of lowly origins, to have less education, and to find it difficult to achieve a position of leadership. It is a combination, an individual rating by multiple systems of ranking, that gives him his final status.

The cases of Dona Branquinha and Raimundo Gonçalves illustrate the weighing of a variety of criteria. Dona Branquinha comes of a "good family"; she is a descendant of the baron of Itá. Although her father was poor, she spent her childhood in companionship with Dona Dora Cesar Andrade and the other girls of the First Class. She was sent to Belém to finish her primary schooling. Although her married life has been insecure (she has been widowed three times by death), she has always maintained a moral life. She made a great effort to educate her two sons, both of whom attended secondary schools in Belém. It was perhaps the unlucky fate of her marriages which turned Dona Branquinha's interest to religion. She has achieved a position as religious arbiter and leader of Itá. When the Brotherhood of St. Benedict fell apart, the records were left with her. When Itá no longer supported a padre, Dona Branquinha began to lead prayers at Vespers and on Sundays in the church. Whenever a visiting padre comes to Itá, Dona Branquinha invites him to stay in her home. The priest stationed in a nearby town asked Dona Branquinha to take charge of the Itá church. Gradually farmers and rubber gatherers, who wished to make offerings to St. Benedict, began to bring them to her house, asking her to add their names to her list of donors. It is said that at one time Dona Branquinha had more than "one hundred *contos*" (approximately $5,-000) in her hands from offerings to the church. With these powers deriving from her position as religious leader, Dona Branquinha also became something of a social arbiter. She criticizes the manners and the morals of the townspeople, and they fear that she will pass on her opinions to the padre. It was Dona Branquinha who reported to the padre that the dancing at the annual festival of Nossa Senhora das Dores celebrated by a small brotherhood in Itá was "nothing but an orgy." With the padre, she opposes the small brotherhoods in the rural zone. As religious leader, Dona Branquinha has achieved a social position in Itá much superior to that of her immediate family.

Raimundo Gonçalves, on the other hand, comes from outside. He moved to Itá only five years ago from the Upper Amazon. Though he is literate, it is obvious from his handwriting, spelling, and vocabulary that Raimundo has had only a year or two of schooling. No one knows anything about his family, but it is clear that he does not descend from aristocracy. First, he does manual labor. In supervising the weeding of the airfield, Raimundo sometimes works alongside the day laborers; and in his gardens, Raimundo and his wife will help to clear fields or to peel manioc tubers for making flour. Second, although Raimundo had a good income by Itá standards, sufficient to support his wife and eight children, he continues to live on Third Street. When Raimundo came to Itá, he moved into a hut. Little by little he improved it until it was better in appearance and in construction than many First Street dwellings. Yet its location is Second Class and it is still a hut. Third, Raimundo and his family continue to behave toward "whites" in a manner which indicates that they are Second Class. He is respected for his hard work and economic position by both the First and the Second Class, yet Raimundo and his wife are retiring and humble before upper-class people. He is apt to remove his hat when talking with Manuel Serra Freire, and his wife is embarrassed in front of Dona Branquinha. It is their way of being polite. Finally, although Raimundo and his family have better clothes than the normal Second Class family, he likes to walk barefooted and his wife seldom puts on her shoes or her better dresses. There is no need, therefore, to consult a family genealogy to know that Raimundo comes from the "people."

These criteria—family, education, manners, and behavior—are of little importance in differentiating between the various strata which form the lower class of the Itá society, that is, between the urban lower class, the farmers, and the collectors. As stated earlier, townspeople of all classes expect rural dwellers to be less polished in their manners. Townspeople criticize the morals of the rural collectors and farmers. They tell with mixed admiration and criticism of the leader of the village of Jocojó, João Povo, who has for years lived openly with his legal wife and with his mistress Ermina, by whom he has several children. They tell stories of the caboclo who found that he might marry twice, once in the Church and once according to civil law. They point out the frequency, in rural neighborhoods, of marriage carried out on the order of the police after the complaint of the father of a minor girl against her lover. In addition, because schools are not available to them, people in the rural neighborhoods are overwhelmingly illiterate. Still, the line between the lower-class town dweller and the rural population, and between the farmer and the collector, is not so sharply drawn. Many people who are collectors move into one of the farming areas, and people from the farming areas have moved to the Islands to collect rubber during years when rubber prices were high. Many townspeople have lived in the rural zones. To a great extent, the difference between these lower strata is a question of occupation, income, residence, and living standards. But the difference between the "whites" and the lower strata is one of deeply ingrained attitudes and behavior patterns which must be learned and practiced if one is to pass from one group to another. Mobility upward from one strata of the lower class to another is relatively easy; there are no serious barriers to it in group consciousness or in the behavior expected of the members of each stratum.

Movement from the lower class into the upper class, however, is difficult and infrequent. Educational opportunities are almost totally lacking for the rural population and the lower classes of town find it difficult to maintain their children in school even for the three year course. For any further education, only those of a superior financial position are able to send their children to Belém, or upriver to Santarém, where schools offer a complete primary education and the secondary course. Economic improvement is more difficult for the rural population than it is for the lower-class town dwellers. The persistence of inefficient methods of "fire agriculture" inherited from the Indians, the lack of modern farming equipment, the relatively poor land, the low prices paid for farm products, and the relatively high prices of all imported objects, the rigid commercial system based on debt, and other difficulties of this almost nomadic agricultural and collecting economy make it very improbable that an individual will rise in the economic scale. Furthermore, should a member of the lower class gain some education and be able to escape the almost inevitable trap of the debt system and improve his economical position, then he is faced with the necessity of learning new manners and new ways of behavior. Such a person would also find the memory of his low family origin a barrier to upward mobility. In Itá society, and in Amazon society as a whole, mobility upward from the lower class into the upper class is a diffi-cult feat. As in other rigid class societies, and especially in small towns, the memory of low origin is an almost impossible barrier to overcome. Generally, the only way for an individual to rise in the social hierarchy is to move away to another town.

The tragic story of João Porto who made a majestic effort to rise both economically and socially, will serve to illustrate the difficulties of social mobility. João was born of poor parents in the agricultural zone near Itá. His parents moved into town when he was a small child, and João was able to attend school for almost three years. He is therefore literate, although he reads and writes with some difficulty. He is at present about thirty-five years old; he is married and has one daughter. As a young man, he was known in Itá as a hard worker, shrewd, and honest. He has worked as a day laborer, as a rubber gatherer, and as an employee of Labato Cesar Andrade, owner of the Casa Gato, who seems to have become rather fond of him. Some ten years ago, with Lobato's financial help, João was able to purchase a small farm situated on the Itapeira Tributary, about a half-hour's walk from town. His land had three rubber trails, some lowland near the Amazon, and some terra firme for manioc. By working the land with the help of his brother-in-law, Jorge Dias, by collecting rubber from his trails, and by work-ing as a day laborer on the construction of the health post, João was able to pay for his land in a few years. During the first years of World War II, when rubber was high and the price of manioc flour was relatively high, João actually had credit or *sobra* (some-thing left) on the widow Cesar Andrade's books. There came a time when the state government took steps to form an agricultural cooperative which would allow local farmers to purchase much-needed tools and sell their produce at better prices. João was a leader in the group which attempted to establish the cooperative. He had plans to purchase machinery for exterminating the *saúva* ant and machinery to produce manioc flour. João had his three children in school, and his family was relatively well dressed. He was on his way up the ladder—at least, economically.

But the cooperative failed for lack of official support. In 1942 João's seven-year-old son died, and the entire family came down with malaria. Since then his wife has been chronically ill. Because of sickness in the family, João missed many days of work; he was not able to plant as much manioc as in former years and he had to leave the exploitation of the rubber trails to his brother-in-law. After one bad year, he was again in debt. By 1948 rubber prices had fallen, and although João and his brother-in-law had planted large manioc gardens João was still in debt. People said that a ghost had put a curse on João's house, for his second son died in 1947 and his wife continued to be ill. He still had his land, but João's entire attitude in 1948 was one of defeat. He discussed at length the impossibility of anyone "improving one's situation" in Itá. His dream of becoming a landowner and a commercial man, of visiting Belém and of educating his children seemed an impossibility. João was a bitter man.

Yet Itá people seem to believe in success stories. At least, they tell of cases in which a simple sailor or a rubber gatherer became a wealthy and important man. Eneas Ramos, for example, told of his own son-in-law who, according to his account, became an important trader on the Tapajoz River. This son-in-law, José Dias da Silva, was a poor sailor who worked aboard one of the numerous river steamers which ply the lower Amazon. He worked his way up to become a steward aboard. Then, through the help of his godfather, Manuel Paiva, the Portuguese owner of a large trading post near Itá, José moved to a better job aboard the motorship *Moacyr*. He appeared in Itá from time to time, generally for his holidays. During one visit he courted and married one of Eneas Ramos' daughters. As he became better known in Belém, he was able to secure merchandise on credit from one of the large commercial houses, and he set himself up as a trader on the Tocantins River. He was successful, and now he has a high social position in a small Tocantins town. His godfather, according to Eneas, has invited José Dias da Silva to return to Itá several times. His godfather offered him the use of a large tract of land with rubber trails, but "he would not work on another man's land; he would return only if he could buy his own land and have his own trading post," said his father-in-law.

All local success stories of economic and social mobility relate how a successful young man was successful elsewhere, but not in Itá, through the help of a benevolent godfather, relative, or employer, or by some other stroke of luck. Migration to the city of Belém or Manaus, or to another small community in the Amazon Valley, not only erases the memory of low family origin but also makes it possible for a person of lower-class family to establish a new set of relationships, escaping those people of the upper class toward whom he has habitually deferred. A few sons of Itá are known to have been successful in the large cities. These few, however, evidently have little desire to return to their home town even for a visit. There is a well known physician in Belém who was born and who spent his first few years of life in Itá. He has not visited the town in over twenty years. Successful sons of Itá in the large cities are rare, however; social barriers in the cities are also rigid, and Itá is unable to furnish young people with a solid early education as a basis for economic and social ascension. Most migrants from Itá to the large cities of Manaus and Belém become factory workers or low-paid laborers, members of the urban lower class.

The difficulties of economic and social advancement in Itá society reinforce the belief, so common throughout Brazil, that only a stroke of luck can lead to economic success. Only by winning in the lottery, by a lucky break in business, or by discovering gold buried centuries ago by missionaries is a man able to gain wealth. Lottery tickets are rarely sold in Itá nowadays, and *jôgo do bicho* (a sort of numbers game, played throughout Brazil, in which animals are drawn instead of numbers) has not been played in recent years in the town. Both forms of gambling, however, are very much a part of Itá culture. People would like to buy a lottery ticket or "draw an animal" if they were available. They tell of friends who won in the "animal game" or in the lottery in the big city. Above all, Itá folklore is full of stories of hidden treasures. There are "real-life" stories of men who spent years digging for treasures revealed to them in dreams. Lobato Cesar Andrade, who was for many years Itá's most important merchant and probably its wealthiest man, is said to have gained his start in life by finding a buried treasure. According to the story, Lobato dreamed one night that there was a pot of money buried just in front of his house. The dream revealed the exact spot, even the depth of the pot of money. Lobato heard the words, "The money is there for you." He went to the spot at night and dug up the money, but he did not tell anyone about it at the time. People knew of his luck because one of his employees saw him counting his fortune. Soon afterward Lobato had a mass celebrated in the church. But Lobato's luck did not stop with the finding of hidden treasure. He was able, because of his money, to marry Dona Dora Cesar Andrade, the daughter of a wealthy merchant, and to inherit from her father. In Itá people have little credence in becoming wealthy by slow accumulation of money. They believe in luck; or, as the Itá saying goes, "Whoever gets rich either inherited or stole."

V

Brazil is well known throughout the world for its racial democracy. Throughout the country racial prejudice and discrimination are relatively subdued, in comparison to the situation in the United States of America, South Africa, and most of Europe. This does not mean that race prejudice is entirely lacking or that physical characteristics are not symbols of social status and thus barriers or aids to social mobility. It does mean, however, that race relations are essentially peaceful and harmonious. The Amazon Valley shares the traditional Brazilian patterns of race relations. Yet the attitudes in regard to different racial groups and the relations between racial groups in Amazon society reflect the distinctive aspects of Amazon history and regional society.

Throughout most of Brazil, Indians rapidly gave way to imported African slaves as the major source of labor. Thus, the descendants of Negro slaves came to form the majority of the lower classes in contemporary society. The Indian, as the memory of his early slave position in colonial society faded, became a romantic figure, and it is today a point of pride for many aristocratic families in South Brazil to number Indians among their forebears. In the Amazon, on the other hand, colonists were not wealthy enough to purchase many African slaves. The few Negroes who did reach such communities as Itá during the colonial period must have been valuable property, men to be instructed and treated with great care—or they were already freemen. In the Amazon the majority of slaves were always Indians. Commerce in Indian slaves, which began early in the colonial period, evidently continued in the Amazon well into the nineteenth century. W. E. Bates describes Indian slavery quite specifically in the middle of the nineteenth century. In the small village of Egá on the Upper Amazon, he saw enslaved "individuals of at least sixteen different tribes; most of whom had been bought when children of native chiefs. This species of slave dealing although forbidden by the laws of Brazil is winked at by the authorities." Bates' own assistant "ransomed" two Indian children who had been torn from their families, and Bates tells us how both died within a short time after their arrival at Egá, despite his effort to doctor them.[10] Indian slavery persisted in the upper tributaries of the Amazon even into our own century. Slavery is therefore a relatively recent phenomenon in the Amazon Valley, and the descendants of Amazon Indian slaves occupy a low socio-economic position, comparable to that of the Negro in other areas of Brazil.

In Itá all three racial stocks which make up the Brazilian population; namely, the European, the African, and the Indian, are represented. All possible crossings of the three races have taken place to such an extent that classification of the population of Itá as to physical race is difficult, if not scientifically impossible. Roughly, however, the population of Itá appears to be about 15 per cent European, about 50 per cent mixtures of Europeans with Negroes

[10] W. E. Bates, *The Naturalist on the River Amazon*, pp. 278 ff.

and Indians in various degrees, about 25 per cent American Indian, and about 10 per cent Negro.[11] It is doubtful whether any of those classed as European, Negro, or Indian are genetically pure; they are classified according to apparent physical characteristics.[12] Our general observations in Itá, as well as the historical evidence, indicates that the American Indian genetic strain predominates in this mixed population.

The people of Itá have their own categories by which they classify their fellow citizens as to physical type. The most frequent ones used are *branco* (white) for those of apparent European or Caucasoid physical type; *moreno* (brunette) for mixtures of various types; *caboclo* for those of apparent Indian physical characteristics; and *preto* (black) for those of apparent Negro physical type. The term *mulato*, so often used elsewhere in Brazil, is only used in Itá in the feminine gender to refer to an attractive woman (for example, *uma mulatinha bonita* [pretty little mulatta] or *uma mulata boa* [good mulatta], but having the meaning of "a well formed wench"). As in most of Brazil, the term "Negro" is seldom heard, and then only in anger. Against anyone who has physical traits suggesting Negroid ancestry, the label *Negro ruim* (bad Negro) is a powerful insult. The term *pardo*, which is so often used in Brazilian newspapers and in official census data to include people of various racial mixtures who are not clearly Negroid, Indian, or European, is not used in Itá except by a few government officials.

The most important criterion for arriving at such classifications in Itá is the quality of the hair and the amount of body hair. The branco has thin straight hair and a heavy beard. The caboclo has black coarse hair. He has "three hairs on his chin for a beard and his hair stands on end despite all efforts to comb it." The kinky hair

[11] In classifying 202 adults as to racial appearance, the results were as follows: 50 per cent *mestiço* (mixed), 17 per cent *branco* (European), 23 per cent *caboclo* (Indian), and 10 per cent *preto* (Negro). An independent census carried out by the health authorities of 305 Itá people listed 71 per cent as *pardo* (literally "brown"), 19 per cent as "white," and 30 per cent as Negro.

[12] *Race and Class in Rural Brazil*, ed. Charles Wagley (UNESCO, Paris, 1952), p. 122.

of the preto is described as *quebra pente* (break-a-comb); people laugh when they tell how such hair strips the teeth from a comb when the preto tries to comb it. Other criteria which are sometimes used as indicators of racial types are a flat nose and thick lips, which are signs of Negroid ancestry; and slant eyes, indicative of Indian parental stock. Skin color is frequently mentioned, but the common diagnostic trait is hair. Itá people say that skin color and facial features are not trustworthy: "They fool one."

The general rule of thumb for Brazil—"The lighter the skin, the higher the class; the darker the skin, the lower the class"—may be said to apply in Itá. The majority of the Itá First Class are in physical appearance either Europeans or mestizos (mixtures) with predominantly European ancestry. The majority of the lower-class groups (the urban Second Class, the farmers, and the collectors) are in physical appearance mestizos with predominantly Indian or Negro ancestry, or they are of apparently pure Indian or Negro physical type. The accompanying chart gives the racial appearance and the social class of 202 Itá adults, the fathers and mothers of the families covered in our family studies referred to above. Of the First Class, 53 per cent (or 16 people) of the total were classified as brancos ("whites"), 44 per cent (or 13 individuals) as morenos (mixed), 3 per cent (or 1 individual) as caboclo (Indian), and none as preto (Negro). Of the 172 people in three lower-class groups taken as a unit, about 10 per cent (or 18 individuals) were classed as "white," 51 per cent (or 89 individuals) as mixed, 27 per cent (or 46 individuals) as Indian, and 12 per cent (or 19 individuals) as preto, or Negro (see Chart, p. 132).

In Itá the descendants of the Indian and the Negro continue to occupy the lower positions in the social hierarchy. Despite the relatively large population of freemen in the Amazon Valley of Indian and Negro ancestry in the nineteenth century, those inhabitants of Itá with Indian, Negroid, and mestizo physical characteristics are derived ultimately from slave ancestry. As a group, they have not, during the last half-century, been able to rise in the social hierarchy. In Itá, where the effects of mass education and industrialism have

CLASSIFICATION OF 202 ADULTS BY RACE AND BY SOCIAL CLASS

CLASS	SOCIAL STRATA	MASCULINE									FEMININE								
		Branco		Moreno		Caboclo		Preto		Total	Branco		Moreno		Caboclo		Preto		Total
		No.	%	No.	%	No.	%	No.	%		No.	%	No.	%	No.	%	No.	%	
UPPER CLASS	Brancos or First Class	7	50.	6	42.9	1	7.1	—	—	14	9	56.2	7	43.8	—	—	—	—	16
	Second Class	4	8.7	25	54.4	10	21.7	7	15.2	46	5	9.6	27	52.	14	26.9	6	11.5	52
LOWER CLASS	Farmers	2	6.9	14	48.3	9	31.	4	13.8	29	1	3.8	16	61.6	8	30.8	1	3.8	26
	Collectors	2	22.2	4	44.5	2	22.2	1	11.1	9	4	40.	3	30.	3	30.	—	—	10
	Total	15	15.3	49	50.	22	22.5	12	12.2	98	19	18.3	53	51.	25	24.	7	6.7	104

not as yet been felt, Indian and Negro physical characteristics are still a symbol of low social status and of slave ancestry. European physical appearance is a symbol of aristocratic slaveowning descent.

Yet there are individuals of all racial types in all social strata. The mayor of Itá, who is, of course, classified as a "white" or First Class, has the copper skin color and the high cheekbones of an Indian. The widow Dona Dora Cesar Andrade, the individual who has perhaps the highest social position in Itá, is a dark mulatta. Her husband was a Negro. The local porter and the town drunk, Oswaldo Costa, at the other extreme of the social scale, is clearly of European descent, having light pigmentation and a heavy beard. His father, some old people remember, was a Portuguese immigrant. There are other cases of dark mestizos and even a few caboclos in the upper class and of European physical types in the lower-class groups. The people of non-European physical types who figure in the upper class are numerous enough to indicate that racial characteristics are not immutable barriers to social advancement. Social position and class membership are economically and socially determined. Physical race is an important but uncertain diagnostic of social position.

Perhaps because of the enormous variety of different racial types in their society, the people of Itá seem acutely conscious of physical characteristics. When one wants to describe a specific person, it is usual to do so by saying "*aquele branco*" (that white) or "*aquele preto*" (that black), and so on, in about the same way that we might say "that short fat fellow." The relative lack of racial prejudice or discrimination does not mean that people are unaware of physical appearance. On the contrary, they seem more conscious of minute details of racial characteristics than people in the United States.

Eleven local people were asked to classify, as to physical type, twenty well known individuals, selected from different social strata, according to the fourfold Itá classification—branco, moreno, caboclo, and preto. The town drunk, the leader of the annual Boi Bumba pageant dance, the schoolteacher, a day laborer of the town hall, and others well known to everyone were included in the list. For a few individuals in the list whose physical characteristics were clearly Negroid or European, there was general agreement as to their physical type. For example, Alfredo Dias, the pilot of a launch stationed at Itá, whose hair, facial features, and black skin leave no doubt that he is a Negro, was classed as preto by nine people, although two thought that he should be called a moreno despite his marked negroid traits. Agreement was also fairly general for those whose social position and physical characteristics, in a sense, coincided. The adopted son of the widow Cesar Andrade was a branco for ten people and a moreno for only one. He has a light complexion and a heavy beard.

On the other hand, people do not always agree on the racial classification of people whose physical traits were not so clear-cut, who were obviously of mixed racial descent, or whose physical characteristics conflict, so to speak, with their expected social position. Thus, Dona Branquinha was found to be a branca by five people and a morena by six. The vice mayor was classed as a branco by three, a caboclo by three, and a moreno by five people. He is a rather portly man whose mixed ancestry is clearly of all three racial stocks, but his appearance is more that of an Indian European mestizo. In classifying Oswaldo Costa, five people out of eleven classified him as a caboclo, despite his marked European features, which the other six took into consideration in calling him a branco. "How can Oswaldo be a branco?" one informant exclaimed, referring to his low social position. Conversely, Dona Dora Cesar Andrade was classed as a morena by nine people, while two others placed her as a branca. Dona Dora had a "white father and a Negro mother," one man reasoned, "but her money whitens her skin." He implied that if Dona Dora were of low social rank she might even be classed as a preta. The conflict between race appearance and expected social position reminds one of the Brazilian expression, "A rich Negro is a white and a poor white is a Negro," and of the story told by Henry Koster, the nineteenth century English traveler to Brazil. When Koster asked if a certain high official (*capitão-mór*) was not a

"mulatto man," his informant replied, "He was but he is no longer."
When Koster asked for an explanation, his informant replied, "Can
a *capitão-mór* be a mulatto man?"[13] Social position tends in many
cases to override observable physical characteristics in the classification of individuals in terms of "race."

A series of stereotyped concepts and cultural values persists in
Itá, reflecting the social position of people of different racial stocks
in the colonial society. Light complexion and the fine facial features
of the European, for example, are considered beautiful. In the slave
society of the past, it was an advantage for children to inherit the
features of their European fathers rather than the Indian or Negroid
features of their slave mothers. In Itá, mothers frequently boast
of the "fine nose, the light skin, and the fine hair" of their children.
Again, as Freyre has emphasized, the Portuguese male seems to have
been especially attracted to the Indian and even the Negro woman;
this attraction, according to Freyre, seems to have its roots in the
idealization of the Moorish beauty.[14] Itá men consider the morena,
varying from dark brunette to mulatta, to be the most attractive
feminine type. They like the "long straight hair of the Tapuia"
[Indian], the regular features of the European, and a dark skin. On
the other hand, women prefer lighter men. In colonial times it was
to the advantage of the Indian or Negro woman to be the concubine
or the wife of a European. Emilia, a young girl of Indian-Portuguese
descent, made it quite clear that she would not marry a Negro "even
if he were perfumed." She would like to marry a "light moreno."
Yet Marcos Dias, the twenty-year-old son of the Negro Alfredo
Dias, who is a dark mulatto, was considered handsome by many
women "in spite of his color and his 'bad' [kinky] hair."

Yet despite their stated preferences, people actually seek mates of
approximately the same physical type. Of 82 married couples known
to us in Itá, 56 couples were of the same physical type—that is,
both brancos, or both pretos, and so forth. The other 26 couples
in which man and wife were classified in different physical cate-

[13] *Travels in Brazil*, 2nd ed. (London, 1816), p. 391.
[14] *The Masters and the Slaves*, pp. 11 f.

gories were marriages between people of those categories which were nearest in pigmentation. They were all marriages of a branco with a moreno, a dark moreno with a preto, or a preto with a caboclo. There were no marriages, for instance, in our sample, between a preto and a branco.

Marriages between people of the same physical type or between people of approximately the same skin color are not determined by any restrictions against interracial marriages. They result from the fact that in Itá people tend to marry roughly within the same social stratum. Since people of a social stratum tend to be generally of similar physical type, marriage in one's own social stratum results in marriage between people roughly similar in physical type. That marriages between people of different physical type are not prohibited, or even discouraged, was attested by our Itá informants, who remembered numerous cases of branco men marrying women of American Indian or Negro physical type and of pretos and caboclos marrying branco wives. In Itá, whatever segregation exists is based on social class rather than on physical or socially defined race.

The fixed ideas which the people of Itá maintain regarding the innate abilities of people of each "racial" category also reflect the position of each of these groups in colonial society. In Itá, people say that the branco is always "good at business," and a man who is physically a branco arriving in the community would be considered per se "intelligent and well educated," obviously a persistence from the time when most Europeans were landed aristocrats, owners of great rubber-producing forests, or important officials from the capital. Our informants in Itá told us with some amusement of strangers who were brancos but who came dressed in poor clothes and who were found to be illiterate. In asking for a favor, people in Itá are apt to address others as "*Meu branco!*" (My white!), a term which indicates high respect.

As in other parts of Brazil and, for that matter, other parts of the New World, people of mixed Negro and Caucasoid parentage (the moreno of Itá and the mulatto of other regions) are considered treacherous, irascible, and difficult to deal with. Especially those with light skin, "who seem almost branco," are thought to have *mau génio* (bad character), a term used to indicate an irritable person whose mood shifts easily to anger, and not to describe a person's moral character. No one in Itá liked one of the public-health physicians, a dark mulatto who spent almost three weeks there waiting for a boat to take him to his post. At first, several families invited him to visit them and men sought him out for conversation, for he was a doctor and thus a visitor of considerable prestige. But people soon found him to be abrupt and somewhat over-aggressive. He was critical of Itá, complaining that it was a dull town. The attitude of the townspeople soon changed. "When a dark moreno becomes a doctor," one man said, "he is proud and he tries to act like a white." People will often overlook their fixed concepts of the different physical types, but when there is reason to criticize a person they soon fall back upon such concepts to justify their feelings.

The number and variety of the stereotypes held in Itá in regard to the preto seem strangely out of keeping with the small number of Negroes in the present population. There is a veritable aura of prestige tied to the "old Negroes" (*os velhos pretos,* as they are called). It was a group of "old Negroes," people say, who were the leaders in the famous brotherhood devoted to St. Benedict, the most famous and most miraculous saint of the whole Lower Amazon area. It was the great devotion and the ability of these "old Negroes" which made the brotherhood of St. Benedict in Itá such a strong one. "The old Negroes began to die and the 'whites' began to take part in the devotion to St. Benedict" is the way in which people of all racial groups explained the relative decadence and disorganization of St. Benedict's brotherhood today. Furthermore, the small village of Jocojó is said to have been inhabited almost entirely by "old Negroes," although the people living there today have about the same appearance as the rest of the people of the Itá community area. This explains to people of Itá why the annual festival on St. Peter's day is always so well celebrated in Jocojó, and why the brotherhood devoted to this local saint is still so strong. "It is due to the knowledge and the devotion of the 'old Negroes of Jocojó,'" people say.

The preto is also known as a fluent conversationalist and a good storyteller. People say that the "old Negroes" who lived in Itá over a generation ago knew more stories than anyone else and told them better, and a local saying has it that "whoever talks a lot is a Negro." Maria, the light morena who is the wife of Juca, is an excellent story-teller, and people directed us to her at once when they heard that we were interested in hearing traditional legends and myths of the Amazon. "She tells so many stories that she is almost a preta," we were told. Others who told us stories would often say that they had heard them from an "old Negro" who was long since dead. And they pointed to Roque, a very black preto who was very articulate about his experiences as a rubber gatherer in the upper reaches of the Amazon tributaries, and who indeed told stories very well, as an example of the Negro storyteller. People excused Roque's somewhat doubtful veracity by saying that he was a "preto who liked to talk."

In Itá the Negro is known, in addition, as particularly witty and crafty. And the Negro male is thought of as especially potent sexually. He has large genitalia and is therefore thought to be much appreciated by women of all racial groups. A series of pornographic stories told in Itá among men illustrate all these qualities of the Negro. In several of these stories, a Negro is having a sexual affair with a white woman, the wife of his master—or of his *patrão* (boss) if the story is placed in modern times. The stories revolve around the skill of the Negro in tricking his master, who suspects the affair but is unable to discover the pair together. Men tell of the sexual exploits of pretos of their acquaintance and of their greater sexual abilities. The Negro woman and the dark morena are also considered to have greater sexual appetites than the cabocla or the white woman. But the craftiness of the Negro is not limited to situations involving his sexual exploits. There are stories of how the preto outsmarted his master who would punish him for not working, and how the Negro equalized matters with a trader-patron who overcharged him for the goods he purchased.

The stereotypes of the Negro as a good storyteller, and of the Negro as especially potent sexually, are similar indeed to stereotypes regarding the Negro encountered in North America. Furthermore, a series of jokes, many of which are pornographic, are told in the North American South about the Negro.[15] Undoubtedly, these similar stereotypes result from the background of Negro slavery which is common both to southern North America and to northern Brazil. But here the similarity ends. The picture of the "old Negro" as a good storyteller in Itá is not that of Uncle Remus who mildly recounts folk tales to a younger audience. In Itá the picture evoked is that of the colorful raconteur of stories of all kinds, both for the family and for the ears of men in the bar.

The stereotype of the sexual ability of the Negro male may well arise from sexual envy on the part of non-Negro males in Itá, as it seems to in the South of the United States. But it does not serve, as Gunnar Myrdal indicates, for the North American South, "as part of the social control devices to aid in preventing intercourse between Negro males and white females."[16] This very situation is part of the plot of many "off-color" stories, and both legal marriages and extra-marital sexual affairs between Negro males and lighter females are commonplace occurrences in Itá. Nor do the stories told about the Negro serve the function of "proving [his] inferiority";[17] on the contrary, they have the function of proving a superior quality; namely, his craftiness. In Itá these stories are not told by a white caste about an inferior caste: they are stories told by people of various racial hues about their fellow citizens. In Itá the stereotypes held in regard to the Negro show him in a favorable light. To be sure, they show the Negro as inferior to the white, but he has many attributes which are highly valued in Itá society.

Yet at the same time people in Itá disparage the Negro in a rather

[15] Gunnar Myrdal, *An American Dilemma* (New York, 1944), p. 39.
[16] *Ibid.*, p. 108.
[17] *Ibid.*, p. 39.

warm and humorous manner. They know and make use of widespread Brazilianisms which disparage and belittle the Negro, such as, "If the Negro does not soil when he enters, he does when he leaves." [18] But these sayings are apt to be used by pretos about themselves, and by people in a light joking manner to chide their intimate friends of obvious Negro ancestry. Juca, for example, whose mother was a well known "old Negro," often blamed his own bad habits on his Negro ancestry. "I talk too much because I am a preto," he said, to the amusement of his visitors. "I would put an end to that race of people" (the Negro), he ad libbed into the lines of a folk play in which he had an important part, "but the devil of it is, I also come from the same quality." Juca's complaints about his Negro ancestry always brought laughter, for people knew that he was proud of his mother. No one in Itá, to our knowledge, is ashamed of Negroid ancestry, and the prestige of the "old Negroes" is high in Itá tradition.

The stereotypes which the people of Itá hold regarding the *tapuia* or the caboclo (American Indian physical type), on the other hand, are not so favorable as those referring to the Negro. The caboclo appears as a good hunter and fisherman. He has a special sensitivity for the habits of animals and he knows almost instinctively where and how to hunt or fish. No one can remember a famous hunter who was not a "caboclo with but three hairs on his chin." Eneas Ramos was known in his earlier years as an excellent hunter. He was born and raised in the rural district near Itá where he learned very early to hunt, but people attribute his skill to the fact that "he is *tapuia*." These concepts are harmless enough, for skill at hunting is something useful and to be admired in Itá. Still caboclo and *tapuia* are used in a sense of dispraisal; people do not use them when speaking directly to people of Indian physical characteristics. "It is not a hard word," said Eneas Ramos, who was pointed out as a typical representative of this physical type, "but it makes a person sad."

[18] Cf. Wagley, *op. cit.*, and Donald Pierson, *Negroes in Brazil: A Study of Race Contact in Bahia* (Chicago, 1942).

The term, as stated earlier, has a double meaning—one indicating low social status, and another indicating American Indian physical characteristics. Furthermore, most of the stereotypes associated with the caboclo or the *tapuia* are derogatory. The caboclo is considered lazy: "They do not plant gardens, but live from the sale of a little rubber and by fishing for their meals." The caboclo is thought to be timid because he lives isolated in the forest. "They prefer to live like animals, away from others, deep in the forest," one man said. The caboclo, however, is thought to be tricky and exceedingly suspicious. A popular local saying has it that "the suspicious caboclo hangs up his hammock and then sleeps under it." Commercial men say that the caboclo must be watched in any business deal; he will insert a rock in the core of a large ball of crude rubber to increase its weight when he sells it to the trader. He will sell *timborana*, a vine which resembles the true *timbó* from which insecticides are produced, but which has no value, to the unsuspecting trader. Such stereotypes regarding the caboclo are not limited to people of that physical type (American Indian) but are often aimed at all rural collectors. As most people point out, the rural collectors are in the great majority *tapuias* or caboclos in a physical sense, but even town dwellers of this physical type are thought to share their timidity, laziness, ability at hunting and fishing, and trickiness.

People of American Indian descent, unlike those of Negroid descent, do not like to be reminded of their Indian ancestry. The children playing in front of an Itá home were heard many times teasing the housewife of caboclo physical type. They called her *tapuia* and *índia*, and she would reply in anger, "Go away, your parents are Indians themselves." In the Amazon the Indian, even more often than the Negro, was the slave in colonial society. In the opinion of the European, the Indian was a nude barbarian and of less prestige than the more expensive African slave. Today, Indian physical characteristics are therefore a symbol not only of slave ancestry but also of a social origin in colonial times lower than the Negro's.

VI

The system of race relations which has taken form in Itá provides a comparatively favorable and fertile basis for the growth of social and economic democracy. In contrast with many colonial areas of the world, neither in Itá nor in other Brazilian communities is there a "color line" which makes for intense and emotionally charged feelings of the native population (generally of Mongoloid or Negroid racial stock) toward the dominant European caste. Brazilian society has avoided developing a "caste society," such as that of the United States, where the strict line between the Negro and the white has been such a costly drain upon the nation and the individuals. If and when the standard of living and the educational level of Itá improve, the people of darker skin now occupying the lower ranks of the society should be able to improve their economic and social position despite their racial origins. People of "color," and all other people in Itá, may raise their social status by improving their educational level, occupation, economic situation, and family connections.

Economic and social change, however, might endanger the persistence of this Brazilian tradition of racial democracy. In the great metropolitan centers of the country, there are already indications that discrimination, tensions, and prejudices between people of different racial types are emerging.[19] There is the danger that, when a large number of people of Negro and Indian racial ancestry improve their educational and economic position, they will challenge the dominant position of the "whites" (even though they are also of mixed ancestry), with the result that race will be emphasized as a criterion of social position. Furthermore, as such rural Brazilian communities as Itá become more closely tied to the Western industrial and commercial world, it will be exposed to a different ideology

[19] "Race Relations in Brazil: São Paulo," by Roger Bastide, and "Race Relations in Brazil· Rio de Janeiro," by L. A. Costa Pinto, *Courier*, Unesco, Paris, Vol. 5, Nos. 8–9, 1952.

regarding race relations. After all, the technicians, the administrators, and even the scientists are the products of a civilization which has in the last four hundred years taught racial inequality. There is a danger that along with their useful techniques, instruments, and concepts they may teach racial inequality. But, aware of these dangers and pitfalls, Itá and other Brazilian communities may well enjoy the benefits of technological change and of greater educational facilities without losing their rich heritage of racial democracy.

The social class structure of the Brazilian Amazon region, however, is a drawback to be overcome by any program aiming at social and economic change. The *alta sociedade*, that is, the descendants of the colonial landholders of the rubber barons, and of successful commercial men, are content with the status quo. They look with suspicion on any program which might result in basic changes in Amazon society. They have been able to draw sufficient wealth from extractive industries to allow them to live in Belém and Manaus or even abroad. They have been able to educate their children elsewhere. Any program of economic development and technical assistance would inevitably have to deal with these "aristocrats" and with the growing middle class of the Amazon region, made up of the professional groups, the public officials and civil servants, the office workers in commercial companies, and the like. In Itá any health program or agricultural program would have to be channeled through the First Class, since they are the government officials and the commercial leaders of the community. Any initiative which depends entirely either upon this "middle class" or upon the regional aristocrats would have but a limited influence upon the region. The Itá upper class and the regional middle class share many of the social values of the old landed gentry. Upper-class Brazilian urbanites look down upon the inhabitants of the small towns and know little about the so-called "interior." The ideal of any state or federal employee who is unfortunate enough to be stationed in a small town in the "interior" is to be transferred to the city. Like the urban upper and middle class, the Itá First Class holds manual labor in dispraisal. They know little about the problems and the values of their lower-class fellow citizens—the Second Class towns-people, the rural agriculturalists, and the collectors of forest products. The chasm between the upper and the lower strata in Amazon society is a wide one. Innovations introduced through these upper- and middle-class groups tend to ignore the mass of people in the lower strata of Amazon society.

Social rank in all human societies is based upon a combination of birthright and individual achievement. Despite many changes since colonial times, Amazon society still places an emphasis upon birthright, and there are few opportunities for individual achievement. The highly crystallized class system which has persisted since the colonial period is changing with extreme slowness. But, as educational and health facilities and economic opportunities are made available to a larger segment of the population, the emphasis will shift from position ascribed at birth to social positions which are achieved. This will bring about a rearrangement of the Amazon social hierarchy and will result in individual maladjustments and disappointments. That is the price that the people of Itá will have to pay for "progress." But modification of the traditional class system will also allow a fuller utilization of the human resources of the Amazon Valley.

5. FAMILY AFFAIRS IN AN AMAZON COMMUNITY

The large and closely knit family is one of the most important institutions of Brazilian society. When a Brazilian speaks of *minha família* (my family), he generally refers to a large group consisting not only of his own relatives but also those of his wife. He is apt to call the more immediate unit "my wife and children" (*minha mulher e filhos*) reserving the word "family" for the larger circle of kin. The family often includes first, second, and even third cousins. First cousins are called "brother cousins" (*primos irmãos*), while second and third cousins are simply "cousins." The term for "uncle" and "aunt" may also be extended to mean one's parents' cousins. Over a hundred relatives may form the family of a middle-class Brazilian city dweller, and a member of the traditional aristocracy may be able to count literally hundreds of relatives. In such large

145

circles of kin, intimacy is greater among those who have a close degree of kinship. An inner circle of aunts, uncles, and "brother cousins" usually has the more frequent and devoted relationships. For many Brazilians social life is lived mainly within this widely extended family. There are birthday parties, baptisms, graduations, funerals, and other occasions on which the family gathers, and there are weddings at which one garners a whole new circle of family connections. In Rio de Janeiro, São Paulo, and even in the Amazon cities of Belém and Manaus, crowded urban conditions make for dispersal of these large family groups throughout the city, yet constant visiting, the telephone, and frequent family gatherings keep the group intact.[1] At any crisis in the life of one of the family members, others gather to offer help and sympathy.

Gilberto Freyre has described the role of the large patriarchal families in the colonial life of the northeastern coastal region of Brazil. In the rural society of colonial times, the aristocrat lived on his plantation surrounded by his married sons and daughters and their children, by a few distant relatives who had come to depend upon him, and by his slaves—all members, in a way, of his family. Marriages were alliances between large families, and marriages of first cousins or of uncles with nieces were frequent.[2] Often, an effort was made to steer a younger son into the church so that the family chapel might be in the hands of a priest who was a member of the family. Political affairs were dominated by family loyalties. The family was so important in colonial society that, in Gilberto Freyre's words, "The family and not the individual, much less the State or any commercial company, was from the sixteenth century the great colonizing factor in Brazil, the productive unit, the capital that cleared the land, founded plantations, purchased slaves, oxen, implements; and in politics it was the social force that set itself up as the most powerful colonial aristocracy in the Americas. Over it

---

[1] There is a tendency in Rio de Janeiro for relatives to purchase apartments in the same large cooperative apartment building.
[2] *The Masters and the Slaves*, p. 261.

the King of Portugal may be said, practically, to have reigned without ruling." [3]

In the Amazon region families were not so wealthy or powerful as the great patriarchal groups of the colonial ·northeast. Nevertheless, they were very important in politics, in economics, and in the social life of the region. Even today most Amazon commercial companies are family-owned, and family connections are important in politics. After each election the bureaucracy is apt to be crammed with the relatives of newly elected officials. The family is the focus of social life. A visitor in Belém or Manaus may find people somewhat inhospitable, since most social events take place within the family circle. Once accepted by a family, however, a visitor's social life may then become quite intense. He will be introduced by a friend to relatives, by these relatives to others, and perhaps even be given letters of introduction to members of the family in other towns.

II

People of all social classes in Itá share the Brazilian ideal of a large and united family group. They speak of important families and they are conscious of the role of family connections. Yet in Itá families are not nearly so large as they are among the urban middle class and the aristocrats of the region. Frequent emigration to Belém, to distant rubber fields, and even to other regions of Brazil results in a loss of contact with relatives. Among the upper and middle class of Brazilian cities with their superior economic conditions, people migrate less frequently than in rural communities. Whenever possible, Brazilians stay within reach of their families. In Itá, however, with one or two exceptions, everyone has a relatively precarious income and at any time may feel the need to move away in search of more favorable and stable circumstances. Without wealth or property, or even economic stability, relatives can be of

[3] *Ibid.*, p. 27.

little help to relatives. The large Brazilian family is therefore less often encountered in rural communities such as Itá.

In such a town everyone has relatives who have moved away. Even Manuel Serra Freire, a descendant of one of Itá's "best families," is the only one of four brothers now living in Itá. He had just returned there in 1948. One of his brothers is a civil administrator in the Brazilian army; another has a position in Rio de Janeiro; and the third "could never settle anywhere, but worked with a commercial company in many places until he died in Belém" a few years ago. Serra Freire's mother and sister live with him in Itá, and he has an uncle (his mother's brother-in-law) and a first cousin who are owners of a trading post not far from town. Nowadays these are his only relatives in the community; most of his family lives in Belém or elsewhere. In his father's time, when Itá was more prosperous, the family was important politically and exceedingly numerous, if the genealogy which he gave us may be trusted.

Eneas Ramos, a Second Class town dweller, also has many relatives who have long since left Itá. His family was a large one consisting of five sons and two daughters. But when Eneas Ramos was about ten years old, they moved from Itá to Monte Alegre, where they lived for a few years. Two of his brothers remained there with an uncle and an aunt when the family returned to take up farming near Itá on the Igarapé Itapereira. He still has family, he says, in Monte Alegre. Another brother left later to collect rubber in the rubber fields of the Upper Amazon and has never returned. His older brother married late and left no descendants. But Eneas has several "nephews and nieces," children of one of his sisters. Anastacio Ramos, the best known flute player in Itá, is his cousin, and through Anastacio, Eneas has several other relatives. Eneas is the father of five daughters and one son; two daughters married and stayed in Itá, but the others have moved away to Belém, to Santarém, and to the Tapajoz River with their husbands. His only son left Itá long ago and seldom writes. Eneas considers himself, however, to be a fortunate man; he says that he has a "large family." He was able to count as many as twenty-five relatives within the

Itá community between close and distant kin. But, as compared to the widely extended family groups of the middle and upper class in Belém, his family is small.

In the farming district of the Itá community, however, the kinship circle is somewhat larger than among the town dwellers. Income from farming in the Amazon is amazingly low, yet farming is still a relatively stable occupation. From their gardens people are guaranteed a minimum subsistence, and they are less dependent upon cash for foodstuffs than the city dweller or the rubber collectors. Farmers are thus less often forced to migrate, and they have large and extended families—closer to the Brazilian ideal than those of the poor townspeople.

In the farming village of Jocojó, genealogies showed that kinship formed a complex web of relationships among the inhabitants. Valentino, one of the leaders of the village, had four married sisters and their husbands and children as neighbors. Furthermore, his wife was the niece of João Povo, the most important man of the settlement, and thus he was tied to Povo's large group of relatives. He was also related, through marriage, to Teodoso, another head of a large family in the settlement. Of the total population of slightly more than one hundred people, this one man, Valentino, was related by kinship to well over half. And João Povo could claim relationship to over eighty of the villagers through direct descent or through marriage.

The Amazon rubber collectors, as already mentioned, are famous for their nomadic habits. They move about frequently, hoping to escape from debt and to find rubber trails where conditions are better than the one in which they work. The collector, therefore, often leaves his relatives behind, and in the rubber-collecting neighborhoods of the Itá community, even more so than in town, the family is small. Sometimes a father lives and works with his sons, or sometimes two or more brothers will exploit a group of contiguous rubber trails; but in general the collector is a man with few, if any, relatives. In this sense he is not an average Brazilian. The economic instability of rubber gathering does not provide a basis for a large kin group. Only among more settled farmers do people in Itá have the security of widespread kinship bonds.

In keeping with Brazilian ideals, however, relatives are no less united in Itá than elsewhere in the country. In normal social relations in Itá, one is aware of moving within small circles of kin. For example, soon after our arrival in 1948, we became quite friendly with the farmer Jorge Porto. When we needed someone to clean our house, he recommended a cousin. Later he introduced us to his brother-in-law, João Dias. Jorge became one of our most trustworthy sources of information on farming techniques and the problems of the small farmer in Itá. His mother-in-law, João Dias' mother, received us at once in her simple home and gave us unsparingly of her time, teaching us local folklore. Whenever we traveled in the vicinity by canoe João Dias' half-brother was always ready to arrange for a canoe and, if necessary, paddlers for us. Both Jorge Porto and João Dias had a few distant relatives (a "cousin," an "aunt," or an "uncle") in the rural neighborhoods, and we were always received at once by them. Likewise, in the village of Jocojó, João Povo asked his family to receive us well, and thus the majority of the villagers welcomed us into their homes. Eneas Ramos said that we might always call on his family. As elsewhere in Brazil, kinship is an important mechanism in Itá for channeling personal relations.

III

As in most of the Latin world, the people of Itá extend their relationships beyond the kinship circle by means of ritual co-parenthood. Because their kinship circle is, for Brazilians, not large, the people of Itá perhaps make even more frequent use of such ritual relationships than do the inhabitants of the big cities. It is almost as if they compensated for their relatively small number of kinsmen by so doing. Like most Latins, the people of Itá are Catholics. In accordance with Catholic ritual, the parents of a child invite a man and a woman to serve as sponsors at their child's baptism. The sponsors become godfather and godmother to the child, and the same rite establishes a strong relationship not only between the godchild (*afilhado*) and its godparents (*padrinhos*) but also between the parents of the child and the godparents, who become *comadres* (co-mothers) and *compadres* (co-fathers) to each other. This three-way relationship—between godparents with their godchild, between parents with their child, and between parents with the godparents—is one of considerable importance in most of Latin America and in many Latin countries of Europe. Godparents accept responsibility for the child materially and spiritually. Children owe especial respect to their godparents—"even more than to their parents" as one person in Itá explained. The parents and their co-fathers and co-mothers have, ideally, a relationship of mutual respect, of mutual aid, and of intimate friendship. They help one another and lend financial and moral aid to one another. It is considered incestuous for a co-mother and co-father to have sex relations; thus individuals of different sex, related to one another in this way, may have friendly relations without being suspected of sexual misbehavior. It is a common sight in the Amazon region to see two men embrace each other, using the common salutation, "*Como vai, meu compadre?*" (How are you, my co-father?), and to hear a man politely say, "*Minha comadre, Maria.*" Children kiss the hands of their godparents, asking for "a Blessing," and the godfather or godmother answers, "*Deus lhe abençoe, meu filho*" (God bless you, my child).

In the upper- and middle-class groups of a large Brazilian city, *compadresco* [4] relationships are often used to extend further an already extensive kinship circle or as a way of reinforcing the existing bonds with a particular kinsman. For example, the director of a company might invite a close business associate and his wife to serve as godparents to his son; or he might invite a wealthy or politically important cousin and his wife to serve. In the former case he establishes new ties both for himself and for his son, and in the latter

---

[4] *Compadresco* (adjective) and *compadrio* (noun) are the terms used for the constellation of relationship between the parents, godparents, and godchild.

he strengthens his kin ties to his cousin. In addition, throughout Brazil there is generally a ritual sponsor (godparent) at confirmation; [5] and at marriage both the bride and the groom invite a couple as their *padrinho e madrinha de casamento* (godparents of marriage). Thus a Brazilian child might normally, in the course of its life, acquire godparents at baptism, another godparent at confirmation, and godparents at his marriage. He or she would also share, in a sense, the marriage godparents of the spouse. An individual by the time of marriage might expect to be related to at least seven people by ritual sponsorship. In addition, any adult might also expect to be invited several times to serve as godparent of baptism, of confirmation, or of marriage, thus adding considerably to the number of individuals with whom ritual kinship ties are extended.

The force of these *compadresco* relations, added to family and kinship ties, are felt profoundly in Brazilian social, economic, and political life. Co-fathers extend political and economic favors to each other and to their godchildren. It is common to refer to someone who is protected politically by an important figure as an *"afilhado político"* (political godchild). A much more durable political maneuver than "kissing babies" is to stand as godparent for children at baptism. An old and practiced politician in the Amazon region, for example, kept a notebook in which he entered the addresses and birthdays of his three to four hundred godchildren. They were strategically scattered over the entire state, and both his godchildren and his co-fathers were certain voters and excellent political campaigners for him.[6]

In such communities as Itá, where so many people are econom-

---

[5] A male acquires a *padrinho* and a female a *madrinha*.

[6] In the rural areas of north Brazil, *compadrio* relationships are not "stripped of their importance and reduced to a mere formula of address" as indicated by Antonio Candido for the central and southern parts of the country (cf. "The Brazilian Family," in *Brazil: Portrait of Half a Continent*, T. Lynn Smith and Alexander Marchant, eds. [New York, 1951], p. 308). My own experience, even in such urban centers as Rio de Janeiro, leads me to believe that although *compadrio* relationships are perhaps less strong, and certainly modified by industrial urban conditions, they still have important functions in Brazilian society. A godfather is no longer "a second father," but he passes on favors, if convenient, to his godson, even in large towns and urban centers.

ically insecure, the *compadrio* system seems to have proliferated. For in addition to *compadres* [7] of baptism, in Itá and throughout the Amazon region, there are also *"compadres de fogueira"* (co-fathers of the fire). Both on St. John's Day and on St. Peter's Day in late June, it is customary throughout Brazil to build large bonfires around which the festivities of the season take place. Paper balloons are launched, fireworks are set off, sweet potatoes are roasted, and special songs of the season are sung. Along the Amazon, as the bonfire burns down into embers, one may also garner new co-fathers, godchildren, or godparents, as the case demands. A man invites a good friend, or an important man who might help him, to become his co-father. A youngster asks an adult to become his godfather or godmother. The relationship is established by a simple rite. The two, with the fire between them, pass their clasped hands over the fire three times, and recite an oath in unison. This oath, of which there are several versions, is as follows: "St. John said, St. Peter confirmed, that Our Lord Jesus Christ ordered us to be co-fathers in this life and in the other also." [8]

Such relationships established "over the fire" are not as binding as those established at baptism. Some people caught by an undesirable invitation go through the rite out of politeness. They sometimes elect to ignore the relationship later on. On St. Peter's Day in 1948, for example, a young married man was invited by three young girls to become their godfather. He accepted, explaining that it would be bad manners to refuse. Later he treated the relationship as a pleasant joke, calling each of them "my godchild" when he met them, and then, after a few weeks again addressed them formally by name. Others, however, take such relationships more seriously, and co-fathership by fire can be as intimate and stable as that formed

[7] The term *compadre* is used here generically to refer to the constellation of relationships of the system; namely, *compadre, comadre, madrinha, padrinho, afilhado,* and *afilhada.*

[8] São João disse,
São Pedro confirmou,
Que Nossa Senhor Jesus Cristo mandou
A gente ser compadre
Nesta vida e na outra tambem.

by baptism. João Povo, to cite one example, invited a man from Itá to become his co-father several weeks before St. John's Eve. The two men arranged to spend the festival together, and that evening they went through the rites of becoming co-fathers of the fire. Afterward, they treated each other with the same respect, the same mutual support, and the same cordiality as if one had sponsored the baptism of the child of the other. The possibility of extending one's bonds of ritual kinship at St. John's and St. Peter's Eve increases the number of people within the *compadrio* circle of any individual enormously. Most people in Itá make use of this mechanism to widen their circle of secure interpersonal relations.[9]

The strength and the degree of intimacy of *compadrio* relationships depend upon several factors—upon the continuity of frequent association of the individuals concerned, upon whether or not the continuation of such ties is of material or social value, and upon the personal inclinations of the individuals involved. In many cases noted in Itá, individuals have lost touch with their godparents or co-fathers; frequently, we were told of a sponsor at the baptism of a child who later moved away and never again wrote letters or returned to visit. Yet in other instances, where there was a reason to continue the relationship (if the sponsor was a commercial man or a politician, for example, to whom numerous relationships throughout the region would be valuable), the godfather did not forget his godchild and his co-father. Several of our friends in Itá told us of their godfathers or co-fathers who had moved to other towns or to Belém and who sent presents on each birthday. Whenever these co-fathers pass through Itá, they visit with their godchildren and co-fathers. *Compadrio* relationships between people within the community, however, tend to be close and intimate. The relationship between two old friends, between two cousins, between a trader and his customer, or between neighbors who are co-fathers is generally a warm, stable, and respectful one. If they live nearby, the godchild visits his godparents daily, asking them for their "blessing."

---

[9] Sometimes, people also "confirm" their kinship or their previously existing co-father relationship "over the fire."

Godchildren run errands for their godparents and are given small presents and sweets. Presents are forthcoming from the godparents on birthdays and at Christmas. Godchildren become intimates in their godparents' homes, and they come to look upon their godmother and godfather somewhat as a "second mother and father." Co-fathers lend each other small sums; they cooperate with each other in cooperative work parties; they aid each other in house repairs; and they are apt to spend many leisure hours together. Co-mothers cooperate in manufacturing manioc flour, watch out for each other's children, help each other in preparing the large meals on birthdays, and visit each other often. There is freer visiting, without fear of jealousy, between couples tied to each other by *compadrio* relationships than between neighbors or even distant relatives, for sexual relations are unthinkable between a man and his co-mother.

Juca and his wife, Anna, have a strong *compadrio* relationship with Ernesto and his wife, Maria. For years the two men had called each other co-father since they had passed over the fire on St. John's Eve; in addition, they were good friends and neighbors, both living on Second Street in Itá. Then, a few years ago, Ernesto and his wife invited Juca and Anna to serve as sponsors at the baptism of their adopted son, thus strengthening and reaffirming their established friendship and existing relationship. Juca and Ernesto plant their gardens cooperatively and they have pooled their resources to build a large fish trap. The two women work together each week preparing farinha, and sometimes Juca and Ernesto help their wives in the task. When Ernesto and Maria undertook to serve as sponsors for the festival of Santa Maria, celebrated by a religious brotherhood in one of the rural neighborhoods, Juca and Anna spent most of a week helping their co-father and co-mother prepare food to be served at the festival. Juca lent Ernesto approximately $5 (cr. $100), and Anna lent Maria cooking utensils and cups and saucers for serving coffee. Juca and Anna attended the festival, working throughout the day, helping their co-fathers to serve the many guests. The two couples visit each other almost daily, and each is aware of the family difficulties and troubles of the other. Maria sent for Juca at once when her husband got drunk and was jailed; Juca knew of his co-father's weakness for rum and was able to persuade the police officer to release Ernesto in his care. Each of these four people has other *compadrio* relationships, both by baptism and by fire, but the bond between the two couples has been singled out among all of them as the most intimate of all. Like the formal structure of kinship, the institution of *compadrio* offers a form through which intimate and secure interpersonal relationships may be channeled; but, as in kinship, the potentiality of the relationship may not be fulfilled. Neither co-fathers nor cousins need have especially close or friendly relations, and certain kinsmen or certain co-fathers are always more closely associated than others.

Juca and Ernesto and their families make use of the full potentialities of the *compadrio* relationship in living out a cooperative and intimate friendship. These two families are lower-class townspeople. Both have approximately the same income and approximately the same social status in the community. Their *compadrio* relationship is therefore a reciprocal one strengthened by mutual aid. Neither co-father has any special power to protect the other, nor has Juca wealth or political power through which he might be of any special aid to his godson. Many co-fathers are, like the two discussed above, members of the same socio-economic stratum and class. On the other hand, the *compadrio* relationship is perhaps more frequently established in Itá between individuals of different economic and social position—between members of the lower- and the upper-class groups. Poor people feel that one way to garner some advantage for their children is to ask a trader, a public official, or anyone with prestige and a relatively superior economic situation to serve as sponsor at the baptism. Perhaps, also, the co-father of higher status and greater wealth will favor and protect his poorer co-father. In such cases the initiative comes always from the lower-class family, who invite the upper-class individual or couple to serve as godparents. That this form of *compadrio* relationship is more common in Itá is attested by the number of such relationships which people of different social classes reported in our household survey. The household heads who were classified as "whites" reported an average of 28.1 godchildren; that is, they were requested to serve that many times as godparents.[10] In contrast, the heads of families classified as lower-class townspeople (that is, *Gente de Segunda*) had an average of only 4.2 godchildren.

In Itá the higher one's prestige and the greater one's wealth, the larger the number of godchildren and co-fathers one tends to have. In fact, it almost might be said that the number of godchildren and co-fathers which an individual can claim is an index of social position. The frequency with which an individual is invited to serve as a ritual sponsor or to pass over the fire on St. John's or St. Peter's Eve is a reflection of economic, social, political, and familial standing in the community. Dona Dora, owner of the Casa Gato, whose income and social position is perhaps the highest of any individual in Itá, claimed 142 godchildren and over three hundred co-mothers and co-fathers, the fathers and mothers of these godchildren. Another strong commercial man of the community reported one hundred godchildren, and a rural trader had as many as sixty-five godchildren. Dona Branquinha, the schoolteacher who lacks financial support for her upper-class position, was able to report only sixteen godchildren. Not all of these numerous *compadrio* relationships reported by people of the upper class were with lower-class families; for among upper class families too there is a tendency to invite someone as a godparent or co-father who stands even higher in the social and economic hierarchy. In this way strong ties are established between important families of the community and of neighboring communities. But mainly, the *compadrio* system provides a means of cementing relationships between the various social strata of Itá society.

Compadrio relationships between individuals of widely different social strata are by nature not as close and intimate as those between people of the same economic and social position. The fact that Dona

---

[10] These include godchildren by baptism as well as godchildren of the fire when the latter were recognized as godchildren.

Dora has so many godchildren and so many co-fathers means, of course, that the relationship is necessarily diluted and weakened by sheer numbers. In fact, Dona Dora cannot possibly remember all of the names of her godchildren and of her co-fathers. She keeps a note-book in which, over the years, she has inserted their names in order to remember them all. On several occasions young men have appeared at the Casa Gato announcing that they are godchildren of Dona Dora and of her late husband, Lobato. Dona Dora refers to her notebook (which is evidently not complete) on such occasions, questioning the young man about his age, the name of his parents, and when he was baptized. If she is reasonably certain that she or Lobato "stood for him" at baptism, she extends him the hospitality of her house and asks the manager of the Casa Gato to advance credit to him if he wishes to collect rubber.

Co-fathers and co-mothers who are steady customers at the Casa Gato are remembered well by Dona Dora. When they come to trade, they are offered coffee or a meal in her house. João Povo, for example, the neighborhood leader on the Igarapé Jocojó, is Dona Dora's co-father. She and Lobato stood as sponsors at the baptism of João Povo's eldest son. Whenever João Povo comes to Itá, he eats a meal at Dona Dora's house. She respects her co-father and will not listen to the gossip regarding João Povo's complex family affairs (he has maintained both a wife and a mistress for years). João Povo sent his son to live with Lobato and Dona Dora so that the boy might attend school in town. For this he paid the boy's godparents nothing, and when the son finally returned to Jocojó to live Dona Dora complained, half in jest and half seriously, "My co-father stole our godchild from us." João Povo has brought many customers to the Casa Gato, and he is a valuable co-father to the owner of the Casa Gato. Nowadays the people of Jocojó tend to buy and sell at other stores and trading posts, and Dona Dora freely complains to her co-father for allowing "his people" to do so.

Many of Lobato's co-fathers, Dona Dora explained of her late husband, always came to ask him how they should vote. Lobato is said by the people of Itá to have avoided politics and to have attempted to remain neutral during some of the rather violent political campaigns and elections which took place before 1930. Lobato always said that politics were bad for his business. Yet everybody says that local politicians always made friendly gestures to him. On one occasion he carried out a quiet but effective campaign against a candidate for mayor who offended him. Lobato, with his numerous co-father customers, controlled many votes. Even today local politicians seek out the support of individuals with numerous *compadrio* relations, and such relationships also serve to cement commercial and political relations. It reinforces relations between the trader and his collector and farmer customers. Between members of the same class, it is a reciprocal relationship of mutual aid; between members of separate social classes it provides a "bridge" reinforcing their economic and social relationship by a personal bond validated by the Church and by tradition.

IV

Unlike the large households of aristocratic plantation owners of colonial northeastern Brazil, with their many numerous relatives and servants, described by Gilberto Freyre,[11] most Itá homes consist of one nuclear family, a man, his wife, and their children. Most people in Itá consider it a real disadvantage to be forced to live with relatives or in-laws despite the value placed on a large circle of kin. Several people told us that they would not like to live with their in-laws. Men, especially, felt that the sharing of a house with their wife's parents would only lead to trouble. A few people, as they do everywhere, realize the value of sharing a household with relatives and of having their help in household tasks and in caring for children. One young mother, for example, told us that she wanted to move away from Itá "to my mother-in-law's house" in another town on the Lower Amazon. "There I will be better off," she said. "She is a good midwife. She will help me with the children. There, if my husband does not behave correctly, his mother will help me

11 See *The Masters and the Slaves.*

talk with him." And in Itá there are households shared by several relatives which are as peaceful as one-family homes. Eneas Ramos shares his small house with his daughter and his son-in-law and their two children; and Dona Dora, owner of the Casa Gato, has her unmarried younger sister, three adopted children, and her younger married sister with her husband and their children living with her. In the rural neighborhoods it is not unusual to find a married daughter and her husband, or even a married son and his family, sharing a house with the parents. But most people prefer to have their own homes and to be economically independent of their relatives.

In these one-family households the father is theoretically the absolute head. One of the main reasons why multiple-family households are thought to be unhappy arrangements is the belief that conflicts inevitably arise between the dominating males. To his immediate family a father's word should be law. No one should question his coming and going. Each evening he should pray before the small altar placed in the corner of one room of the house; he stands as he prays for the family while his wife and children kneel behind him. Only the father is thought to understand the family finances. He should make all purchases, even the daily groceries, and Itá stores are points of reunion for men who chat and have a drink as they buy the food for that night's dinner. Only men should make business decisions. A father should fully support his family, and a disparaging remark about a husband is to say "his wife is fishing"—that is, that she must work for food for the family. A man should be the father of sons, for sons are symbols of a man's masculinity. A husband and father is rather expected to have extra-marital sexual affairs, and he may even have illegitimate children. Women smile and hint at the wicked and very masculine activities of their husbands. João Povo, for example, is known as "a good father and husband," although everyone also knows that he has two families—one by his legal wife and another by a mistress who lives only a few kilometers away. Itá husbands are expected to be extremely jealous, sometimes beating their wives for any signs of flirting. Confronted with adultery, a husband would be expected to kill both his wife and her lover. One case, related to us, concerned the dual murder perpetrated by Joviano Gomes several years ago. One night Joviano returned from his garden and found his wife in her lover's arms. Joviano "went blind" and killed both with a knife. Joviano gave himself up to the police, and months afterward a judge and jury absolved him of any guilt. His wife was dishonest and "he was fully right in what he did," our informants said.

In keeping with this stereotype of the dominating and aggressive husband and father, the wife and mother in Itá should be mild, quiet, and passive. She should never talk too much, at least in the presence of her husband. She is a hard worker within the household, and even in the fields, if necessary. The wife never sits at the table with her husband for meals, but stands to serve him and any other men present. A wife should never participate in economic affairs. She is thought to be entirely dependent economically upon her husband. Even Dona Dora, the well-to-do widow, would never set a price nor complete a business transaction. These are men's affairs to be carried on between men. Thus, when we discussed having our meals in her house, she agreed that we might do so but stated that only her brother-in-law would be able to set a price. In making studies of family budgets in Itá, it was always necessary to have both the husband and his wife present at interviews. The wife would know the amounts of food used in preparing dishes, but only the husband knew the prices they paid for food, clothes, and other items. Women are expected to be virgins at marriage and to know nothing at all about sex. Men feel that a wife should be taught what she knows about sex only by her husband; and during her life she must be absolutely faithful to him. Good wives should not be seen too frequently in the street, nor should they pay visits, even to feminine friends, too often without their husbands. Such freedom might cast some doubt on their moral behavior.

In Itá, as in all communities throughout the world, however, there is a great distance between the ideal and reality—between what people say they should do and what they do. Yet such ideal patterns of behavior, regarding the ideal father and husband and the ideal wife and mother, determine to a large extent actual behavior. Such ideals provide a set of rules toward which people think they should aspire—but never quite achieve. As elsewhere, there are few ideal husbands and few ideal wives. Few men are able to be the dominating central figure of their nuclear family, and there are few women who are able to be the quiet, passive figures of the ideal picture. Most men go through the motions, publicly issuing orders to their wives and children; and women serve their husbands meals, especially when there are visitors. Women refrain from commercial activities, asking men to buy the groceries, and they avoid meeting men in the streets. In public, both sexes act the roles which their society assigns to them.

In the intimacy of the family, things are different. Men and women talk over business deals. Women actually know prices well. Dona Dora, despite her public protestations to the contrary, is the real power at the Casa Gato, and her brother-in-law, who is the manager, discusses business with her frequently and often waits patiently for her decisions. Juca even gives his money to his wife, Anna, to keep for him. Only in public does Juca hold the family pocketbook, for Anna tells him what to buy at the store and gives him money for the purchases. With the exception of a few office holders, who have salaries, and a few storekeepers and traders, most men need their wives' help to make a living. Among the lower-class groups of the town and of the rural neighborhoods, most women help their husbands in the garden at such jobs as planting and harvesting, and they do most of the task of manufacturing manioc flour. There are many women who even collect rubber, taking over a husband's rubber trail when he is ill or indisposed. Women sometimes even do the job of smoking the latex, and most rubber gatherers' wives fish while their husbands make the round of his trails.

Women even hold a few public jobs in Itá and participate in its business life. Dona Filomena is an office worker at the health post. The post office in Itá has a postmistress, the wife of the state tax collector. Dona Branquinha and her cousin are the schoolteachers.

Dona Maria, the wife of Bibi Marajó, is a notary in charge of civil records. Women also participate in business. The baker's wife took an active and equal part in his business, and although women do not normally sell from behind the counters in stores Dona Deborah, the wife of Itá's only remaining Jewish merchant, always took part in the buying of merchandise and the selling of products to the city exporters. After her husband's death she managed the business until her son was old enough to take over.

Widows are especially capable in what is ideally the man's world. Dona Catita Dutra, whose first husband died over ten years ago, is known as a leader in one rural neighborhood. She is a major producer of manioc flour. For several years she hired men to clear gardens for her on the banks of the Igarapé Baca, and she was able to make a living for herself, a small son, and her adolescent daughters. Now the daughters are married and the son is an able-bodied young man. Her son and her two sons-in-law still work with Dona Catita clearing and planting gardens, and she and her daughters work hard at the manufacture of manioc flour, which they sell at the trading post. It is well known that Dona Catita directs the activities of her family group and of the hired workers; the flour they produce is known as "Dona Catita's *farinha*." The actual sale of the flour, however, is made by one of the sons-in-law.

Dona Veridiana, the mother of João Dias, is also a leader in her family circle. During her life she was married twice. Both of her husbands died leaving her with children to support. She has raised four children by dint of her own economic enterprise. She worked as a domestic servant for the local public officials and she and her children planted gardens. As the children grew up, they contributed through their work in the garden and by taking temporary jobs in town. Three of these children continue to live in Itá and they tend to follow Dona Veridiana's directions in most economic affairs. On one occasion, when an inquiry was made as to whether her twenty-year-old son might be willing to work as a canoeman for a three-day trip, she replied for him in his absence. "He will agree," she said. "I shall send him tomorrow morning ready to travel."

It is well known that widows tend to dominate their children. This is true of Dona Catita, of Dona Veridiana, of Dona Dora, and of Dona Maria. The mother of José and Bibi Marajó, Dona Veridiana, took the wages of her unmarried son when he worked with the public-health services, returning to him only what she thought he should spend. Dona Dora holds absolute sway over her twenty-seven-year-old adopted son. He works in the Casa Gato without regular pay, receiving only what she decides he needs for spending money. She provides him with clothes and food. He is said by gossips to "steal enough for his pleasures." Dona Dora watches over his affairs to the best of her ability. When she heard that he was having an affair with a woman from one of the rural neighborhoods, she refused to allow him to visit that neighborhood. She also sent word to the woman to stay away from town. Both of the Marajó brothers complained that they remained in Itá only because of their obligations to their widowed mother. Both said that as soon as she dies they will move away. Bibi complained that he once had a good job in a bar at a resort near Belém and that he would never have returned to Itá if his mother had not written him demanding that he do so. Both Bibi and José, who are thirty-eight and forty years of age respectively, feel they must follow her wishes.

Other people in Itá told us of how "strong" their mothers were. They described a picture of family life in which an old widowed mother came to dominate the family scene. Juca, for example, remembers that his mother, Efigenia, had nine children, and that although only three boys lived to be adults, "We respected her and always did what we were told." She was crippled in one arm, having been burned severely with kerosene when she was a child. "But she worked to raise us," explained Juca. He hardly remembers his father, who was constantly traveling to the rubber fields before he died. Efigenia was an excellent cook, and as such she worked for the "whites." She was severe with her sons and made them serve as "slaves for St. Benedict," performing tasks for the Church and for the saint's festival. She made them attend school and she arranged odd jobs for them, collecting the pay. "She died at eighty-eight years of age when a vampire bat bit her on the toe," Juca told us, with considerable admiration for her longevity and strength of character.

Eneas Ramos also remembers his mother as the central figure in his family and the dominant figure in his early life. He said, quite bluntly: "She was the head of the family. When my father was alive she decided everything with him. After my father died, my older brother, Paulo, helped her. She did nothing without consulting him." The other children came to see her "when they were called," and they "stood when they talked with her." Each morning she asked that they come to stand before her and "ask a blessing," and each evening at vesper she prayed for her family—even before her husband died. Eneas's mother even decided when the time had come for him to marry, and she made arrangements for his first betrothal, which Eneas later, however, broke off. When he did marry, he took his wife to live in his mother's house and he and his elder brother lived near their mother, working with her until her death.

The picture of family life acquired from observation of the facts of family affairs and from the life stories told by people of Itá differs strikingly from the ideal picture of family relationships. Rather than the dominant male controlling and fully supporting his family, a woman is just as often the central figure of the household. Few men in Itá are as aggressive, even in the moment of discovered adultery on the part of their wives, as the picture of the dominant jealous Latin male has it. Casemiro Oliveira, to mention but one case, did nothing violent, although his wife carried on an affair quite openly. He finally made her leave to live with her lover. "It is a sad story," he told us. "She did not behave correctly, and I feel sorry for our children, who live with her, because they are not learning to read and write." Casemiro had lost face; he knew that men laughed at him as a *cornudo* (cuckold), and he continually refused to allow his wife to return to him. Still, he did not resort to violence. Despite the Latin and Brazilian ideal of the dominant male, the *macho*, as they like to say, in such societies as Itá the women must share a great portion of the responsibility and authority in the family. When men are absent, as they often are in societies where the economic situation is insecure and unstable, women have no choice except that of taking over. When men are away for months working in the rubber fields, or when they migrate looking for work, leaving their families behind, women tend to become the dominant figures within the family.

The ideal roles of behavior which are held in Itá are those of the old landed gentry of Brazil. They were only possible of full realization in the stable plantation society of the nineteenth century and among the aristocrats of Brazilian cities—never by the majority of the Brazilian people. Such ideals are obviously out of keeping with the reality of Itá society, just as they are also impossible in the modern urban life of Rio de Janeiro and São Paulo.

V

The difference between ideal and actual behavior patterns is also apparent in courtship and marriage in Itá. Throughout rural Brazil the ideal picture of courting is one of a formal set of arrangements finally leading to marriage. Girls should be carefully protected; they should never be allowed to be alone with men who are not close relatives. A mother should accompany her daughters to a party, watching carefully while they dance, never allowing them out of her sight. Young men should not call casually on a girl. Only after some secret understanding between the two reached by passing notes or through quick snatches of conversation during the promenade in the evening in the public square will a young man find some excuse to call at her house. After several visits from a young suitor, parents expect some formal declaration on his part. With the acceptance of a young man's proposal by the young lady and by her parents, the two become *noivos* (fiancés) and actual courting begins. Now that they are engaged, the young man may call on his fiancée, sitting with her in the parlor in the company of some member of her family. They may be allowed to walk in the public square in view of the populace. They may converse through the window—

the girl leaning out of the window which opens onto the street and the young man leaning against the wall underneath. As their engagement continues, the young suitor may be invited to meals with his fiancée's family and he may visit with them after dinner in the dining room, where family life traditionally takes place in rural Brazil. Their engagement should be relatively lengthy, lasting for a year or two or even more. The young lady accumulates her *enxoval* (trousseau), and the young man works to establish himself economically so that he will be able to support a family.

In Brazil marriage is legally a civil affair. By law a marriage must be performed by a civil official before it may be celebrated in the church. There is thus, ideally speaking, a civil ceremony performed by a judge followed by a second ceremony on the same day (or next day) celebrated by the Catholic priest in the church. In rural Brazil, however, most people put greater emphasis on the Church ceremonies than on the civil ceremonies. A marriage is not fully recognized socially as a proper union until after the wedding in church. As in most of the Western World, the wedding ceremony is an occasion for considerable festivities and there is often a reception at the home of the bride. Pictures are taken of the bride in her white wedding veil. Presents are given. Altogether, it is a high point in the life of any Brazilian girl. She is expected to be a virgin—even innocent of the facts of sexual life. Traditionally, the groom is considered to have been "finally caught," so to speak. Marriage is a point in his life where he has decided to "settle down" and to raise a family. He should have had considerable sexual experience during his bachelor days. The idea that a man marries in order to care for his sexual needs is not a logical one to most rural Brazilians.

This ideal picture of courtship and marriage is shared by most people in Itá, but only a few of the First Class come even close to carrying out the pattern described. As Dona Branquinha tells of her first marriage, it seems to have conformed rather closely to the ideal, and other people in Itá remember that her husband made formal arrangements with her parents, that she had a formal courtship which lasted almost a year, and that she was married both by the civil judge and by the padre. People do not doubt that she was a virgin at marriage; but they add that she was somewhat too gay as an unmarried girl. She "danced the samba in the public pavilion" when the drums beat for dancing during the festival of St. Benedict. This was considered doubtful behavior for an unmarried virgin of a good family. Other upper-class marriages described for us seem always to have fallen short of the ideal pattern in some way. When one of the high public officials of the municipality married in 1948, all of the proper forms were carried out, but it was rumored that the bride was not a virgin and that the groom was willing to overlook this inexcusable fault "because her father is rich." "The whole thing is a joke," said one townsman. In 1948 Serra Freire's sister was engaged to be married, and he was somewhat irritated because her fiancé had never taken the trouble to "speak to the family," that is, to make formal arrangements with her parents. Only a religious ceremony was planned, and the townspeople gossiped that the prospective groom, who lived in a small town downriver, was already married by civil ceremony. Of fifteen couples of the First Class interviewed during our household surveys, nine of them claimed to be married both by civil and by Church rites, three by civil code only, and three only by the Church. Of two or three of those claiming marriage both by civil and by religious ceremony,[12] townspeople informed us that civil marriage had been entered into long after the religious rites and even after children had been born. In others the religious rites had followed the civil rites and the consummation of the marriage by several months, since the Catholic priest visits Itá only two or three times a year.

Among the lower-status groups of the Itá community, both of the town and of the rural areas, marriage diverges more strikingly

---

[12] I have said "claimed" advisedly, for one cannot be certain of such statements without verifying them by records in the state capital or those in the hands of the bishop in another Amazon town. It is our opinion that if careful verification of all statements against both civil and Church records had been made, the figures would have shown more couples married by religious rites only and more couples living *amasiado* ("in friendship," by consensual marriage) in all strata of the society.

from the ideal or "normal" patterns of rural Brazil. Ninety-one couples of the lower-class groups (the Second Class town dwellers, the farmers, and the collectors) were interviewed regarding marriage. The marriages of all the couples interviewed were of at least several years' standing and apparently stable at that time. Of these, only twenty-two claimed both civil and religious rites at marriage. Eight couples were married by civil law alone and thirty-eight only by Church marriages. Twenty-three of the ninety-one couples admitted readily to consensual marriage, that is, they lived together "in friendship," without benefit of formal wedlock. Among those who reported formal marriages, many had lived "in friendship" for years before either the religious or civil wedding was celebrated. The greater frequency of Church marriages over civil ceremonies reflects the values of older people in Itá and in other Amazon communities. It also indicates, as most people in Brazil already know, that the Church in its zeal to sanctify consensual unions often marries couples before the civil rites have been performed. Young people in Itá are fully aware that the civil ceremony is legally binding, establishing obligations enforceable by the police, and there is a growing tendency for brides, and especially their families, to insist upon a civil ceremony.

Throughout Brazil the idea is commonly held that men do not wish to marry. Several people explained that a young man does not willingly take on the heavy responsibilities of a permanent union and renounce the pleasures of sexual adventure. Sometimes the efforts of his own family are enough to push him into a marriage. Eneas Ramos told us that when his mother heard that he was visiting a prostitute in Itá and that he had become "sick" (gonorrhea), she called him to say that "the time has come for you to marry." She took immediate steps ordering him to speak to the father of a neighboring girl, asking her in marriage. As in many cultures, marriage is thought of in Itá as a way of settling a young man down. Generally, however, it is not the youth's parents who are able to persuade or force him into a marriage but the parents of a girl with whom he may have formed a liaison.

Itá fathers, probably from their own youthful experience, are quite certain that all young men have dishonorable designs upon their daughters. They are equally sure, and certainly with less reason, that a girl cannot resist the advances of any man unless she is chaperoned. Daughters, therefore, must be watched with vigilance and all men who approach them eyed with grave suspicion. Young women in Itá have thus little or no liberty of action or movement. They cannot dance unless accompanied by an adult member of their family. They are not allowed to leave the house after dark. They cannot walk freely about the town or about the neighborhood even in the daytime, unless they do so in pairs or in groups. Needless to say, young women are irritated by such curbs. They tend to look forward to marriage as the only way of obtaining a minimum of freedom. They have little opportunity to be courted by young men and they are apt to do so secretly. The necessity of secrecy in courting, at least until the young man is ready to "officialize their courtship" by formally proposing marriage to her family, very often leads to a premarital sexual affair.

A typical case is the personal history told to us by Maria Silva, who now lives in Itá as a respected widow. Maria was in love with Raimundo Amazonas. She exchanged notes with him. She met him secretly to talk for a few minutes as she walked in the early evening to a relative's house. As arranged, he came to her house to visit her family, but her parents did not approve of him. They did not believe that he really intended to marry Maria nor that if he did he would make a stable husband. As in most tragic love stories, her parents forbade her to see Raimundo and they took to meeting secretly in the forest. He promised to marry Maria. "To force my father to allow us to marry," Maria gave herself to Raimundo. Shortly afterward, she became pregnant. Then she began to feel "morning nausea" and headaches, and her mother noticed that her menstruation did not occur. A *curandeira*, who gave herbal medicines for irregular menses, was called to attend her. The old woman immediately recognized that Maria was pregnant and forced a confession out of her. "Medicines will do no good," the old midwife reported to Maria's mother; "we must wait to see if it will be a dressmaker or a hunter!" Maria was "so ashamed that she wanted to die." The old midwife defended her, saying, "This happens to many young women, even the daughters of the 'whites.'" According to Maria, her father whipped her until she fell to the floor, and he called her all of the vile names in his vocabulary. "I felt relieved after the beating," Maria says today.

Later she explained to her father that Raimundo had offered marriage but that they did "not want to be married by the police" (that is, by order of the police). When her father sent for Raimundo, he came at once. Her father threatened him with arrest and even with physical violence. Raimundo promised marriage. For a time Maria lived on with her family. She was never cursed or disowned by her parents or by her godparents. She avoided walking in the streets to hide her condition, but soon everyone was aware of what had taken place. Maria continued working in the garden with her parents until her father would not allow her to do heavy work any longer. At first she avoided Raimundo because she "was angry with him" for not carrying out his promise of marriage at once. But finally Raimundo found a thatched hut and they took up residence together. Two or three months later, during the festival of St. Benedict, when the padre came to Itá, they were married in the church. Maria was within a few days of giving birth. The child was born and it was a girl. Her father became very attached to his granddaughter, and he was extremely sad when the child died two years later. Maria told us that she "intended to give the child" to her father, for he was more interested in the child than Raimundo was.

Like so many of these marriages, Maria's marriage to Raimundo did not last. Raimundo was soon called up for military service. He left to serve in Belém and never returned. Maria heard that he began "living with" another woman (she was also called Maria) whom he married later in a civil ceremony. Maria later lived for several years with another man but she was not happy. After a time, she left him. She decided "never to take up with another man." Today Maria

Silva is one of the leaders of a religious brotherhood and is much admired for her housekeeping abilities. She deviated from the ideal patterns of her society but in a direction in which women of her class are expected to deviate.

Marriages are forced upon the groom in Itá with such frequency that it can almost be said to be normal behavior. During our last visit to Itá, in 1948, five marriages of couples from the rural neighborhoods were celebrated before the manager of the Casa Gato, who also serves as the temporary justice of the peace. All five marriages, as it happened, were "by the police." Each had been arranged by the bride's father with the backing of the local police officer after the girl had been deflowered. In all cases the young man had agreed to the marriage only after the family had complained to the police officer.[13] Such a complaint is generally sufficient to bring about the marriage, for the girl is anxious for marriage and the young man has generally been attracted to her. Marriage satisfies the parents of the girl, and the community soon forgets the distasteful details. On the wedding day the bride wears a white veil if she can afford to buy or can borrow one, and the groom will spend considerable money buying drinks and food for friends celebrating the marriage.

In town, people say that three-fourths of the marriages among farmers and collectors take place "by the police." Juca explained to us, citing innumerable cases of such marriages among our common acquaintances, that sometimes the cost of a civil marriage is a factor. The justice of the peace and the civil registrar (*tabelião*) do not charge fees when the marriage is ordered "by the police." If a couple marry "by request" (*de pedido*), then "they must work for almost a year to save money to pay," although the fee amounts to only about ten dollars. "If they marry 'by the police,' it is cheaper and they do not have this expense," said Juca.

Not all cases of deflowering of a minor, however, are reported

---

[13] The Brazilian penal code makes deflowering of a minor a prison offense, but it would be difficult for the Itá police officer to enforce this law. Often the girls involved are not legally minors (i.e., under 18 years of age). Thus, about all the police are able to do is to threaten the man with jail.

to the police officer.[14] In many instances, such as that of Maria Silva, the couple have already agreed upon marriage and when the girl becomes pregnant a few tough words from her father are enough to bring about the marriage. The girl's family keeps the matter quiet. The couple then take up residence together and the marriage may never actually take place. Sometimes, years afterward, when several children have been born, such a couple will be married in a Church or civil ceremony.[15] Many of these unions are as stable as marriages fully validated and enforced by both Church and state. Other consensual unions, however, are stormy and brittle affairs. In some cases there are bitter quarrels between the father and his daughter and her husband. Often the young man, who is forced into a marriage for which he has little desire, uses almost any pretext to break with his bride. As in the case of Maria Silva, the husband finds some excuse to move away, looking for a more lucrative occupation and an excuse to leave his bride behind.

The common-law marriage of Anna Botelho and João Inácio, for example, led to bitter quarrels with Anna's father. João Inácio and Anna had been having sexual relations secretly for several months when her father learned of their affair. Anna wanted to leave home to live with João Inácio, but the father refused to allow her to do so. One night João Inácio, accompanied by his four brothers, came "to get the girl." Her father resisted, and rather than harm him the brothers left without her. The next day, however, Anna slipped away by herself in a canoe to join her lover. This occurred in January. In June she was still living with João Inácio, without a marriage

[14] The rather haphazardly kept police records of Itá showed only 41 cases of "deflowering a minor" for a ten-year period (1933–1943), although from local informants we heard of more than ten taking place in 1948.

[15] The legalization or sanctification of long-standing unions is a widespread phenomenon in Brazil recognized both by Church and by civil officials. A charming story, making use of this situation, is told of a well known Brazilian who was marrying a widow with a ten-year-old daughter. It seems that the widow neglected to inform the officiating priest that she was a widow. During the wedding her small daughter interrupted the ceremony by calling out for her mother. The priest hesitated. The quick-witted groom, not wishing to have the ceremony stopped for an explanation, simply whispered to the padre, "We are legalizing an old situation, Father," and the ceremony was completed.

ceremony having taken place. Her father complained to the police officer, who sent word that he would jail João Inácio unless the couple came to Itá for a civil marriage. In June, when João Inácio appeared alone in Itá, the police officer jailed him for twenty-four hours to frighten him, and the marriage was set for August. Most people doubt whether the couple will ever marry, for they live too far up a small tributary on the far side of the Amazon for the threats to have much effect. Anna's father, however, still rages at João Inácio and at his daughter. "She is nothing better than a prostitute," he told us, and he refuses to have her in his house. Yet when a younger sister was ill, Anna returned home to visit her. People told us that on this occasion she asked for a "blessing" from her father and received it. Although the father says that he will never receive either Anna or João Inácio in his house until they are married, most people predict that within a few months they will be on close family terms.

Men often resist civil or Church marriage with women with whom they are living in consensual marriage on the basis that they were not virgins when they met them. A man may even hesitate to marry the young girl who he is certain has given herself only to him. One man in Itá reasoned rather brutally that if a girl allows one man to have her without wedlock, then she may well do so again. She might therefore easily succumb to temptation as she did with him. Only in exceptional cases may a girl who is known "not to be a virgin" (*não é moça*, literally, not a girl) expect either a civil or a Church wedding. Likewise, a man who discovers that his bride is not a virgin on their wedding night may be expected to leave her at once. This happened to Pedro Silva, a sailor on the public-health launch stationed at Itá. Pedro married Clara "with all the apparatus," as they say in Itá. He spent almost $125 on the wedding, including clothes for himself and his bride, fees for both the civil and Church ceremonies, and celebrations. It was a voluntary marriage "by request." On his wedding night, however, Pedro found that Clara was not a virgin. "She had been used," he said. Next morning Pedro denounced his bride to her father and refused to live with her. After more than a year, Pedro was still disillusioned with women in general and would have nothing to do with Clara. Other cases were told to us of women who "had been returned to their fathers" because they were not virgins at marriage, and three women, now living by consensual marriages of long standing and who are the mothers of children by their common-law husbands, were pointed out as girls abandoned on their wedding night by their legal husbands. Only as long as she is a virgin may a girl hope for marriage according to the ideal pattern.[16]

The frequency of consensual unions in Itá,[17] the large number of marriages performed against the grooms' desires, often under police pressure, and the high value placed on virginity, and even the "act of returning a bride to her father" make for instability of marital relations. Although consensual unions are recognized by the community, people also realize that they lack both legal and religious sanction. Men desert their common-law spouses, or even wives whom they have been forced to marry, with frequency. The economic instability of the lower-class townsmen, of the farmer, and especially of the rubber collectors contributes to marital instability, and it is perhaps the fundamental cause of the reluctance of so many men in Itá to accept the responsibility of a legally sanctioned family. Economic necessity forces many men to leave the Itá community to collect rubber in the district of Acre or in another upriver rubber

---

[16] Those cultural attitudes and values are reflected in the terms used for women in Itá: *moça* is used for a woman of almost any age above puberty who is virginal and thus still marriageable; *rapariga* for any non-virginal woman, ranging from a respectable woman living in consensual marriage to a prostitute; and *viúva* for a widow who was once married either by civil or religious rites.

[17] Of 3,360 people over 20 years of age in the municipality of Itá, according to the 1940 census, only 1,577 were reported as "married" and 190 as "widows" or "widowers." Of 5,124 people in the entire municipality listed as "single," only 3,721 were under 19 years of age, thus leaving 1,503 of 20 years of age and over. I am not aware of the criterion used for "marriage," but it was probably legal union. If so, this indicates that the number of people who enter marriage either on a consensual basis or only by religious ceremony amounts to almost 50 per cent of the total population. Few people in Itá over twenty years of age live without some form of marital alliance. Women are expected to get married when they are 18 or 19 years old, and men by the time they are 20 years old, or slightly afterward.

field; they often find themselves bound by debt or attracted to the new community, and they may never return. Others migrate to Belém, and even eventually to the metropolitan centers of South Brazil, seeking employment. Women are therefore often left with children to support by husbands searching for a better economic situation. Thus in Itá women often become the heads of families without adult males. Such women may have a series of common-law husbands during their lifetimes, each of whom moves on—or dies—leaving children for them to raise and support. Such was the case of Dona Catita, Dona Veridiana, and Dona Efigenia, mentioned earlier, widows forced to take a dominant and active role as the heads of their families.[18] It is clear that the values and the ideal patterns of behavior held in Itá are not adjusted to the realities of Itá society.

VI

The picture which the people of Itá give of the proper manner of educating children and of the treatment of children by their parents is very similar in many ways to the one we are accustomed to in the Western World. Parents are supposed to love and to protect their children, and in turn children must respect their parents. Both men and women in Itá told us that they wanted children. Men want males, and they told us of the pride of a father in having a son to carry on the family name. Women profess to want a large family of children of either sex. Our friends in Itá pointed to the

[18] T. Lynn Smith, in *Brazil: People and Institutions* (Baton Rouge, 1946), mentions the tendency for the frontier regions of Brazil to have a high ratio of males to females. There were as many as 171.3 males to each 100 females in the District of Acre in 1920 and 117.5 men per 100 females in the state of Amazonas in the same year (*op. cit.*, p. 213). The Amazon Region is traditionally an area where men have come, leaving their women folk behind. This has been especially true during the years when rubber prices were high. Itá, however, is not a frontier community in this sense. The 1940 census showed a sex ratio about equally balanced between males and females (i.e., 3,557 males to 3,524 females) in the municipality. The rubber-producing zones, especially during periods of high rubber prices, attract male migrants, but in turn the agricultural zone loses population by emigration.

frequency of adoption among childless couples in the community as proof that everyone desires children. Parents seem proud of their children; they like to dress them in satins, laces, and ribbons. On the first birthday of her child, one Itá mother gave a party for her friends at which there was a huge cake with one candle, sweets and cakes for the guests, beer and rum, and dancing with music through the night for her friends and relatives. She was proud of her infant son. Theoretically, people feel that children should be given warmth, care, and protection. They do not believe in corporal punishment. Although they showed us the *palmatória* (small paddle) to be used to slap the open palm of a disobedient child, none of us ever saw one used. One man told us indulgently how he made such a paddle to frighten his little grandson and how the boy cut it up into pieces.

In Itá people say that children should never do heavy work, for "their bones are soft." Eneas Ramos felt, for instance, that boys should not be allowed to work in the fields with an ax or with any other heavy instrument until they were seventeen or eighteen years of age. He claimed that he did not allow his son to work in the garden until the boy was fifteen years old. Even then the boy did only light jobs such as planting and harvesting manioc. Not until he was eighteen, Eneas said, did he allow his son to help in the heavy jobs of clearing the garden site and of digging out the roots. Eneas' nephew, on the other hand, had to do heavy work "as early as fourteen years of age." For that reason "he never built his body," Eneas explained to us. Eneas also told us that his own mother made him study music (he learned the flute by ear) until he was almost twenty years of age, and she would not allow him to do heavy work. The same is true of girls; they should not carry heavy burdens until after they are married at eighteen to twenty years of age. Children should be protected from heavy manual labor and surrounded by affection. If they are given such treatment, later they will repay their parents. They owe the parents a debt and they should support the parents in their old age. In Itá, as elsewhere in rural Brazil, children are taught to ask a "blessing" of their parents each morning and evening; and an ideal child continues to ask a "blessing" of his father and mother throughout life and continues to submit to parental authority long after he is adult.

Such ideal patterns of the "protected child" and of the "respected parent," however, differ considerably from the norms of behavior. The idea that a child should not be allowed to do manual labor is essentially aristocratic. The insecure economic plight of most people in Itá, the instability of marital relations, and the resulting broken families do not create a situation favorable to protecting children. In a few upper-class families where there are servants, children are free from household tasks. In all upper-class families children are shielded from any manual labor—for that is a mark of lower-class status. People of all classes would like to achieve the ideal of protecting their children from work; but the best they can do is to indulge their children from time to time by spending relatively large sums for clothes, for presents, or for a birthday celebration. Actually, most children work hard, and begin to do so at a relatively early age. Girls, as early as six or seven years of age, carry water from the river for household use. They help in the kitchen washing dishes, grinding coffee, helping to cook and keeping the house clean. Juca's daughter, who was eleven years old, helped wash clothes, did much of the ironing, worked with her mother in the fabrication of manioc flour, peeling the tubers, passing the dough through a sieve, and turning the larger wheel of the grater. Between her school hours (from approximately 8:00 A.M. to midday) and her numerous chores, Chiquinha had only a couple of hours, snatched at the end of the day, for play.

Boys are equally occupied. They generally begin working with their fathers in the garden when they are ten or twelve, and they may fish at night to help fill the family larder. Eneas Ramos, for example, criticized his neighbor, Raimundo Mendes, because he allowed his small ten-year-old son to paddle the canoe when the boy fished with his father and because he allowed the boy to fish alone until almost midnight. In most rural families small boys of twelve years of age commonly do a full day's work in the garden, and they often take the father's place in making the rounds of a rubber trail when he is ill. Above all, little boys are asked to run innumerable errands and to perform a variety of small tasks which adults find trying. The observation, made in jest by a Brazilian, to the effect that "the last slave in Brazil is the small boy," is valid for Itá. Adults keep boys from about nine to thirteen years of age busy scurrying about. "Fetch me my tobacco!" "Take this package home for me!" "Let Joãozinho fetch an umbrella for you. It is raining!" "Go to the garden and get the ax I forgot"—these are but a few of the innumerable orders given by parents, relatives, and even friends of the family to a small boy in the course of a day. Boys only have time to play if they can escape from adult company. For play, they therefore meet at distant parts of the town, late in the afternoon.

The frequency of adoption in Itá is, in fact, directly related to the usefulness of children. Many of our Itá acquaintances had *filhos de criação* (adopted children). Juca and his wife, who were childless, had adopted their daughter when she was but one year of age. Another childless couple, Ernesto and Maria, adopted an infant just before our visit in 1948. Domingos Almeida, one of the public-health-center employees, whose wife was pregnant, also had an adopted son four years of age. Orlando and his wife, Diquinha, whose house also served as the local *pensão* (boardinghouse) had two adopted children—a boy and a girl. Bibi Marajó and his wife have an adopted son ten years of age. The schoolteacher, Dona Branquinha, had raised several adopted daughters in addition to her own two sons. Dona Dora, whose only son died a few years ago, had during her lifetime adopted twelve children. In 1948, three of her adopted children lived in her house under her care. These were a ten-year-old girl, Raimunda, whose parents, distant relatives of Dona Dora, lived in another state; Liberato, a boy eight years old, whose parents had died; and Catarina, a girl eleven years old, whose rubber-collector father had asked Dona Dora to take her to raise. In addition, Filomeno, who was a man of all work at the Casa Gato, and Manuel, the clerk in the same store, were both adopted sons of Dona Dora and had been raised in her house. Her other adopted children were then scattered, some living in the rural areas and others in Belém. Practically without exception, all families with any financial stability in Itá had adopted children. In nearly all of the trading posts in the rural neighborhoods of Itá, the trader and his wife showed us their "adopted children."

These children are in general treated well. When they are adopted by a childless couple, they are treated as if they were the parents' own children. This was true of Juca and Anna's adopted daughter and of Ernesto and Maria's treatment of their adopted son. People in the Amazon region have a great respect for education. In most cases the foster parents see to it that their adopted children attend school, if facilities are available. People also feel that in addition to "instruction" (formal schooling) they have an obligation to give their adopted children "education," meaning training in manners, and they are strict with them, teaching them "respect" and formal manners. Foster parents also have the obligation to see that their wards have some religious training, and they insist that they pray each evening with the family. If possible they give them some formal religious education through the Church. Thus in Itá they send the children to vesper service led by Dona Branquinha and to catechism and to Mass when a padre is in town. It is also an obligation of the foster parents to "teach adopted children to work." Since such children usually come from a lower economic and social status than their foster parents, frequently from poverty-stricken families, they are given tasks involving manual labor—carrying water, cutting firewood, washing out the house, and other menial tasks.

In upper-class Itá families, where there are both adopted children and the parents' own offspring, it is the adopted children who do the chores. Dona Dora's ten-year-old adopted son, Liberato, for example, had to watch over her small nephews. He spent many hours patiently rocking them in a hammock and watching over them in their play. During the few hours Liberato had free from school and from his younger charges, he was constantly dispatched on errands by his adoptive mother or by the manager of the Casa Gato. The family whose back yard adjoined our own in Itá included an adopted son five years old. He was constantly occupied with chores —chopping firewood, carrying water, emptying bedpans, fetching his "grandmother's" scissors, and so on. The mother of the family scolded him constantly in a tone of voice that easily carried over into our house. From time to time his "grandmother" rapped the boy hard on the head because he was slow to learn, an act which is rare in Itá. Sometimes she threatened to return him to his father "if he did not correct his ways." In most upper-class households such adopted children are given a definitely inferior status in the family. Their position is midway between that of a poor relative and of an unpaid servant. In fact, in the city of Belém, it has long been an established custom for families of some means to "adopt" children from the small towns of the interior. They thus provide their homes a servant, and at the same time give a child some schooling and often training in a trade or craft. But in poorer families of Itá, all children must work hard. Thus the treatment of adopted children is no different than that of the offspring of the parents.

The frequency of adoption in the Amazon region is related directly to poverty and to the high mortality rates among the population. Human life is uncertain in the Amazon. It is not uncommon for malaria or another epidemic to cause the sudden death of a man and his wife, leaving two or three minor children. Lacking public institutions, and without the backing of large circles of kin, other families must take the orphans to raise. As described above, the uncertain economic situation of most men leads frequently to the disruption of marriage. Women abandoned by their husbands often find it necessary to "give away" one or more of their children. Sometimes a poor farmer or rubber collector and his wife have "more children than they can support," and they "give away" their children, hoping to gain material and educational benefits for them. Many travelers to out-of-the-way areas of the Amazon have been offered children. "Take the child back to your country [to Rio de Janeiro or to Belém], where he will get an education," said a woman near Itá, offering a cringing little boy, one of several small children. Dona Dora told us of a rubber gatherer and his wife who had traveled several days to give her their daughter because they had heard of her kindness and interest in her adopted children. They told her of their desperate economic plight and said that the little girl did not have enough to eat and that they had no possibility of giving her any schooling. They begged Dona Dora to take the girl, and would not let her refuse. When Dona Dora finally accepted, the couple left for an upriver rubber station never again to return.

As a system of caring for orphans and abandoned children, this system of adoption depends upon the presence of a favored socio-economic group able to assume the care of numerous children and on social conditions which make children useful members of the household. As these conditions disappear, as they have in southern Brazil and in the more industrialized nations, public institutions are provided. Yet in Itá, as elsewhere, adoption is also motivated by sincere parental yearnings for children. One childless couple of Itá's First Class, for example, asked a rubber-gatherer's wife, while she was pregnant, that they be given the child when it was born. The baby was given to them only a few days after its birth, and they were sad, they said, that it would be necessary to tell the child when it was older that it was adopted. Many foster parents remember their children with great affection even after they have left home. Dona Branquinha told us how much she suffered when her adopted daughter ran off with Samuel, the son of one of Itá's storekeepers. Dona Dora used every opportunity to send fruit, fish, and other presents to one of her adopted sons who had moved to Belém to work for an air-transport company. Likewise, many adopted children remember their foster parents with real warmth and respect.

One of the most striking cases of adoption in Itá illustrates this sincere desire for children, as well as the rather free manner in which people "give away" their children. The case occurred only a few months before our visit to the community. Maria, a young woman of about nineteen years of age, was abandoned by her common-law husband after she had become pregnant. During the last few days of her pregnancy, according to the report of the public-health doctor in Itá, Maria had serious hemorrhages. He was able to send her downriver hurriedly to the hospital in the delta region, where Maria gave birth prematurely to a child which at once died. Although she had no husband, and a child would have been a real burden to her, Maria was heartbroken. A woman in the next bed, who had just given birth to her seventh child, commiserated with Maria. Finally, the woman told her that she and her husband "could not feed so many" and offered Maria the newborn boy. To the surprise of the physicians (who were newly arrived from South Brazil), Maria accepted the child with alacrity. She returned proudly to Itá with her baby. For almost a year she worked as a domestic for one of Itá's "first families" in order to support the child. She then went to live "in friendship" with a young farmer who had manioc plantations near the Igarapé Itapereira, not far from town, telling us that he would "help support my son."

The frequent adoptions in Itá and the free way people allow their children to be adopted cannot therefore be explained entirely in terms of poverty or of the usefulness of children to their foster parents. Adoption has the same human basis in the Amazon as it does elsewhere. But, in many parts of the world, a mother who would give up her child so easily as the one mentioned above would be considered lacking in maternal feelings, and in many societies even poverty-stricken mothers cling desperately to their children.[19] In the Amazon, the "giving away" of a child is understandable behavior motivated by the acquisition of benefits for the child. And in Itá the attitudes of foster parents toward their children differ from those of foster parents in other Western societies. In the United States of America, for example, foster parents are generally anxious to know something of the "antecedents" of a child considered for adoption, and they sometimes fear that an adopted child might "turn out badly" because of its biological heredity. In Itá people never predict that an adopted child may become a social deviant or be un-

[19] In Itá, no strong stigma, such as exists, for example, in the United States of America, attaches to illegitimacy or to the unmarried woman to force her to give up her child.

successful in life because of its parentage. More credence seems to be given to social environment than to biological heredity in Itá. Further, these attitudes toward adoption and toward allowing children to be adopted seem to reflect a fundamental attitude of parents toward children in Itá. People love children, but they can allow them to be taken by others when their own poverty makes adoption beneficial. People are able to consider and to love their children as independent personalities, and not as projections of their own personalities and desires.

VII

Knowledge of the family life of any society is of foremost importance to any program of planned social change. This is especially true of any program involving the modification of habits, values, or attitudes. It is within the intimacy of the family that habits, values, and attitudes are inculcated. Attempts may be made to bring about changes in a community, and in its individual members, through schools, through health centers, or by various governmental means; but if these efforts run counter to patterns of behavior and values held within the intimacy of the family they will have little chance of final success. Hygiene, for example, may be taught in the schools and the health center may carry on a skilled program of public education; but unless such knowledge filters into the family and is taught by the family also, it will tend to be accepted only "theoretically" and will have little effect upon the lives of the children. Furthermore, the people carrying out such programs must be cognizant of the ideal roles assigned to the various members of the family as well as of the actual behavior of its members. In Itá, for example, the ideal pattern has it that the husband, controlling completely the family purse, does the family shopping. He therefore has an important voice in what the family eats, and any educational program aimed at establishing better food habits in Itá must educate both the husband, who buys the food, and the wife, who cooks it. Yet one must be aware of the disparity between the ideal and the normative behavior. In Itá wives have, in fact, greater powers over family affairs than the ideal pattern indicates, and many women are in reality the mainstays of their families. This means that any educational program calling for cooperation of the family group must aim at both the man and his wife.

Again, in laying plans and putting into effect any program of social change in a community or in a region, the different forms which a particular institution or a set of attitudes and values takes in the various socio-economic groups must be considered. In the Amazon region the ideal form of the family, the ideal patterns of behavior for its members, and the values attached to family life are those of the aristocratic upper class of the region. Among the regional aristocracy—a class not present in Itá—these ideals are more nearly realized than in Itá. Among the descendants of the regional landholders, among the commercial class, among the political leaders and the higher bureaucrats, the large extended family with hundreds of relatives is a functioning institution which is basic to their social, commercial, and political relations. A knowledge of the surnames and the familial affiliations of one's associates is very necessary for successful participation at this level of Amazon society. If one knows that one's associate is a da Gama Martins or a Costa Azevedo,[20] much is at once explained in regard to his social, economic, and political position in regional society. Such large families control the social, economic, and political life, and they have intermarried until a web of kinship unites large groups of people in business and government circles.

In the small towns and in the rural neighborhoods of the Amazon region, this widely extended and united Brazilian family is an ideal seldom achieved. Because people are poor, they lack the property and the common economic interests which tend to hold large kinship groups together. Kinsmen move away and lose touch with one another. The poor townspeople, the small farmer, and the rubber gatherers of Itá have relatively circumscribed family circles. Lack-

[20] These names are, of course, fictitious, but during a visit to Belém or Manaus one soon learns the surnames of the important families.

ing the security of a large kinship circle, they place great emphasis
upon ritual kinship. The lack of economic security in Itá has led
to brittle marital relations that are in basic conflict with the ideals
derived from the aristocratic tradition. Among these rural Brazilians,
the family is indeed a weak link in their social system, and the
source of many of the community's social ills.

6. PEOPLE ALSO PLAY

In Itá the winter months of rain from January through April are tedious and monotonous. People are held at home by the hard winter rains. The streets of the town are muddy and sometimes even partially flooded. The river and the small tributaries are swollen and overflow their banks. Like the cold winter of temperate climates, the tropical winter of the Amazon region makes people in Itá stick close to home. And, as in the Temperate Zones, the end of the dull winter months is marked by a series of festivals. In fact, this analogy in the cycle of the climatic year assured the continuation of the old spring festivals of Portugal in North Brazil. In particular, the festivals of June (St. Anthony's, St. John's, and St. Peter's), which are so important in Portugal, were transplanted to the New World, where they now mark the end of the winter rains, just as in Portugal they mark the arrival of spring. In May and in June of each year in the Amazon Valley, as the rivers return to their banks and as the rains diminish in frequency, the season begins, and during the whole dry season there is a series of festivals in the Itá community which reaches a climax with the festival of St. Benedict on December 24th. Between June 13th, which is St. Anthony's Day, and December 27th, when the festivities for St. Benedict officially end, there are more than fourteen religious festivals in the Itá community. Only three of these festivals take place in the town, the others being celebrated in the rural neighborhoods. Although all of them are celebrated in honor of a saint, only two of them, St. Anthony's and St. Benedict's, are recognized by the Church. The others are considered "profane" by the priest who visits Itá periodically.

These "profane" festivals are organized in each rural neighborhood by religious brotherhoods (*irmandades*). These brotherhoods resemble the "Third Orders," which are so common in Brazil, but they are not beneficial associations and they are not subordinated to the official Church. Since they do not conform to Church rules, the Catholic priest opposes them. Yet, despite his opposition, these brotherhoods thrive in the rural districts. More than a mere association of the devotees of a particular saint, the brotherhoods give formal organization to the rural neighborhood. Since most of the inhabitants (both male and female) of a neighborhood are, at the same time, members of the brotherhood, the officers of the brotherhoods are also the leaders and the individuals of highest prestige in the neighborhood. The officers of a typical brotherhood are generally the *procurador* (attorney for the saint), the *tesoureiro* (treasurer), the *secretário* (secretary), the *zeladora* (keeper of the image), the *mestre sala* (master of ceremonies), and the *andador* (offi-

cial in charge of the saint's errands). Each brotherhood is devoted
to a particular saint. The brotherhood owns an image of the saint,
a banner on which there is the symbol of the saint, and also the
musical instruments—the drums, rattles, and *raspador*, or "scraper"
—used by the *folia*,[1] whose obligation it is to go from house to house
each year singing and asking for contributions toward the celebration of the saint's festival. The "saint" is housed in the residence of
one of the officials or, by some of the better organized brotherhoods,
in a small chapel. Members pay a small membership fee, usually no
more than one *cruzeiro* (five cents) each year. There is a registry
book in which the rules and regulations of the brotherhood, the
names of the officers, the list of members, and, irregularly, the
minutes and financial accounts are inscribed.

The principal function of these rural brotherhoods is the organization of the annual festival of the saint to which they are
devoted. This festival is sometimes anticipated by a *folia*. On these
occasions, the officers of the brotherhood take the image of their
saint in a decorated canoe to visit other neighborhoods and villages.
As they travel, they stop at each house, where, to the rhythm of the
drums, the rattle, and the scraper, they sing in honor of their saint
and ask for donations. Such a *folia* may last as long as a month or as
little as a few days.

The festival itself fills ten days, beginning nine days before the
saint's day and ending the day after it. Although this lengthy festival
is the responsibility of the entire brotherhood, individuals are chosen
each year as judges (*juízes*) and as major-domos (*mordomos*) to
take over the expense and the responsibility of the various phases.
For each phase of festivities, there are two judges or two major-
domos—a man and a woman, usually a married couple. The couple
responsible for the first day of the festival, when an enormous
votive mast is raised, are known as the judges of the mast. The
judges of the festival are responsible for the festivities on the vespers

---

[1] *Folia*, which has the literal meaning in Portuguese of rapid dancing to the
accompaniment of the tambourine, is used in this region to mean both the
group of musicians and devotees who seek contributions for the saint and for
their activities.

of the saint's day itself. The major-domos, also known as *noitários* (owners of the night), organize the activities and the expenses of the days between the raising of the mast and the saint's day.

The major-domos are expected only to offer coffee and a small manioc cake to those who attend the *ladainha* (evening prayers). On the rare occasions when a dance is offered during the nine days preceding the saint's day (the novena), a flute and guitar played by two of the brothers provide the only music. But the costs of the judges of the festival are exceedingly high in terms of the average income of the people concerned. They are the sponsors of that part of the festival attended by the largest number of people. The actual saint's day is the climax of the festival, and it is fitting that the occasion be most elaborately celebrated. The judges must have food for all who come; they must purchase dozens of rockets; they must pay musicians to play through the night for dancing; and they must provide rum for at least the officials and more important guests. The average expenditure for a couple serving as judges of the mast is between $25 and $40; for a couple serving as major-domos, about $10; and for the judges of the festival, between $40 and $100 or more.

These rural festivals, while built around religious observances in homage of the saint, are gay social occasions for the whole family. Typical is that held in Maria Ribeira each year in honor of the patron saint, St. Apolonia. Maria Ribeira is a village-type neighborhood. There are some twelve palm-thatched houses clustered around an irregularly shaped plaza. In the plaza there is a large shed with open sides and a hard beaten clay floor, called the *ramada*, which is used for dancing during festivals. The local brotherhood does not support a chapel, and the image of St. Apolonia is housed in a portion of an official's residence. St. Apolonia's day is celebrated on August 28th in Maria Ribeira; following local custom, festivities are initiated on August 18th. On that day people from nearby and even from the town of Itá begin to arrive early in the morning for the raising of the mast. They come in canoes loaded to the gunwales with their small tin trunks containing their party clothes, with hammocks, and other baggage, with food and sometimes a bottle of rum. Each canoe-load announces its arrival by shooting off fire rockets, or simply by shouting. As each canoe ties up in the little port of Maria Ribeira, the men first hide their paddles securely in the brush, for it is well known that at the end of the day's festivities, or at dawn after a night of dancing, property rights in paddles are not respected by people in a hurry to return home. As more and more visitors arrive, separate groups of men and women may be seen going to bathing spots along the small stream. There they bathe leisurely, perform their toilet, and change for the late afternoon's and the night's recreation. Among the men a bottle is generally taken along, and as they change into their shoes, clean trousers, white shirts, and suit coats, they laugh and talk and have a few early drinks.

Such baths are repeated as often as twice a day during the festival. One of the strongest impressions an outsider takes away is the cleanliness of the people. There is a smell of clean clothes and of the natural perfumes from the Amazon woods. Even on a hot day it seems cool, for people are freshly bathed and dressed for each prayer service and for each dance. Only the cheap manufactured perfumes, with which men and women alike are apt to sprinkle themselves, mar the very pleasant atmosphere.

By noon the *folia*, made up of musicians and singers of the brotherhood, begin the round of the houses of Maria Ribeira itself. Earlier they have visited other neighborhoods asking for contributions. Now, they go from house to house asking for donations from the residents. Before each house, they sing a verse asking permission to enter. The lady of the house kneels before the image of St. Apolonia, takes the image from its bearer, and carries it into her house, placing it upon a temporary altar improvised for the occasion out of a sewing machine or a wooden box. The housewife then kneels and prays to the saint. Following her prayers, the *folia* sing again in praise of the latter. The woman of the house then presents them with an offering—money, a chicken, a pineapple, a few pounds of manioc flour, or something else that may be auctioned on the saint's

day. The official in charge of the brotherhood accompanies the *folia*
in order to collect the offerings at each house. By sundown the
folia have visited each household in the small village and the time
has come for the official opening of the saint's festivals.

The festival officially opens with the raising of the mast. A pole
about eight meters long has been prepared and placed in readiness
a short distance away from the village in the forest. This mast is
decorated with green leaves and with whole pineapples which have
been tied to the long pole at regular intervals along its entire length.
At sundown, the mast is shouldered by a group of young men.
Accompanied by the judges of the mast and the musicians of the
folia, they carry it to a spot in front of the residence which serves
as a chapel. There the long pole is planted upright. Rockets are
set off and the *folia*, followed by the judges and by members of
the brotherhood, march around the mast several times, singing the
praises of their saint. Following these ceremonies the saint's image
is returned to the altar in the chapel and the master of ceremonies
calls everyone to evening prayers.

The evening prayers, and all other religious services during these
festivals, are led by a lay member of the brotherhood. The leader
of religious services is usually the master of ceremonies. A Catholic
priest is never present, nor is his presence wanted. On one occasion,
it was explained, the padre was determined to attend one of the
festivals, despite all the difficulties which the brothers of the association had put in his way. They explained that there was little food
and that the tributary would not allow travel in anything but a very
small canoe which would be uncomfortable for him. They could
not promise him a decent house. Still he persisted in his determina-
tion to attend. So they sent a canoe which leaked so badly that the
padre had to give up and turn back after several hours of travel.
Had he been present, they explained, there would have been no
dancing and no drinking at the festival.

At Maria Ribeira the master of ceremonies led the services in
Latin, and each short verse was repeated by the members of the
folia. Then a young women led the prayers. When she had finished,

the master of ceremonies continued to pray in Latin. This consisted of several repetitions of *miserere nobis* while the *folia* beat softly on the drums. This was the pattern, in general, of the evening prayers, which were held each evening during the entire novena, and of the other religious services held in the chapel on the saint's day. After the religious services were over, the group in the chapel formed a procession which moved to the pavilion. There the master of ceremonies invited the judges of the mast to be seated while the *folia* group sang a series of verses thanking the judges for providing the festival. The judges then opened the dancing. They danced a *"mão de samba"* (literally, "a hand of samba," but meaning "a dance") together and the festivities were under way. The drummers beat out samba time and everyone joined in. After the first dances, which must always be samba, an orchestra consisting of a flute, a guitar, one or two *cavaquinhos* (ukuleles), and perhaps a *sacudidor* (rattle) substituted for the drums. Dinner was served first to officials of the brotherhood, together with the judges, major-domos, and the *folia* group; then to the orchestra, and then in a series of tables to all the guests. Dancing continued throughout the night until dawn.

During the night the men slipped away furtively from time to time to their cache of rum for a drink—"to take the dust out of your eyes," as they explained. Rarely, however, did anyone drink to excess. Violent and noisy behavior is unusual. Women left the dancing at intervals to have a look at their children who were asleep in their hammocks hung around the edges of the dance pavilion or in nearby houses. Sometimes an adult relaxed into a hammock for a quick nap or a rest, but the noise of the music, the shuffle of feet over the rough boards, and the laughter and chatter of people continued throughout the entire night. The next morning, after a small black coffee and a piece of *beijú* cake, the visitors took their leave.

During the next eight evenings of the novena, there were evening prayers each afternoon at sunset. The major-domo of the day provided rockets to be set off just before and after the prayers, as well as coffee and cakes for the participants. Only twice during the novena did the major-domos pay for music for dancing, and this lasted only a few hours. The days of the novena were gay, but generally only a few visitors were present. The people of Maria Ribeira were busy preparing for the climax of the festival.

On August 27th, the day before St. Apolonia's day, more than a hundred visitors from other rural neighborhoods and from the town of Itá arrived during the morning and early afternoon. As evening approached, the *folia* group took the image of St. Apolonia from the chapel and placed it in a canoe highly decorated with paper banners and flags. It was time for the "Half-Moon," a nautical procession of canoes which weaves in and out, forming a figure eight in the stream in front of the village. The *folia* group, carrying the saint in the leading canoe, played their drums and led the singing. Rockets were set off in profusion. Following the Half-Moon, the *folia* group carried the saint's image to several houses where visitors were staying to ask for additional donations. By eight o'clock the master of ceremonies had announced evening prayers. After the services, which were more elaborate than usual, a *círio* (a procession in which each participant carries a candle) was formed. It moved slowly from the chapel to the dance pavilion. That evening the judges of the festival danced the first samba while others watched. The social dancing in the pavilion which followed was especially animated, continuing throughout the entire night and until the sun was well up in the sky next morning. And on that day, after a brief rest, the dancing started up again. It was the morning of St. Apolonia's day, and dancing extended throughout the morning until about midafternoon.

More people were present on the vespers of the saint's day than on the first day of the festival when the mast was raised. The dinner given by the judges of the festival, which was served with the aid of their co-fathers and close relatives, began as early as 9:00 P.M. and continued with consecutive tables throughout the night. Some visitors were not invited to the table until well after midnight. Four pigs were killed and great amounts of manioc flour, sugar, coffee, and rum were consumed. Including the cost of the musicians, who played throughout the night and the next day, the cost of the festival to the judges was well over $100 (cr. $2,000). The judges, a man and his wife, had made a vow that they would undertake the responsibility. The husband had planted a large garden the year before to provide manioc flour for the occasion and he had raised the pigs in anticipation of the feast. He was certain, however, that with St. Apolonia's protection he would be able to repay the debts he had contracted at the trading post to provide rockets, coffee, sugar, kerosene, and other articles. He had also borrowed money to pay the musicians. It is a point of honor for the judges that nobody goes without food and that there is music as long as people wish to dance—even though in doing so a judge may acquire debts which will take two or three years to repay.

About midafternoon, the master of ceremonies stopped the dancing to announce the auction to sell off the objects and the food which had been donated to the saint. The officers of the brotherhood conducted the auction. One of them, a person noted for his wit, served as auctioneer, and another took note of all sales. Bunches of bananas, pineapples, bags of manioc flour, a pedigree hen, a bottle of rum, a shaving kit wrapped in tissue paper as a "surprise," two cakes in brightly colored boxes, and numerous other small items were auctioned off. On this occasion the proceeds from the auction were only $2.50 (cr. $50), but at times men are known to compete ardently for desired items (especially for "surprises"), raising the bids far beyond any expectation.[2] The funds go to the brotherhood to be used in repairing and decorating their small chapel.

Following the auction, the officers of the brotherhood retired to select the sponsors for next year's festival. Candidates for judge of the mast, for major-domos, and for judge of the festival had already been approached. Some of those present had made vows to the saint, and they came forward volunteering to serve. In Maria Ribeira, in 1948, the selections were easy, for Dona Dora Cesar Andrade, who attended during the last days, offered to take the obli-

[2] At an auction held in the town of Itá of donations contributed for a health club, people bid as much as $2.50 for a watermelon, $1.00 for a pineapple, $3.00 for a simple cake, and so on. Competing with each other, men bid far more than they could afford.

gation of judge of the festival for the next year. Another merchant and his wife agreed to be judges of the mast, and other couples accepted as major-domos for the nights of the novena. The names of these new judges and major-domos were copied into the minutes, and at evening prayers the new judges and major-domos were asked to stand along with that year's sponsors so that all might see them. Dancing began again after the evening religious services, and as usual lasted until morning. The last night was considered the high point of the festivities, and a few additional visitors came only for the dancing.

The next morning people began to leave. A few stayed for the felling of the mast, which took place in midafternoon as a symbol of the end of the festivities. While the *folia* sang to the rhythm of their percussion instruments, men stepped up to take a swing with their axes at the mast pole until it was finally cut down. People then removed the foliage and made it into brooms to be used in a symbolic sweeping of the plaza and of the homes of the officers of the brotherhood. When this had been done, canoe-loads of people started for home. They floated slowly down the tributary, paddled leisurely up or down the Amazon, and then up the small streams where they lived, to return home. They paddled slowly, for they had used considerable energy dancing for two nights. Some of the men had hangovers. After such a festival, both the visitors and their hosts sleep throughout the next day.

During the summer months, a typical family of the Itá community might participate in several of these rural festivals which are held in nearby neighborhoods. In the concentrated village of Jocojó alone, there are four during the summer. No one needs an invitation to attend a festival, for one always has friends, relatives, or co-fathers in each neighborhood. Townspeople also attend and, as in the case cited above, they often serve as judges or major-domos for the saint's festivals in the rural neighborhoods. People seldom go to festivals held outside the area of the Itá community. They believe that dances in more distant neighborhoods often turn into *farras* (orgies) with drunkenness and numerous fights. Within the community area, however, the festivals are attended by "our own people." Such festivals not only provide recreation for town and rural inhabitants of the area, but they also serve to bring unity to the community. They bridge a gap in social relations between the people of the town and those of the rural zones. Both the brotherhoods and the festivals they sponsor are important social institutions in the community of Itá.

II

The patron saint of Itá is St. Anthony, the patron saint of Portugal. But the saint who is most loved, most famous, and most worshiped is St. Benedict, known in Brazil as the "black saint." The image of St. Benedict in Itá is famous throughout the Lower Amazon. He is known as a special protector of rubber gatherers. In Itá St. Benedict is considered "the people's saint," while St. Anthony is the saint of the First Class and the "whites." The latter, selected by the Iberian founders of Itá, did not find favor with the people who came to make up the bulk of the population—the Indians, the mestizos, and the Negroes. Yet, since St. Anthony is the official patron of the town, the Catholic priest encourages his devotion; and with the full support of the padre St. Anthony's day in June is one of the major festivals of the town. The festival of St. Benedict, however, celebrated in December, is by far the most important and the best attended festival in Itá. It is a festival famous throughout the entire region.

About a generation ago, the festivals in honor of these two saints were organized by brotherhoods similar to those which exist today in the rural neighborhoods. The brotherhoods of the town were richer and larger in membership than those in the rural districts of today. Both the Irmandade de São Benedito and the Irmandade do São Antonio maintained cemeteries in which the members were buried. These are still in existence. In keeping with the social position of the people devoted to each saint, the Brotherhood of St. Anthony was made up of "whites" and First Class, while the

Brotherhood of St. Benedict consisted of the "people"—the town Second Class, the farmers, and the rubber collectors. Especially were *Os velhos pretos* (the old Negroes) devoted to St. Benedict, and they are said to have been the leaders in the brotherhood. Today both brotherhoods exist in name only. Each year before the festivals of St. Anthony and St. Benedict, an announcement is printed listing the officers of the brotherhood sponsoring the festival and the names of the judges and the major-domos. The Catholic priest is always listed as attorney for the saint for both brotherhoods. The other officers are always people of some official position, such as the mayor, the schoolteacher, or the federal tax collector, or important merchants. The judges and the major-domos are always the same each year, and all are of the upper strata of Itá society. The festivals are actually organized by Dona Branquinha, the devoted schoolteacher, with the help of a few other upper-class ladies. The cost of the festivals is met to a great extent by a collection made among the townspeople. Substantial donations are expected from the merchants of the town, who stand to profit by them. The names of those who contribute most are listed as major-domos of the brotherhood. Actually, however, these associations have ceased to exist; there is no membership body, and the directorate consists only of the upper-class sponsors listed on the printed announcement.

Of a once strong brotherhood, only the *folia* group of St. Benedict remains as an organized body. The *folia* is composed mainly of lower-class mulattoes and Negroes, descendants of the "Old Negroes" once so devoted to St. Benedict. There is a master of ceremonies, an official in charge of saint's errands, and musicians (drummers, a rattle player, and a scraper), all of whom learned their duties and the traditional verses and songs from men who held the positions when the brotherhood was an organized association. These members of the *folia* of St. Benedict feel that the image of the saint belongs to them: "It has been taken away from us by Dona Branquinha and the padre." Nowadays, the padre no longer allows the *folia* group of St. Benedict to take the image out of the church. The long journeys throughout the Lower Amazon on which they once took their saint, singing his praises and collecting contributions, are now reduced to a short procession through the town, supervised by the padre and Dona Branquinha. Only on the actual saint's day is the *folia* group allowed to follow behind their saint's image in the procession. The *folia* may not nowadays go from house to house carrying the image and asking for donations, nor may they play and sing inside the church as they once did. The festival of St. Benedict, once directed and organized by the brotherhood, has now been expropriated by the official Church.[3]

The festival of St. Anthony is rather a formal affair. The Catholic padre, who comes to Itá for the occasion, does not believe in mixing religion with pleasure: thus the recreational aspects of the celebration are minimal. In form the festival follows the pattern described for rural festivals. In the past there was the day of raising of the mast followed by a novena for the saint ending on the saint's day. A mast is seldom raised now, but the upper-class devotees still celebrate a novena. On St. Anthony's Day, there is a Mass and a procession. Numerous baptisms and marriages are performed, for this is one of the two days of the year when a Catholic priest is certain to be present in the town. Several hundred people are generally attracted to Itá for the occasion. Business is brisk in the town stores, and the merchants put up a few stands to sell soft drinks and sweets. Sometimes a dance is furtively organized, against the wishes of the priest, by some of the townspeople. There is generally an auction where the few gifts offered to the saint are sold. According to Dona Branquinha, the festival of St. Anthony "does not pay the expenses of decorating the church."

On the other hand, the festival of St. Benedict not only pays for the decoration of the church for both festivals but also provides the cash to pay for repairs on the church throughout the year. Since St. Benedict is the special protector of rubber gatherers, most collectors donate the first day's harvest of each season to their saint. In a normal year this amounts to more than one thousand pounds

---

[3] Eduardo Galvão, *The Religion of an Amazon Community* (unpublished Ph.D. dissertation, Columbia University, 1952).

of crude rubber. Boats passing by Itá fire off rockets in honor of St. Benedict and frequently stop to offer a donation to the saint. Both the townspeople and the rural dwellers of the Itá community present gifts to their favorite saint during the year in return for his favors. As St. Benedict's festival approaches, the voluntary offerings increase. They consist of rubber, a calf, manioc flour, chickens, pigs, and almost any salable product. Dona Branquinha receives the offerings and lists them in a book with the name of the donor and, later, the amount they bring when they are sold at auction on St. Benedict's day. In two years Dona Branquinha was able to pay the expenses of decorating the church for the festivals and to accumulate approximately $2,000 (cr. $40,000) used for repairing the church. "St. Anthony lives in St. Benedict's house and at St. Benedict's expense," people complain. Dona Branquinha considers that these funds "belong to the Church," and she makes an accounting of them to the padre, but the people feel that the money belongs to their saint.

In the past, St. Benedict received even more donations than he does now. During the years of the rubber boom, the saint's annual income was fabulous in terms of Itá's economy. In those days the brotherhood sent the *folia* group with the saint's image on two long trips to collect contributions and offerings. The saint's image was placed on a temporary altar in a large sailing vessel manned by members of the brotherhood. They sailed almost 125 miles upriver, stopping at each settlement or trading post, singing and praying to their saint, and collecting offerings. Returning to Itá, the group unloaded their cargo of rubber, cattle, pigs, manioc flour, and other gifts and then proceeded downriver, returning only on the eve of the raising of the mast to inaugurate the festivities. The return of the *folia* was always anxiously expected, and the stories of the miracles performed by St. Benedict on these expeditions are told with pride by older men. Nowadays, "because the padre no longer allows the image to go out of the church with the *folia*," one devotee explained, "St. Benedict is poor."

In the past the celebrations for St. Benedict, like those for St.

Anthony, followed the traditional pattern of the raising of the mast, the evening prayers during a novena, the social dancing, a Half-Moon nautical procession, the *folia* group playing in front of each residence, and the cutting of the votive mast and the sweeping of the houses. St. Benedict's festival differed from those held today in the rural zones only in that it was more elaborate and attended by many more people. Today many phases of the saint's festival are abbreviated, even omitted, because of the greater controls of the Catholic Church. As before, however, people begin to gather by December 1st, and the crowd increases each day until December 8th, when the mast is raised. At least one thousand visitors from the rural districts and from neighboring municipalities attend the inauguration of the festival. By December 25th and 26th, during the climax of the festivities, there are generally more than two thousand people in Itá—almost four times the normal population of the town. To feed the many visitors, there are stands in the streets serving foods, assai juice, sweets, and soft drinks. In every Itá household there are guests and even paying boarders. Other people sleep in the boats that bring them, and still others, braving the possibility of rain, hang their hammocks outdoors under the trees.

Each night there are dances. Admission to these dances is five cruzeiros for men. Ladies enter free of charge. The music is furnished by an orchestra consisting of a flute, a guitar, a ukulele, and a scraper. And every night and all day long during the last days of the festivities, there is samba dancing in the pavilion to the beat of drums. The samba, as danced on this occasion and at the rural festivals, differs from the characteristic Brazilian samba of the city, both in tempo and in the movements of the dance itself. The old-style samba of Itá is danced by couples, but the partners dance apart without touching each other. Their steps are short and shuffling; their bodies are stiff with only the arms swinging for balance. The tempo is fast, and the drummers are replaced at intervals; the dancing is almost continuous. Samba dancing in the pavilion is traditional during St. Benedict's festival, and people gather to "dance a hand" and to watch the better dancers. Order is kept by the *folia* group, the remnant of the brotherhood, who do not allow men to dance with their hats on and forbid drinking in the vicinity. The pavilion is a central attraction of the festival, but nowadays people are beginning to prefer the *baile pegado* (joined dancing), as modern social dancing is called, and these commercial dances attract many visitors away from the pavilion.

Under the direction of the master of ceremonies, Benedito Torres, a descendant of one of the "old Negroes," the *folia* of St. Benedict still meets to practice in the evenings for several weeks before the festival. There are several good drummers as well as players of the scraper and of the rattle. All of them know the *versinhos* (quatrains)[4] to be sung on each specific occasion during the festival. They still hold forth in front of the church on the occasion of the raising of the mast, and from time to time during the festival they sing an *alvorada* (morning serenade) at the break of day, and at sunset an Ave Maria. Only on the vespers of St. Benedict's day, however, do they sing in front of people's homes asking for donations. The padre allows them to carry only the *esplendor* (the saint's crown) as a substitute for the image itself. On December 24th the *folia* sings for the Half-Moon procession, occupying the first canoe with their saint and accompanying the image back to the church. Afterward they sing its praises from the church doorway.

In Itá Christmas is hardly celebrated at all, except for a midnight Mass. It is overshadowed by the climax of the festivities for St. Benedict, which continue from December 24th through the 28th. On the 24th there are the processions and the singing of the *folia* group, and on the 25th there is samba dancing. The activities of the *folia* group are nowadays suspended on Christmas day at the request

---

[4] These quatrains are introduced by the leader, the master of ceremonies, who is known for his good voice. The instrumentalists join him in the refrain. An *alvorada*, to give but one example, has the following words:

> Alvorada! Alvorada!
> De manhã de madrugada
> ainda o folião canta "Madrugada"
> Grande tino tem o galo
> para cantar "Madrugada!"

of the padre. Early on the 26th there is an early Mass for St. Benedict, and in the afternoon the traditional auction of the donations
to the saint begins. This generally continues well into the next day.
Samba dancing and social dancing are continuous on the 26th and
27th. On December 28th the mast is cut down as the *folia* group
sings again. The leaves used to decorate the mast are much sought
after by townspeople and visitors alike as medicine. A large crowd
rushes to gather them as the votive pole falls. The custom of sweeping out the houses of the judges and the major-domos at the end
of a festival is still maintained in the town of Itá, although these
people are sponsors in name only. On New Year's Eve, after the
influx of visitors is over, the merchants offer the townspeople a
dance "because they have made a great deal of money." Coming
just before the heavy rains of "winter" begin, St. Benedict's day is
the climax of the year.

III

The festivals of June, St. Anthony (June 12th), St. John (June
24th), and SS. Peter and Paul (June 28th), are among the most
characteristic and traditional of Brazil. Like most traditional elements of Brazilian national culture, the northern portion of the
country preserves these celebrations in their characteristically Brazilian form. Throughout North Brazil, St. Anthony's, St. John's, and
St. Peter's are the occasion for numerous social gatherings and celebrations, following customs inherited from Portugal but modified
in the process of adaptation to new conditions. On these occasions
there is always the large *Fogueira de São João*, the bonfire around
which a Brazilian family and their friends gather to eat sweets,
roasted sweet potatoes, manioc cakes, and other traditional delicacies.
Around the bonfire it is traditional to set off firecrackers, rockets,
and fireworks and to send up paper balloons into the night. Old
folksongs are sung. In cities and towns these days are occasions for
dances and parties. In the larger metropolitan centers, such as Rio
de Janeiro, Recife, and Belém, people come to parties and balls in

costumes of rural dress—in simple gingham dresses and in trousers similar to blue jeans worn with cotton shirts and straw hats. These festivals, especially St. John's, are characteristic of the rural country-side and of small towns, and it is traditional for city folk to dress as country people and to imitate old rural tradition, just as in North America we dress as country folk at square dances.

In Itá, as in other communities of the Amazon Valley, the festivals of June are celebrated in their characteristic and traditional manner. St. Anthony's, as noted earlier, is an important religious festival. Thus there is little merrymaking on this day. On the eve of St. John's and of St. Peter's, however, there are bonfires in front of most Itá homes. Few fireworks are set off, since only rockets are available locally and these are used mostly for religious processions. But people gather around the bonfires visiting and singing. On these occasions people seek co-fathers over the bonfire, widening their circle of personal security. Generally there are social dances in the town. In the village of Jocojó, St. John's Day is celebrated by the brotherhood of the neighborhood. During these days, also, the *Boi Bumba* company, and on occasion a group enacting the *Cordão de Passarinho* (The Bird Chain), enliven the scene. *The Bird Chain* has not been enacted in Itá for several years; it is a rather mild tale of a bird that was killed by a hunter and brought back to life by a fairy. It was always played by a company of young girls and young men recruited from the better families, and it was never very popular among the people. Everyone prefers the *Boi Bumba*. This traditional folk comedy is performed by local actors in many towns of North Brazil and in almost every Amazon community during this season of the year. Even in Belém numerous companies enact the *Boi Bumba* during June and July.

Everyone knows the plot. It is the story of the shooting of a cowboy's favorite ox by a simple farmer. Old Francisco, as the farmer is called, is the central figure in the drama, and he is usually dressed in the garb of a northeastern backwoodsman. In Itá, Francisco, a comic character, wears a mask with a notably long nose. The head cowboy and his companions cry over the ox's death and try unsuccessfully to capture Old Francisco. Finally, the head cowboy calls in the Indians, played in Itá by younger men, who are decorated with paint and red macaw feathers and who each carry a bow and arrow. After these caboclos (the term is used to signify Indians) are baptized, they are sent out to capture Francisco. Since they are famous warriors, they are able to do so. The cowboy demands that Francisco cure his ox, so Francisco calls the "doctors"— Dr. Rum, Dr. Woodtick, and Dr. Medicine. The latter gives the ox (at least in the Itá version of the play) a purgative of peppers, woodticks, rose leaves, and various other herbal medicines. Then he orders Old Francisco to look under the ox's tail to see if the purgative is working. As Francisco looks, the purge suddenly works. The ox rises full of energy and life as the play ends.

In the past, Itá supported two or three companies who played *Boi Bumba* during the festival season of June. In those days there was a competition (*desafio*) among them for the most luxurious costumes and the originality of the actors. Formerly each company had a *curral*, something like an open-air theater. Nowadays there is only one company, and it performs in the open street. This company, known as the Deuce of Diamonds (*Dois de Oiro*), is led by Paulo Azevedo, whose position is called the *amo de boi* (owner or attendant of the ox) or sometimes the *mestre de boi* (master of the ox). Paulo also plays the important role of the head cowboy. In 1948 Paulo had just returned to Itá after several years' absence, motivated by his irritation at being jailed when he drank too much during a performance. For the performances of 1948, therefore, Paulo had to train several new actors. During his absence several regular performers had moved away. He began rehearsals in early May, teaching his actors their lines from a notebook into which the entire play had been copied. He carefully explained their roles with the wisdom of many years of experience. Several actors, however, had played the same part year after year. Juca, for example, who played Old Francisco, and Paulo himself were old hands at their respective parts.

The lines of the play are both sung and recited. They are similar to those used by other *Boi Bumba* companies, but Paulo has written many of his own variations into his version of the play. Furthermore, the actors often elaborate upon their lines or ad lib in accordance with the occasion. Juca, who is known for his wit, is famous for his improvisations, and he overacts constantly. He explains coyly, for example, that his wife Catarina (played vulgarly by a man) caused him to shoot the ox: "She is pregnant and would eat only fillet of ox." A high point in the play is the exchange of insults between Francisco and the Indians. Sings Francisco:

> I don't like Indians
> even if they are my relations;
> For Indians have the habit
> of stealing all one's possessions.[5]

And the Indians answer in chorus:

> Whoever wants to catch Chiquinho
> need only make a fire in his sight.
> For Chico has the habit
> of always asking for a light.[6]

These are traditional lines, and they are always good for a laugh no matter how many times the audience has heard them. But the brightest moments come when Juca departs from his lines and comments upon a local matter or singles out someone in the audience as the butt of his ready wit. "The only thing that is useful about

[5] In Portuguese it makes a neat little verse:

> Eu não gosto de caboclos
> nem que seja meu parente.
> Todo caboclo tem de costume
> de roubar os teréns da gente.

[6] "Chiquinho" and "Chico" are nicknames for Francisco. In Portuguese, the Indians' reply reads:

> Quem quizer pegar Chiquinho
> Faça fogo no caminho.
> O Chico tem de costume
> ascender seu cachimbo.

the SESP," he remarks as the physician approaches, "is DDT." As an American anthropologist was sighted, he ad libbed, "I am also an American and Americans can't be Negroes." [7] The ox itself comes in for considerable fun. It is constructed of papier-mâché and starched cloth stretched over a bamboo frame. It has horns on its crude head and is decorated with garlands of bright paper flowers. The words "Deuce of Diamonds" are painted on its sides. Two young men play the ox, and as usual the head sometimes gets out of coordination with the hind parts to the great amusement of the audience. A particularly hilarious performance was given one evening when the two young men under the ox were slightly intoxicated, stampeding about and chasing the young women in the audience.

The Deuce of Diamonds Company plays almost each night from June 11th, the vespers of St. Anthony, until after St. Peter's festival on June 29th. Each year their leader invites someone of prestige in Itá to serve as sponsor of his *Boi Bumba* company. In 1948 the sponsors were Orlando and his wife, Diquinha, the owners of the Itá boardinghouse. It was in their house that the company rehearsed and the sponsors paid for the construction and decoration of the ox. The company's first performance of the year took place in the street in front of Orlando's house.

Following the first performance, any who wish may invite the company to perform for them in front of their dwelling. All First Class families feel obligated to request one performance, and many other families are anxious to have them play at their homes. On certain evenings, especially on the three saints' days, the company performs several times. In payment, the host at whose home the play is performed offers the company a donation, "the tongue of the oxen," as it is called. The "tongue," generally wrapped in an envelope, varies from fifty cents (cr. $10) to $2.50 (cr. $50), depending upon the financial position of the family. And it is con-

[7] Juca is a dark mulatto but he calls himself a *preto* (Negro). He makes fun of the so-called weaknesses attributed to the Negro.

sidered proper to invite the principal performers into the house
after the play ends for a glass of beer, a glass of sweet homemade
liquor, or even a drink of rum. A large audience gathers at each
performance. The host brings chairs and offers refreshments to his
close friends, to relatives and to co-fathers. Others crowd about in
the street watching the performance.

The funds collected as donations from these performances are
not paid to the performers. Each performer pays the cost of his own
costume, and participates for the pleasure the acting gives him.[8]
Antenor Porto, for example, who played the role of an Indian,
spent over $5 (cr. $100) for the materials for his costume and lost
several days' work as an employee of the health post in order to take
part in the play. The donations given to the company go to the
sponsors, who thus recoup the cost of the construction of the ox
and the other expenses (such as drinks for the performers during
practice). Furthermore, the funds collected from performances are
expected to pay for a party offered to the performers and to their
many friends on the day of the *matança do boi* (slaughter of the ox)
following the final performance of the season. At this party the
sponsor kills the ox with a knife and the guests "drink its blood";
that is, the sponsor ·by tradition punctures a barrel of wine placed
under the ox and the wine (ox blood) is caught in jars to be consumed by the participants. In Itá wine is expensive, but at least one
bottle must be spilled before beer and rum are substituted. There
is music and dancing at the "slaughter" party, which usually takes
place just after St. Peter's Day in late June. The exact date for the
party depends upon the pleasure of the company's sponsors. The
Boi Bumba is a much-appreciated part of the festivals of June, but
by late June people are somewhat bored by the repeated performances. Each year in May, however, they look forward with renewed enthusiasm to June and to the *Boi Bumba*.

[8] Compatible with the Itá ideals of feminine behavior, women do not participate in the *Boi Bumba*. A man, as indicated above, enacts the only feminine
part in the play. Young girls did participate in *The Bird Chain*, which was
mainly an upper-class affair closely supervised by their families.

IV

In addition to these regular festivals and holidays, families in Itá offer parties, dinners, and dances for their friends and relatives throughout the year. One manner of entertaining one's neighbors and relatives is the work party for clearing gardens in the early summer. The cooperative labor, the large lunch, the drinking, and sometimes a dance when the work is done turn hard work into recreation. The majority of these social gatherings, however, are offered, as in most of Brazil, on the occasion of a wedding, a baptism, a first communion, and especially on birthdays. Throughout Brazil birthdays are important occasions to be remembered and celebrated by one's family and friends. In the cities people receive telegrams and visits from friends and relatives. Housewives keep a notebook listing the various birthdays and take care not to forget them. On the birthday of any one of its members, many Brazilian families expect visitors late in the afternoon. Relatives and friends come bringing their children; and, even though a small child's birthday is being celebrated, adults pay the family a visit. There is a table sumptuous with tiny sandwiches, cakes, pastries, and such traditional sweets as *bala de ovo* (balls of eggs), *trouxinhas de noiva* (brides' little packages), *toiçinhos do ceu* (pieces from heaven), *olhos de sogra* (mother-in-law's eyes), and *bombocados* (good mouthfuls). Soft drinks, chocolate, and tea are also served. Children run about in their best clothes, stuffing themselves with sweets from the table. The late afternoon reception is often extended into dinner when a buffet supper with wines is served, and sometimes there may be dancing in the evening for younger members of the family. When families cannot afford such elaborate entertainment, there is a lunch or dinner in honor of the anniversary, with several plates served with beer or wine. No matter how modest the family, a birthday in Brazil is an occasion for entertainment.

The people of Itá, like other Brazilians, go to considerable expense and work to celebrate birthdays. If the family can afford it at all, there is some kind of a commemoration for each member of the family. The food served in Itá is not as elaborate or as plentiful as that offered in the upper-class homes of Rio de Janeiro, but many of the traditional delicacies and sweets are present on the table. Midday lunch is a common manner of celebrating a birthday; sometimes people offer a party at night with music for dancing and a table of meat-filled pastries and sweets with *guaraná*, beer, wine, liquors, and other beverages. On such occasions people are apt to be excessive and ostentatious in their hospitality. They spend more than they can afford, often going into debt heavily in order to offer a *festa* or a lunch at which nothing is lacking. Always at such luncheons and parties, the hosts ask to be forgiven for the poor quality and the lack of quantity of the food served, while going to extremes to offer more than the guests can consume. People are exceedingly hospitable in Itá, but their hospitality is never really modest and unassuming.

On the first birthday of her adopted son, for example, Maria, the young unmarried mother·whose history was mentioned earlier, had musicians play a morning serenade for the infant. She and her friends set off several rockets in the child's honor early that morning. She gave a large luncheon for more than twenty friends, with beef, duck in tucupí sauce, numerous other dishes, and a variety of beverages. In the afternoon visitors poured into her small house. Later she paid the local orchestra to play for dancing until after midnight. At the time Maria was working as a domestic in the home of a state government employee, and her income was hardly as much as five dollars per month, including food. She went in debt almost fifty dollars for the festivities. Though people felt that Maria's behavior was extreme, and they could not understand why the stores allowed her so much credit, everyone admired her hospitality and her free-handed way of doing things.

On another occasion, Orlando offered a luncheon for his wife, Diquinha, on her birthday. It was to be a small luncheon for a few friends, Orlando announced, but he invited twenty-three guests, selected only from among the First Class. The mayor, the federal tax collector, the secretary of the municipal government, the public-health physician, and other local notables were invited. Friends of lesser importance and his neighbors were invited to a *festa* with dancing that same evening. Although the luncheon was given in her honor, Diquinha did not sit at the table. She and her sister worked steadily all of the day before and throughout the morning preparing. The table at lunch was literally smothered with beef, with duck in tucupí sauce, with fish, and other edibles. Numerous bottles of beer were opened, and more than a dozen bottles of wine were consumed. There were three desserts. The meal was followed by flowery toasts and speeches. Each male guest rose to speak in honor of Orlando and Diquinha, offering felicitations for her birthday. Finally Orlando spoke, asking to be forgiven for his limited hospitality, and toasted his guests. At four o'clock, after more than three hours at the table, the guests departed to fall into their hammocks to sleep, only to be invited to return that evening for dancing. The cost of the luncheon and of the evening party which followed was the equivalent of several months' income for Orlando and his wife.

Some fifty or more guests came for the *festa* at Orlando's that evening. A local orchestra played *choros, marchas,* and sambas until well after midnight. People came in their best clothes, and although it was a warm evening men danced in their coats. Mothers came escorting their daughters. The women sat in chairs and on benches on one side of the room, and the men stood in a group on the other side. As each dance began, the gentlemen crossed the room to invite the lady of his choice to dance. Everyone behaved with rigorous formality. About ten o'clock the ladies were invited to partake of *pasteis* and vermouth which had been laid on the table in the dining veranda. Later the men went to the table to drink beer, and vermouth mixed with rum. Afterward the party became gayer. Zeca Marajó announced a quadrille (a square dance), which he "called" in a mixture of Portuguese and confused French—the manner he had learned from his father. After an hour of the quadrille the guests seemed to have relaxed, and dancing in couples was resumed.

Everyone spoke of Orlando's and Diquinha's party as *muito alegre*
(very gay), but compared to other birthday parties offered by Itá
families living on Third Street and living in the rural neighborhoods
it was obviously a rather ceremonious affair. At some of the parties
given by people of lower social status, dancing continues until
dawn and neighbors and friends drink frequently to their hosts'
health and to many more birthdays. Birthday parties are perhaps
the most frequent type of social gatherings held in Itá. They satisfy
a basic human need of response from others and considerable recreation for all who attend.

V

In the city of Belém, Itá is known as a dull town. People from the
city passing Itá on a river steamer, or even after visiting there for
a few days, wonder how people can live in such a humdrum community. There are no movies. The town does not support a social
club where the upper class might hold dances and congregate in
the evening as do many larger Brazilian towns and cities. The occasional Sunday-afternoon soccer matches between the two recently
organized local teams are of little interest to Brazilian urbanites,
who are apt to be impassioned fans of a professional team which
plays for thousands of spectators in a huge stadium. In Itá even
the pre-Lenten carnival, which Brazilians of the cities celebrate in
such a colorful and joyous manner, tends to be relatively dull. A
few members of the upper class dance in the streets in weak imitation
of the dancing they have seen in Belém, and on one night during
Carnival there may be a ball limited to upper-class participants.
As compared to the annual *círio* in Belém, even the festival of St.
Benedict provides little excitement. As in most small towns, the pace
is slow in Itá and the forms of amusement are few. The way people
entertain themselves would seem quaint and old-fashioned to most
city people.

The people of Itá, however, do not find their community dull.
They seek pleasure, as they understand it, by means of their tradi-

tional forms of recreation. Although recreation is an important aspect of community life everywhere, in the Amazon Valley, where a sparse population is spread over an immense area, recreational gatherings are of even greater importance in breaking the solitude of human existence. Furthermore, in Itá people do not seek pleasure alone, but mix their pleasure with their work. They organize work parties and they drink and sing as they work. Their saint's festivals and their birthday parties provide the basis for important group and individual incentives. People will spend all of their savings, or go into debt, to serve as a sponsor for a saint's festival or to offer an elaborate birthday party. And recreation is closely related to their religion and to the social organization of their community; the rural religious brotherhoods have as their principal function the celebration of a saint's-day festival and are also basic social units in the rural neighborhoods. Any educator, technician, or administrator charged with planning or implementing a program of social and economic change should take into consideration the meaning and the function of these traditional forms of recreation in Itá society.

In opposing the neighborhood brotherhoods and festivals, the Catholic priest and the official Church organization are combatting an important social institution, unaware of its great potential value to themselves and to the community. It is well known that the cooperation of community leaders is necessary in any program of community action. The officials of these rural brotherhoods are important leaders in the rural neighborhoods. Their cooperation would be of the utmost value to the Church or to any other organization dealing with community problems. The brotherhoods of rural Itá might easily be given new and additional functions; the leaders of these neighborhood organizations might, for example, be persuaded to support programs in health, in agriculture, and in education. The Brazilian government and its various administrative agencies should be aware of these leaders and their power. In fact, in any effort to stimulate the relatively weak sense of community cohesion in Itá, it might even be advisable to attempt the reorganization of the decadent town brotherhoods dedicated to St. Benedict and to St. Anthony. Such associations could furnish a basis for community organization in a form already well known to the people.

One frequently hears city dwellers and people from abroad complain that the Amazon caboclo is lazy. Such people cite their experience. "When caboclos are paid higher wages, they will work fewer days," they say. They complain that the caboclo neglects his gardens and neglects rubber gathering because of the "orgies" at religious festivals. Unquestionably, the season of festivals is the time when new gardens must be cleared and planted and when rubber is harvested. Amazon festivals, therefore, conflict with the season of most intensive economic activity; but as long as the present economic patterns continue the people will necessarily divide their time during the dry summer months between work and play. Such festivals, however, are major economic incentives. In the Amazon people are anxious to improve their material life, but even more important to them is the prestige and the response from others which they receive when serving as sponsors for a saint's festival or as hosts to family and friends at an elaborate birthday party. To earn the money for such purposes, people work to earn more than their minimal necessities. Material improvements such as radios, electric fixtures, mechanical farm tools, cheaper clothing, and imported foods, are generally not available to the Amazon rural worker, or are beyond the scope of his earning power; therefore such material improvements provide little incentive. When people are deprived of their own forms of recreation and hospitality, as they are in many Amazon communities, there is little desire to accumulate beyond their immediate physical needs. People do not value material improvements alone, and such intangibles as recreation and hospitality may be valued as highly as a better material standard of living. It is just such incentives and values that are often overlooked by "practical" administrators responsible for programs of economic development.

7. FROM MAGIC TO SCIENCE

In our own civilization scientific and naturalistic explanations have gradually replaced magical and supernatural explanations for phenomena and for events. This basic change in our world view began centuries ago and is still taking place with ever increasing velocity. Only a relatively short time ago, rainfall was thought to depend upon the supernatural, and malaria was believed to result from bad air or bad "humors." Magical means and prayers were used to ensure sufficient rainfall for the crops. Often harmful precautions, such as sleeping in a room tightly closed to keep out night airs, were used to prevent malaria. Nowadays rainfall is attributed to natural causes and can even be produced by scientifically controlled experiments. Today it is known that the anopheles mosquito transmits malaria; science has shown us how to control the disease through control of the insect. Similar examples might be taken from almost any sphere of our way of life. As the field of science expands, the segment of human experience depending upon magical or even "common sense" explanation is steadily reduced.

This process of change has not taken place with equal velocity in all segments of our culture nor is it as complete at any time as it might be. Even in our large metropolitan centers magical beliefs persist in the face of the most modern scientific concepts. We avoid using the number "13" in public buildings and some of us still do not walk under a ladder. Science has not fully penetrated "downward" to great masses of people nor has it diffused "outward" to those living in marginal areas of our civilization. In London, Paris, New York, and Rio de Janeiro large numbers of people have a very vague idea of the bacterial concept of disease. In out-of-the-way portions of any Western country, countless magical folk beliefs persist regarding agriculture, health, and other aspects of human affairs. Lacking a knowledge of soils, of plant genetics, and other scientific principles of agriculture, the farmer sees a relationship between the phase of the moon at planting and the success of his potato crop, and a mother relates the illness of her child to the stare of a stranger who she concludes must have "an evil eye." Both science and magic depend upon cause and effect. In magic, however, the relationship is by analogy, a fabrication of the human mind, while in science the relationship is in the natural world and can be experimentally determined. Thus as greater scientific knowledge becomes available, magic and fortuitous relationships established by tradition slowly give way before scientific knowledge. But magic does not give way easily to science. People do not give up their traditional beliefs with ease even in the face of more rational explanations, because their own experience validates their view of the universe. They hesitate to take over the new and untried. Therefore new concepts, to be accepted, must be introduced in comprehensible terms of the world view of the people concerned. Without a knowledge of this world view, the social innovator may have difficulty in introducing what he considers rational thought.

Brazil, with its cultural heritage formed out of the fusion of the cultures of Europe, of Africa, and of the American Indian, has its very distinctive set of folk beliefs and magical practices. The Amazon region, isolated for so long from the centers of technology and science, has retained many folk beliefs and magical practices from all three of those cultural backgrounds. There are medieval Iberian beliefs which have persisted long after they disappeared in Portugal. Numerous concepts and customs of American Indian origin are retained today by the Amazon rural population. And despite the relatively few African slaves who came into the region, African custom has also influenced Amazon folk belief. In many cases the origin of a particular set of beliefs may be easily assigned to one of the three cultures. For example, the concepts and practices surrounding the shaman or medicine man, or *pagé*, as he is called in the Amazon, are clearly of American Indian origin. But other elements and complexes seem to have their origin in more than one cultural heritage. They seem to be fusions of beliefs and custom from two or all three of these traditions, and to have taken new forms distinctive of Amazon folk culture. The belief in Matintaperera, a person who becomes a dreadful ghost at night, to cite one example, is probably a merging of the European belief in werewolves with Amazon Indian concepts of dangerous forest spirits. No matter what their origin, Amazon folk beliefs are an important aspect of the world view of the simple rural inhabitant of the region. Such beliefs, and the customary behavior associated with them, often determine the acceptance or rejection of scientific concepts crucial to technological change in the Amazon Valley.

II

The people of Itá, like most other Brazilians, are Catholics. There is one Jewish family of Moroccan origin, the remnant of a group which settled there during the rubber boom. There are only five or six *crentes* (believers), as Protestants are called, among all the inhabitants of the community. This homogeneity in religious faith is an important factor in creating solidarity and uniting people of various social classes and of all races. The regulations of the Roman Catholic Church provide people with ideal patterns of behavior for many life situations. Ideally, all people meet on an equal basis in the Church. In Itá, however, there is no resident priest. The sacraments of the Church are available to the members of the community only when the padre from an upriver community visits the town during the annual festivals of St. Anthony and St. Benedict. Confession, communion, mass, baptism, confirmation, marriage and the last rites may be performed only on these occasions. Furthermore, the parish priest, when he visits the community, is an outsider. In many Amazon communities he is apt to be a foreign missionary—a Franciscan from Germany, a Salesian monk from Italy, a Dominican from France or, in recent years, a Maryknoll Father from the United States. The priest who visits Itá regularly is German, and his severe concept of Catholicism makes it difficult for the people to accept him fully. But even in the past, when the padre who attended the Itá church was a native Brazilian, there was considerable suspicion of him. Men suspect a priest's motives when he closets himself too long in confession with their daughters and their wives. They suspect him of using the funds of the Church for his own purposes. Thus in Itá, as in many Brazilian communities, the people have little connection with the official Church. Men, especially, are apt even to be antagonistic toward it. Although any padre is respected ex officio, and wields considerable power, priests are generally not strong leaders in most Brazilian communities, as they so often are in other Latin Catholic countries.

The religious activities of Itá, as of many other Amazon communities, are left mainly in the hands of the people themselves. Leadership and direction are provided by local devotees. Dona Branquinha, the schoolteacher, cares for the church, leads evening prayers, and teaches the catechism to children. In the rural neighborhoods it is the religious brotherhoods, described in an earlier chapter, who organize and promote religious activities. In all Brazilian communities, there are always *beatas*, women devotees such as Dona Branquinha (and sometimes a few *beatos*, their male counterparts) who are the important religious leaders in their communities. Such women "live in church," people say. They are the religious, and often the moral, arbiters of their community. In Itá,

Dona Branquinha is the treasurer for the Church, receiving donations to the saints. She gives most of her time and attention to religious affairs, even mixing religious instruction with her regular lessons in the school. Some people laugh and say that she is attempting to make up for sins committed when she was a young lady, and a few malicious gossips cast some doubts as to the nature of her relations with the padre. It was said, half seriously, that a former padre was the father of her second son. But Dona Branquinha, ignoring gossip, looks over her flock and complains of their lack of religion and of their "profane" religious activities.

The lack of control by the formal Church organization over the religious life of Itá does not mean that its people are unreligious. On the contrary, they profess to be "good Catholics," and in their own way they are. But the content of their religion includes many local variations of archaic Iberian beliefs which, while not in direct conflict with contemporary orthodox ideology, often overshadow many of its main precepts. God and Christ are worshiped, but more important in local religion are the Virgin and the saints. Furthermore, local devotion focuses upon those saints whose images are found in the local church and in the small chapels in the rural neighborhoods. St. Anthony, St. Benedict, St. John, St. Apolonia, and the Virgin are identified by the people with their local images. Each saint is considered a local divinity. St. Anthony and St. Benedict, whose images share the main altar in the town church, have even been seen walking at night in the streets. Juca's father told him of seeing the two saints strolling one night under the mango trees of First Street. They were dressed as monks, and they walked in the direction of the church. He saw them enter. A light went on inside and then the church was dark again. The next day he went to the church and inspected the images; both St. Anthony and St. Benedict had sand on their feet. On another occasion a soldier saw two men walking in the street late one night. When they did not halt at his command, he fired. They did not stop, and he recognized them as the saints. The next day the keeper of the church found a bullet hole in the image of St. Anthony. Other images of the same

saints in nearby towns are not thought to be identical. The church
in Arumanduba has a St. Benedict, but "it is not the same as ours,"
said an Itá informant. "It may be the son of the one that stands in
our church. Ours is a *pretão* [a big Negro], and he never smiles as
does the little one" (in the Arumanduba church).[1]

To the people of Itá, the saints are protectors, benevolent powers
to whom they may go for help and protection. Adultery, theft,
murder, and other crimes are not punished by the saints, and people
seldom feel the need to ask forgiveness for such sins. These are
matters controlled by the law and by public opinion, and they are
judged by secular standards. The proper attitude toward the saints
is *respeito* (respect); and the only sin punished by them is "lack of
respect." By this, people mean that the saint must be offered prayers,
must have his or her day celebrated in the appropriate manner, and
must be offered vows which must be fulfilled. No one in Itá could
remember when a saint had punished anyone for breaking one of the
Ten Commandments, but everyone could remember instances when
punishment was meted out for not fulfilling a vow.

The vow is the principal means of securing the saint's protection
or aid in a crisis. In a sense even the *ladainhas* (evening prayers), the
processions, and the other collective ceremonies carried out in honor
of the saint are vows. The community, the neighborhood, and the
brotherhood of devotees have a standing vow to perform them in
order to ensure the welfare of the group. Without these ceremonies
the protection of their saint would be withdrawn. Most vows in Itá,
however, take the form of individual contracts. A devotee promises,
for example, that if his son is cured of a serious disease he will offer

[1] The story of St. Benedict's life, as told in Itá, pictures him as of dark skin
and as "a slave in the house of our Lord"—of the same color and status of the
ancestors of most of the lower-class people. One story has it that Benedict
worked in the Lord's kitchen and served the table for the Lord and the other
saints. He was sorry for the many beggars who came to the kitchen door, and
he gave them bread. The other saints told the Lord that Benedict was stealing.
The Lord hid himself behind a door, and when he saw Benedict go out with
a parcel containing bread for the beggars He ordered him to open it. Benedict
was frightened and said that his parcel contained flowers, and when he opened
it, the bread had changed to flowers. The Lord was pleased. "He was a good
employer, and he lectured the other saints for gossiping."

a novena or will serve as judge for the saint's festival day. One man promised St. Lucia that he would offer her a novena each year if she would help him stop drinking. He asked that she strike him blind if he ever again touched alcohol.

Another example was related by Juca. When Juca was a small boy, he suffered from a large open sore caused by an insect bite. His mother, a very devout follower of St. Benedict, offered Juca as a "slave of St. Benedict" if he got well. The open infection had resisted cure for three years, but six weeks after his mother's vow Juca was cured. As a slave of St. Benedict, Juca must all his life offer a day's work each year for the saint, performing such tasks as repairing the church or even cleaning the pavilion where the dancing is held on St. Benedict's day. In Juca's youth, the slaves of St. Benedict were subjected to rigid discipline. If they did not work or pray to their saint, they were ordered by the leaders of the brotherhood to kneel with bare knees on a jagged rock to ask penitence. To offer a son or a daughter as a slave of St. Benedict was a very serious vow in the past, and it is rare nowadays.

One seldom hears in Itá of the more exotic and dramatic vows which are so common in other parts of Brazil. In the arid northeastern region of the country, it is common for people to vow to walk hundreds of miles, sometimes as long as for twenty days, to visit famous and miraculous shrines such as those of the Bom Jesus da Lapa or of São Francisco de Canindé. Individuals of high social status make a vow to walk barefooted in the candle procession of the Virgin of Nazareth in Belém. They sometimes crawl on their knees up the 365 steps leading to the Church of Our Lady of the Rock in Rio de Janeiro. In Itá vows are apt to be less extravagant. One vows to make a donation, to serve as a judge for a festival, to pray a novena, or to offer an *ex-voto*, a present to the saint in the form of an effigy of the organ of the human body which the saint has cured. In Belém and in other large centers of northern Brazil, replicas of arms, legs, heads, fingers, breasts, and even internal organs are cast in wax to be offered to a saint in fulfillment of a vow. In Itá such replicas are carved out of wood. Until the German missionary priest had them removed as profane, carvings of various parts of the human body were to be found on the altar of the Itá church.

Delinquency in fulfilling a vow arouses the saint's anger. It shows lack of respect. The saint expects a return for his favors and his protection. Instances are told in Itá of people who were punished because they did not carry out their vows. João Mendes, for example, promised to give his own weight in crude rubber to St. Benedict if he were cured of his headaches. João Mendes was cured, but the next year, when the *folia* came to his trading post asking for donations for St. Benedict, he modified the terms of his vow. He said that he had promised only the "weight of the saint" (that is, the image) in rubber. No one questioned João Mendes' statement. But when the image of St. Benedict was placed on the scales with the rubber which João gave, it was found to weigh as much as João Mendes himself. The saint had performed a miracle. St. Benedict had forced João Mendes to fulfill his original vow. Another man, who had promised the saint a steer, presented the smallest and thinnest from among his herd. As the canoe carrying the image left the ranch, the strongest beef in the herd broke away and started swimming after it. The members of the *folia* took the second steer into their canoe. They understood that St. Benedict was dissatisfied and had punished the man by making him give two animals instead of one.

Sometimes the saints are not so mild in punishing broken vows. They send sickness, they cause damage to one's garden, and they send bad luck in business dealings. Sometimes the slighted saint sends a warning. Once when the image of St. Benedict was being sent on a large river steamer to Abaeté, where there are specialists in repainting images, the ship's captain placed the saint in the hold as he would any baggage. Shortly after leaving Itá the pilot found that he had no control over the rudder. The steamer was caught sidewise in the river current, and the crew felt certain that the boat would crash into the bank. A man from Itá, however, remembered the saint and informed the captain of the saint's powers. The image of St. Benedict was hurriedly removed from the ship's hold and placed on an improvised altar in one of the cabins. The boat began to steer accurately at once. The saints cure ills, give good crops, protect the rubber collector on the trail, and safeguard boatmen against the dangers of navigation. They help people find lost objects, aid young women in securing husbands, and return wandering fathers to their wives and children. They perform a multitude of other benevolent deeds, but they are also jealous of their rights, expecting a return for their favors and protection.

As in all Latin American communities, certain saints are believed to have special attributes and powers. St. Anthony is a *casamenteiro* (a marrying saint) who is especially appealed to by women wanting a husband. St. Christopher, as elsewhere, protects travelers. St. Thomas favors the farmer. St. Apolonia is a patroness of teeth, aiding people with toothaches. Our Lady of Sorrows protects women in childbirth, and St. John and St. Peter are favorable to lovers. St. Benedict, as mentioned earlier, is the special protector of rubber gatherers, and each year many rubber collectors donate their first day's harvest to their protector. In addition, almost every individual in Itá has a saint who has proved to be especially indulgent to him or to his family. Each household has at least one small image, or sometimes a large picture, of the saint or saints who are its special devotion. Our Lady of Sorrows is Maria Silva's. She appeared to her one night in a dream when numerous families in Itá were ill with fever. Because of Our Lady's protection, neither Maria nor her family became ill during the epidemic. As a result Maria and her friends have organized a small brotherhood to honor her. Juca has the special protection of St. Lucia, the saint who helped him break away from rum. Many people feel that their special protector is the saint of their birthday or the saint whose name they carry. In fact, people name their children after the saint who they feel is their special guardian. In Itá the number of Beneditos and Beneditas attests to the fame of St. Benedict. Indeed, even though they are devoted to another saint, everyone in Itá turns now and again to St. Benedict. Rather than St. Anthony, the official patron of Itá, people feel that it is St. Benedict who really protects the community, and his fame extends far and wide. Stories of St. Benedict's cures are legion. The number of presents which appear before the image, the amount of the donations offered each year, and the influx of people to attend St. Benedict's festival are evidence of the widespread devotion to the saint in the entire Lower Amazon. Not a day passes in Itá without the noise of skyrockets, set off by a passing boatman, in honor of St. Benedict.

III

In addition to this body of Catholic belief, the people of Itá believe in supernatural powers and perform magical practices of aboriginal origin. The Portuguese learned how to survive in this new land and how to exploit the strange environment from the native peoples, but in the process they acquired many aboriginal beliefs. These were perpetuated in the new culture formed as native groups were detribalized and dominated by the newcomers. Thus the world view of the Amazon mestizo and the caboclo came to be an intricate blend of native and European ideology. And it is not surprising that those aspects of native religion which dealt with the forest, the mighty river, the fauna, the flora, and the activities of man in exploiting their environment are today a part of the folk belief of Itá and other small Amazon communities.

The religious system of the Tupí tribes, who influenced Amazon folk culture so strongly, did not stress highly organized rituals led by a priesthood, as did the religions of the more complex native peoples of Mexico and Peru. Theirs was a loosely constructed religion without a well defined pantheon or a highly systematic religious ideology. The origin of natural phenomena and of useful arts was ascribed to a series of mythical culture heroes. One of them, Mairá-Monan, taught mankind the techniques of agriculture, and another, Monan, created the sky, the earth, the birds, and the animals. Still another, called Tupan, who was later identified by Christian missionaries with the Christian God, was a secondary figure accounting for lightning, thunder, and rain. These ancestor figures were not worshiped as active supernatural forces. Instead, a series of forest spirits and ghosts of the dead were believed to bring bad luck, sickness, defeat in war, and general misfortune, and it was this category of supernaturals who had to be pleased, placated, and controlled. One of them, Yurupara, described as a dangerous forest goblin, was equated by Christian missionaries with the Devil. He was believed to attract hunters deeper and deeper into the forest until they were irreparably lost. Another was Curupira, a small man-like creature with his feet turned backward, who protected forest animals and punished hunters. The Tupian peoples were deathly afraid of the spirits of the dead, and believed that they took the form of animals—a toad, a bird, or a lizard—and roamed abroad at night.

These native religious beliefs clashed inevitably with the ideology of Christianity, which offered other explanations for the origin of things. The missionaries set about eradicating pagan beliefs and teaching the people the orthodox Catholic concepts. The names of the Indian culture heroes disappeared and in their place came God, the Devil, and the saints. But the European colonists and missionaries of the seventeenth and eighteenth centuries themselves believed in werewolves, witches, and demons; their own view of the supernatural world was in many respects similar to that of the natives. Since the forest demons and malevolent ghosts referred to a new and strange world and did not directly contradict orthodox Catholic ideology, it was not difficult for the colonists and the missionaries to add dangerous and fearful entities of the forest and the river to their own cargo of magical belief. The new demons and ghosts, as described by the natives, corresponded roughly with those of medieval Iberian belief. Thus the native and the European world views reinforced each other and blended together to form the world view of Amazon folk culture.

The Tupí-speaking Indians of the Amazon forest depended upon their medicine men or shamans, whom they called *pays*, to protect them against the demons, to cure sickness, and to relieve them of the misfortunes caused by the spirits. These shamans were characterized by personal traits which set them off from the laity. They are said to have been highly excitable and of nervous temperament. In communicating with the spirits which they controlled, they went into trance states, even into cataleptic seizures. These trances were induced by swallowing large quantities of tobacco smoke, and by dancing and singing to the rhythm of a gourd rattle. The Indians believed that all disease had a magical or supernatural cause. Sickness resulted from punishment by a forest spirit or by a ghost or from the malevolent magic of sorcerers. The shamans cured such ills by massage, by blowing tobacco smoke over the patient's body, and by sucking out the small object (a bone, a stone, or even a lizard) induced in the body of the patient by the offended supernatural. Shamans had tremendous powers over their people. After 1500 there were several revivalistic movements among the Tupían tribes led by shamans who promised a return to "the mythical land of the culture heroes," where people need not work and where they were assured of eternal youth.[2] Several groups migrated up the Amazon to points above the mouth of the Rio Negro in order to escape the European and to search for this mythical land.

Shamans may even today be found among the mixed populations of the Amazon. In fact, they practice today among the Amazon rural population throughout most of the Valley. They control, as in native times, ghosts and the dangerous spirits of the forest. People have continued to believe in the supernaturals, and it is to be expected that religious practitioners able to cope with these powers would be necessary. They are found in Santarém; Óbidos is a well known center for them, and even in the working-class districts of Belém and Manaus men calling themselves pagés practice a mixture of aboriginal and modern spiritualistic belief. No pagés live and work today in the town of Itá, but there are several in the surrounding rural neighborhoods. People from town sometimes seek their advice and ask them to perform a cure. Sometimes they persuade

[2] Alfred Métraux, "Les Migrations historiques des Tupí-Guaraní," *Journal de la Société des Américanistes de Paris* (1927), XIX, 1–45.

a pagé to come secretly to town. Secrecy is necessary because a physician stationed in Itá several years ago undertook a campaign against the pagés, charging them with practicing medicine without a license. One of them was jailed. As a result the pagés nowadays practice secretly, in fear of the authorities. In turn, the latter claim that the pagés are "superstitious barbarians and uneducated," and criminals to be driven out of the community. Most people deny they have ever sought the help of a pagé. Still, a few pagés who live in the rural neighborhoods of Itá are well known figures, and they are always busy. A municipal official was known to have gone to one of them for a cure. In fact, the pagé is feared and respected both by the town and by rural people, and in general the authorities close their eyes to his activities.

None of the shamans living in the Itá community, however, is a great pagé. The great ones, everybody in Itá agrees, lived about a generation ago. They were called *sacacas*. Such famous men as Joaquim Sacaca, who was said to have been an Indian born on the Upper Rio Negro; Fortunato Pombo, who lived in the neighborhood of Jocojó; and Lúcio, who died about ten years ago, were pagé *sacacas*.[3] These powerful shamans had numerous spirits with whom they were on a familiar basis, and who helped them in their cures; they were also able to travel enormous distances under water and to remain under water for days, even weeks. Their capacity for traveling and remaining under water distinguished these *sacacas* from the less powerful pagés who serve the people of Itá nowadays. People say that the *sacacas* wore the skin of a giant water snake (*cobra grande*) during their travels under water. Each of them had a particular place on the riverbank, called his "port," from which he embarked into the enchanted kingdom in the depths of the Amazon River or on his under-water travels. The port, for example, of Joaquim Sacaca was a log covered with thorns on which only he could walk barefooted. Another *sacaca* used a hollow log as a tunnel

---

[3] I do not know a translation for the term *sacaca*, although it is a name given to an Indian tribe which once inhabited the Island of Marajó, from which famous shamans may have come.

to enter the water. Fortunato Pombo frequently visited other towns. He traveled from Itá to Santarém in a few minutes, and in an instant he would make an under-water trip to towns further down the Amazon. Joaquim Sacaca would often hear Luandinha, a female spirit said to have been a large water snake, call him, and he would disappear to spend a few hours with her in the depths of the Amazon. People saw bubbles rising to the surface as he descended to the bottom to join her. The spirits addressed Joaquim as "Father," and people said that the pagé *sacacas* did not die. According to local folklore, they lived forever in an enchanted kingdom under water just as the shamans of the Tupían Indian tribesmen lived on in a mythical land in the west.

It is said in Itá that a great pagé may announce his future capacities by crying aloud in the womb. As a small child a pagé is unlike other children; he or she—for women may also be pagés—suffers from tantrums and seizures. Such individuals show early signs of supernatural powers. As a boy, Fortunato Pombo loved to wander along the riverbank shooting at shrimp and small fish with his toy bow and arrow. One day he disappeared. His mother found his shirt hanging on a pole close to the pier, and she was certain that he had drowned. She wept for three days, but at the end of the third day Pombo appeared again. At first he would not tell of his experiences. Then he told of the companion spirits he had seen in the depths of the water, and of the food, and of the large, beautifully painted *tauari* (cigar) which he had been offered, but which he did not accept for fear of never returning.[4] By twelve, Fortunato had already performed a cure. One day, while paying a visit with his mother to a dying boy, Fortunato announced that the boy would not die. He picked a few herbs in the back yard and ordered his mother to prepare a medicine for the boy to drink. Remembering Fortunato's earlier visit to the depths, the mother did as he requested.

---

[4] The Orpheus in Hades theme involving the danger of taking anything in the underworld for fear of not being allowed to return reoccurs in all stories told of the under-water visits of Itá shamans.

Shortly afterward the sick boy recovered, and thereafter Fortunato's fame as a pagé and curer spread.

Other pagés do not announce themselves quite so early. Often the parents of children who show signs of possessing such powers do not want them to become pagés, and take preventive steps. They may take a child who shows such symptoms to a pagé and ask that he dispel the spirits attracted to the child. Others, who wish the child to become a pagé, take the child to a well known pagé who will establish the relationship between the spirits and the child. If one of these two procedures is not adopted, a child showing such symptoms may not be able to withstand the spirits, and he may die. Nowadays people profess, at least, that they do not want their children to become pagés. The pagé is persecuted by the authorities, called "pagan" by the padre, and publicly criticized by the upper class. But often the individual cannot escape. Dona Benta, for example, told of her daughter who became a pagé despite the efforts of an old pagé to send the spirits away. The pagé was not certain of the results of his cure and warned the parents to watch the girl carefully when she reached the age of about fifteen. The girl led a normal life until she was sixteen, when her father died. The shock caused her to take to her hammock, crying and moaning in grief. Then, filtering through the moaning of her daughter, Dona Benta heard a man's voice saying that his name was Nerto, a spirit from the depths. Other voices joined that of Nerto, and speaking through the girl each one announced its name. Some of them were females and others were males. Afterward, the daughter told of conversations she had had with her spirits. She was able to foretell the future and she performed several miraculous cures. People advised Dona Benta to take her daughter to a well known pagé for instruction, for it was dangerous to deal with spirits without knowing how. Dona Benta did not allow her to receive full instructions from the pagé for fear of the police and in fear of public opinion. People are convinced that the girl's death several years later was caused by "being taken away by her spirits."

Sometimes the symptoms appear later in life. Eneas Ramos told us of his surprise when his eldest daughter suddenly showed such symptoms when she was over twenty years old. The young woman had been having serious headaches. At night she cried and sometimes moaned in her sleep. Several praying women and blessers, women who add to these methods by a variety of herbal remedies, had tried to cure her headaches, but none was able to help her. Then one night she rose from her hammock and ran pell-mell toward the river. She would have plunged in if her father and brothers had not held her back. Her compulsive behavior occurred several times before Eneas decided to call a pagé. The pagé was able to send the spirits away temporarily, but they soon returned. The young woman soon married, moving away to Belém, and there she became a pagé. Rumors from Belém have it that Maria José, as she is called, is now a well known pagé and spiritualist medium in a working-class district of that city.

Although there have been many changes since aboriginal times, modern Amazon shamanism shows the remarkable persistence of Indian religion despite more than three centuries of Christian influence. Like the Indian shamans before them, the modern Amazon pagé has a retinue of spirit helpers; he has powers of divination, he becomes possessed and falls into a trance, and he cures. Nowadays his friendly supernatural powers are mainly "spirits from the depths of the river" with modern Brazilian names, a saint, or an "Indian" (that is, the ghost of an Indian shaman) rather than the old Tupían demons of the forest or ghosts. Today alcohol is used, together with tobacco, to stimulate trance. A pagé may dance and sing holding a sacred rattle in his hand, as the Tupían *pay* did; or he may make use of a bunch of red parrot feathers, a wand of herbs, or even a crucifix for the same purpose. But the old techniques of curing—namely, the process of blowing clouds of tobacco smoke over the patient's body, of massaging, and, in the end, of pretending to suck a small object out of the patient's body—remain essentially the same.

One of the members of our research party was treated by a pagé named Satiro. Satiro is not a powerful pagé. He has not been practicing many years. Ascendino and Maria de Lourdes, both of whom also live within the Itá community, are better known. Satiro's methods are not as traditional as those of the better known pagés, but he began his cure in the traditional manner. He prepared a table by covering a small box with a white cloth. Then he placed upon the table several long cigars prepared from locally grown tobacco rolled in the bark of the *tauari* tree. Next he fumigated a glass by blowing clouds of smoke into it; then he filled it with white rum. Satiro then asked his patient to lie in a hammock stretched near his table, and he began to sing, calling each of his spirit helpers by name. Suddenly one of them possessed him, and his voice and his posture immediately changed. The spirit helper was obviously a female, because he began to sing in high falsetto and his movements were dainty.

At this point Satiro might well have made use of his divinatory powers, for pagés, while they are in a trance, announce who their next patients will be and may even read the mind of the patient being treated. Ascendino, for example, read the thoughts of one of his patients: "You believe that I am ignorant and you do not believe in me," he said. The patient was embarrassed but admitted that what Ascendino said was true. Satiro, however, did not make use of such powers. He began to smoke, to drink frequently of the rum, and to sing in the voice of his "companion," who, he announced, was Mariquinha—a female from the depths. He left us and went down the path from the house to the nearby stream. There, standing in the water he called other companion spirits. Though Satiro did not use a rattle, he held a wand of twigs in his hand; with this he made the sign of the cross over himself and over his patient when he returned. He blew tobacco smoke over the patient's body and massaged the patient's back where the latter had complained of pains. Ascendino or Maria de Lourdes would have sucked with their mouths near the painful area. Finally, Satiro announced his diagnosis. The pains were not the result of witchcraft performed by an enemy; thus he did not have a beetle or a small piece of bone to show. (On another occasion a pagé announced that he had removed a beetle placed in his patient's body by witchcraft, blew into a glass filled with rum, and then quickly covered the glass with a saucer. The next morning a large black beetle was found floating in the rum.) Satiro, however, said that his patient's pains were from natural causes—an *ataque de ramo frio* (attack of cold twigs), and he recommended a special diet and a series of herbal remedies. Finally, he dismissed his spirit helpers and returned to a normal state. Afterward he complained of being exhausted.

Satiro is still learning his profession. Though he wanted a rattle very badly, he told us that first he must have the power to travel under water. In the depths he expects to receive his *maracá* (rattle) from the very mouth of a giant water snake. A more powerful pagé told Satiro that he also needs a "virgin mirror"—one into which no one has ever looked—so that he could see his spirit companions without danger to himself while traveling under water. He has tried unsuccessfully several times to buy such a mirror, but someone always looks over his shoulder as the box containing them is opened in the store. Satiro is certain that he will one day be a strong pagé. He apologized because he could not as yet distinguish all his "companions" one from another. "In the beginning," he said, "it is like a forest in which one knows there are rubber trees. But, because a trail has not yet been opened, one cannot see the rubber trees or how to get to them. Later on, when a trail has been opened, one knows them tree by tree." He believes that he will one day be able to travel under water and visit the great water snake, and that he will have an "Indian" among his companion spirits as does Maria de Lourdes and Ascendino. Perhaps Satiro will even become a *sacaca* with all the prestige of those great men of a generation ago.

The modern shamans of Itá have been influenced by Catholicism and, as the reader might suspect, to some extent by spiritualism, which is practiced in the large cities of Belém and Manaus. Yet most pagés make a distinction between spiritualism and true *pagelança* (shamanism). They say that the spiritualistic mediums from the city work with "spirits of the air" vaguely thought of as disembodied souls, while the true pagé works with "beings of the water." The pagés do not distinguish so sharply between Catholicism and shaman-istic belief. In curing they freely use Catholic and pseudo-Catholic prayers; they make the sign of the cross; and a saint may be in-cluded among "companion" spirits.

All pagés protest with great vigor that they are good Catholics and stanch devotees of their particular patron saint. But in the Ama-zon Valley, unlike the situation among the Indian populations of Peru, Guatemala, and Mexico, there has not been a thorough fusion between Catholicism and the remnants of the native religious rites. Instead, belief in pagés and their spirits exists simultaneously with Catholicism and the cult of the saints. The two sets of belief, shamanism and folk Catholicism, do not oppose each other. Each serves a different purpose. The saints protect the general welfare of the community, and through the mechanism of vows, they give favors and even cure. Shamanism deals with magical influences; it cures illness due to malignant supernaturals and to witchcraft.

IV

Like the beliefs surrounding the pagé, the series of dangerous supernaturals who inhabit the forest and the river, about which people in Itá tell, are also mainly of Indian origin. As in shamanism, old Indian religious belief has been modified by, and fused with, anal-ogous European concepts which the Portuguese brought to the Amazon. A few people in Itá protest that these spirits and super-naturals do not exist, particularly the upper class, who have heard outsiders scoff at such ideas, calling them superstitions and "the nonsense of the caboclo." Especially in the presence of city people, the more sophisticated members of the Itá community are ashamed and pretend to laugh at such ideas. But in reality almost everyone in Itá, even most of the upper class, retains some credence in these dangerous supernaturals. When it was reported, for example, that the giant snake with luminous eyes had been seen in the river near Itá, none of the upper-class doubters would go out in a canoe at night. Far from being old superstitions now discarded, belief in these old Indian-European supernaturals is alive in Itá today.

Many of these powers are related directly to hunting and fishing—to the exploitation of the natural environment. This is true of Anhangá,[5] a ghost or demon who hunts people in the forest, according to the reports of hunters and rubber gatherers. Anhangá appears to them generally as an *inhambu*, a forest fowl, but it may take the form of almost any animal. However, since the Anhangá so often takes the form of an inhambu, the latter is considered *visagento* (magically malignant). The only difference between the normal inhambu and the inhambu Anhangá is its actions and the white down breast feathers and the red head feathers characteristic of the Anhangá. Both Jorge Porto and Juca have met up with Anhangá in the form of the inhambu fowl. Jorge Porto and some companions were camped deep within a forest cutting timber when they heard a thin whistle which came nearer. Finally, it seemed to issue from right above their heads inside their hut. Jorge Porto recognized the sound as that of the Anhangá. He sprinkled himself and his companions with holy water, frightening the Anhangá away.[6] Juca's experience was more according to pattern. He had been hunting inhambu fowls with unusual success. Each afternoon, after working in his garden, he would hunt for a few hours, almost always killing a bird or two. One afternoon, however, he saw an inhambu Anhangá; before he recognized it, he shot. The bird fell on Juca's head, and it was so heavy that he was knocked unconscious. He was lucky, he told us, that the Anhangá did not "steal his shadow," which would have made him very ill. Juca gave up hunting. His narrow escape thoroughly frightened him.

Like the inhambu, monkeys, especially the guariba, or howler monkey (*Alouatta caraya*), are to be feared in the forest. The guariba is also a *bicho visagento* (magically malignant animal). Certain guaribas, with the same appearance as any normal animal,

[5] *Anhangá* in *língua geral* and the native Tupí language means "ghost" or "shadow."

[6] He did not explain just why he was equipped with holy water, but men do often take a bottle of holy water with them on long trips just for such contingencies.

have powers to "steal a man's shadow." Antonio Dias, a rubber gatherer, told of an encounter with a guariba monkey which was malignant. One day Antonio heard his name called as he walked alone deep in the forest. He turned to see a large howler monkey advancing upon him. Antonio fled in panic. Women are especially afraid of the guariba, who they believe will invade their houses to rape them. Many people believe that such malignant animals are the same as the "mother of the animal" (*mãe de bicho*), a supernatural which protects the animals of each species against hunters or fishermen who kill too many of them. These mothers punish the hunter or fisherman by stealing his shadow.

The most famous of the forest spirits, however, is the Curupira, a small man-like creature whose feet are turned backward. Curupiras live deep in the forest, from which their long shrill cries are often heard. They are said to be especially fond of rum and tobacco. They attract hunters deeper and deeper into the forest, until they are lost and never return. The Curupira can imitate a man's voice. They call out to a rubber gatherer or a hunter who believes the voice to be that of a companion and thus is drawn off his path. Everyone in Itá knows of the Curupira, but no one in town has ever encountered one. In the rural neighborhoods a few men have heard them call out in the forest, but no one has actually seen one. However, people tell many stories of their grandfathers meeting the Curupira face to face. Eneas Ramos told one, as he heard it from his grandfather, who was already an old man when Eneas was a youth. In those days the Igarapé Arinoá was bordered by an impenetrable forest. It was "a place of Curupiras." According to the story, a newcomer arrived in the Itá community. Eneas' grandfather told him of the wild game which might be found in the upper reaches of the Igarapé Arinoá, and the man decided to go hunting there. He went armed with a "cross of holy wax" hung about his neck and a supply of holy wax in his ammunition bag. Later the hunter told of his encounter. As soon as he beached his canoe on the first night, he saw the Curupira. It was a dark creature "no bigger than a child," and "like a small caboclinho" (that is, like a little Indian).

But the Curupira could not come close to the hunter, for the holy wax repelled him and kept him at a distance. The Curupira asked the man to remove the cross from his neck; and when the hunter did so the Curupira closed in. The stranger knocked the Curupira to the ground with a hard blow, but with a simple move the Curupira threw the hunter so high into the air that his leg was broken when he fell. The hunter grabbed his ammunition bag, which contained holy wax, and the act saved him. The Curupira was made harmless, but he did put the stranger to sleep with a powerful *catinga* (bad smell). When the man awoke he was floating downstream in his canoe, a magic arrow by his side. From that day forth, the hunter was an excellent shot, never missing his target. Since those times the Curupiras have left the Igarapé Arinoá. As men have moved in, they have retreated deeper into the forest.

Unlike the Curupira, the giant snake (*cobra grande*) is still seen even by Itá townspeople. The giant snake is believed to be one of the constrictors, a *sucuriju* or a *giboia*, which has grown larger and heavier than normal and has supernatural qualities. A giant snake may be 135 or 165 feet in length. It is so large that "the furrows which its body leaves as it crawls about become creeks." Such giant snakes are believed to live in the deepest parts of the river. Thus many people think of them as the *boiúna*, the giant snake of which some pagés have spoken. Sometimes a giant snake appears on the surface for everyone to see. For an entire week during our 1948 visit to Itá, no one dared fish at night because a giant snake had appeared on two successive nights in the river just in front of the town. Two fishermen had actually seen its great luminous eyes closing in upon them as they sat in their canoes. They went to their hammocks sick with fright. Giant snakes usually appear on stormy nights during the winter, or rainy season. "Its eyes shine like the spotlights on a river steamer." In fact, people say that sometimes a giant snake becomes "an enchanted river boat." Such a ship was seen several times by Antonio Noronha, who was the *trapicheiro* (public dock-man) in Itá for many years. A *"cobra grande navio"* (giant-snake ship) came directly upriver toward the public pier with all lights ablaze. When it came close it turned back downstream. Another informant, a rubber gatherer who was traveling to Itá in a canoe, confirmed Antonio's statements. He was resting at an old abandoned *barracão*, he explained. He heard the beat of a river boat's engines. Then he saw the ship approaching the abandoned pier. It was a big boat all lighted up, and "a man in red clothes" was standing at the steering wheel (probably the Devil). Then suddenly it sailed away in the direction from which it had come. The connection between the enchanted ship and the giant snake was never fully explained by the people of Itá, but all of them felt that they were manifestations of the same dangerous power.

Another dangerous apparition is Matintaperera. While Curupira and Anhangá inhabit the deep forest and giant snakes are of the river, Matintaperera appears in the town itself. It is appropriate, therefore, that the beliefs relating to Matintaperera are mainly European in origin. The description of Matintaperera is much like the Old World concept of werewolves. Some say in Itá that Matintaperera is always a woman, but others say that it also appears in male form. It is agreed that a person becomes a Matintaperera through his own destiny. Such a person is unaware of his fate at first. But then he begins to have nightmares, grows thin, and takes on a yellowish skin color. Matintaperera appears at night in the streets or near people's homes, always accompanied by a coal-black bird which is Matintaperera's pet. Some people say that they "leave their heads at home when they go out." All people are afraid of it because it "steals your shadow," bringing illness and even death. One may capture such an apparition, however, by reciting prayers and locking the door as Matintaperera approaches. The next morning, the person who is Matintaperera will be found seated in human form on the doorstep. Or one may attack Matintaperera with switches. The next day the person will have welts on his face. One of our friends in Itá claims to have captured one by the first method about ten years ago. The young woman who appeared on our friend's doorstep the next morning was arrested and jailed by the police.

The fresh-water dolphin, which inhabits the Amazon Basin, is called the *boto;* is also enchanted and is thought to be endowed with magical and supernatural powers. The people of the Amazon have noted a series of physiological similarities between the dolphin, which is a mammalian, and man, and likewise many physiological differences between the dolphin and fishes. There are two types of botos recognized in Itá—the large *vermelho* (red) and the *tucuxi,* a small black one. The latter is considered to be somewhat benevolent. It is said to save drowning people by helping them ashore, and it frightens away the large red botos when they attack a canoe or bathers. Despite the good reputation of the smaller black boto, however, people feel that it is better to avoid all botos, both red and black. They are all creatures with high magical potency.

In fact, almost the entire body of the boto may be used for some magical or medicinal purpose. The skin may be dried in order to prepare a fumigation used to treat snake bite or the wound of a sting ray. Another treatment consists of grating the teeth or a bone of the boto into a powder to be placed inside the snake bite or in the wound. A tooth of the dolphin hung around an infant's neck will cure diarrhea. The boto's ear made into a charm to be tied around the wrist of a child will guarantee good hearing. The fat from the boto is an important ingredient of a preparation for rheumatism, and the meat of the animal is thought to be a specific for leprosy. The brain is extremely potent and dangerous. A small piece— "enough to fit into the hole of a needle"—placed in a dog's food will make the animal an excellent hunter and immune from panema. The same amount given to a man will allow the giver to gain control over the victim just as a man controls a good hunting dog; but a slightly larger portion of the boto's brain placed in a man's food will drive him crazy and cause his brain to wither away. The penis and the left eye of the boto may be dried and grated to form a powerful aphrodisiac. A powder made of *carajuru* [7] and the grated penis may be spread on a man's penis just before coitus. It is thought to cause such a large and continued erection that the woman will reach orgasm many times and "almost go crazy over her lover."

[7] A wild plant, *Arrabidaea* sp. A red liquid is extracted from the leaves.

A man who uses this preparation will be able to have the woman whenever he wishes her. The left eye of the boto also may be grated into a powder and used as a magical love potion to be placed in a woman's food by a man who desires her. According to many people, the socket of the left eye may be dried to be used as a "sight" through which a man may peer at a girl whom he desires, causing her to become impassioned of him.[8]

The boto has strong sexual associations in the minds of the people of Itá and of other Amazon communities. The animal itself is thought to have great sexual potency and magical powers. It is said that fishermen have had intercourse with boto females which they killed on the beach. The sexual organs of the female are strikingly similar to those of a woman, and they give a man such intense pleasure, it is said, that if his companion does not pull him away he will die in continued intercourse. In Itá, however, people think that the human female must be protected from the advances of the male boto. Women are thought to be unable to resist a man if they are tempted; thus, in the same way that an unchaperoned girl in Itá often falls prey to a human lover, she also cannot resist the male boto. It is believed that the male boto may appear in the form of a handsome young man, generally dressed in a white starched suit. He appears unannounced in homes to seduce women, especially virgins. Sometimes he may take on the likeness of a husband and have sexual relations with the wife, who is unaware of the deception. The boto male in human form can only be discovered by the fact that his feet are turned backward on the body. In any case, it is impossible for women to resist him. But, as women continue sexual relations with a boto, they become thin and yellow, and may even die if the relations are not interrupted. If a girl gives birth to the boto's child, it must be immediately "returned to its father" (that is, thrown in the

---

[8] A rather amusing Amazon anecdote hinges upon this belief: A young city dweller traveling on a large river steamer fell in love with a young lady aboard. Passing the town of Santarém, he bought the eye socket of a boto and decided to sight the young lady through it. As he attempted to do so, however, she moved out of range and the burly captain stepped into view. The young man spent the rest of the trip avoiding the amorous attentions of the captain.

water) so that the boto father will not harm the mother.[9] Numerous cases of illegitimate children have been charged to the boto in the Amazon region.

Juca told us of a friend's wife who was seduced by a boto. The friend, who lived in a rural neighborhood near Itá, was accustomed to fish at night. One night while he was away a handsome stranger came to his house and seduced his wife. The stranger returned night after night. The husband was not suspicious, but then he noticed that his wife was becoming overtired, and that her color was a sickly yellow. Then he began to notice that each night as he went off in his canoe to fish, a boto followed him for a distance, surfacing frequently and then suddenly disappearing. The husband became suspicious, and one night he returned early and rushed to his house. As he entered, he thought he saw a man running to the water's edge making a snorting noise as the boto does. The next night, when the boto followed him he shot at it. He saw a red stain of blood on the surface and he was sure he had killed the boto. The wife began at once to gain weight and to lose her yellow color; but the poor husband, Juca related, became ill with a fever and died a short time afterward, bewitched by the boto lover of his wife.

Several instances of boto men seducing, or attempting to seduce, virgins have taken place in Itá. Raimundo Dias told us how a boto man seduced his sister who died a few years ago. They lived at the time in a hut near the river. For several nights the whole family heard a strange whistling, as if some one were calling. One evening his sister began to sing a strange, unintelligible song. They rushed to her room. She was nude, and struggled violently with them in an attempt to jump into the water. Raimundo saw the flash of a white figure as it entered the water and then he heard a boto snort out in the river. Raimundo's father rubbed the girl's body with garlic, a substance offensive to all botos, and she became calm. People believe

[9] There were no local cases of infanticide for this reason known by our Itá informants, but several cases have occurred in the lower Amazon region in the last decade. One well known case reached the courts in Belém. Both the pagé, who had advised the mother to kill her child, and the mother were charged with murder.

that the boto men want to take women with them to the depths, and this seems to have been the case with Raimundo's sister. She could not be saved, however, for she had lived with her boto lover too long, and she died soon after he left her.[10]

The boto is especially attracted by a menstruating woman. Women therefore should not travel by canoe in this condition. If they do, boto males will follow and try to upset their canoe. Sometimes women need not even be menstruating to attract them. A woman should never look at the botos when they surface near a canoe in which they are traveling. If she does, the boto will try to take her away. Only by sticking a knife into the bottom of the canoe, cutting the water with a large cutlass, or rubbing the stern of the canoe with garlic or garlic vine will the boto males be forced to leave the canoe alone. Other people add that the boto cannot stand the smell of pepper. In Itá people who live on the edge of the river sometimes burn garlic and pepper when women in the house are menstruating, to keep away male botos. The boto, more than any other animal, is "enchanted," and the male is a dangerous sexual competitor to man. At each great festival, some people say, two or three boto men attend, dancing with the girls and finally seducing them.

V

To the visitor the people of Itá seem unusually preoccupied with disease and with the dangers of pregnancy, childbirth, and other physiological processes. They spend a large proportion of their incomes on patent medicines such as *Saúde da Mulher* (a preparation to ease the pains of menstruation), Carter's Little Liver Pills, and other concoctions which may be found in almost any store or trading post. Everyone knows a long list of herbal remedies, and innumerable folk methods of treating disease. In any long conversation with a person from Itá, the subject of disease and of cures and

---

[10] If a girl sticks her boto lover with a pin, he will become disenchanted, remaining a human male and never returning to his boto form.

remedies is almost certain to come up. In our notebooks we wrote down hundreds of local specifics, numerous methods of treating the sick, and many ways to avoid catching disease. Until a decade ago Itá (and most other Amazon rural areas) lacked scientific medical assistance almost completely. From time to time a physician from Belém stopped over in the town, attending patients and dispensing medicines. On occasion a male practical nurse was in attendance at the health post which was maintained for short periods by the state government. Until 1942, when the SESP stationed a physician in Itá and provided him with up-to-date pharmaceuticals, the people of Itá depended almost entirely upon patent medicines, household remedies, herbal specifics, and their own folk practitioners for protection against disease and physical accidents. With their poor diets, without adequate public-health facilities or medical assistance, without a scientific knowledge of the transmission of disease, and living in an environment which is amenable to disease, the people of Itá have always suffered from ill health. It is no wonder that they are preoccupied with the subject.

The concept of disease held by the people of Itá is, in a sense, dual in nature. They believe in natural causes, and are often quite willing to accept a physician's explanation of the cause of illness; but they also believe that disease is caused by the dangerous forest or water spirits, or is even the result of punishment by a saint. Their own folk medicine reflects this dual concept. The pagé cures by magical means, by removing an extrusive particle with the help of his friendly spirits; but he also advises special diets and herbal medicines. Similarly, though people pray to their patron saints asking for their intervention in a cure, they also take patent medicines and local remedies. Many of the Itá beliefs regarding the treatment of disease have a sound basis in observed fact, but others are based on supernatural and magical concepts. Some of the methods of treatment and medicines used by Itá people and by local practitioners are at least scientifically well grounded; but many others are actually harmful to the patient. Still, whether good or bad in the light of modern scientific medicine, the people have been able to survive in the Amazon environment for several centuries.

Birth is a dangerous process. Although statistics are not available for the number of women who die during childbirth or for the number of stillborn children, numerous cases of deaths in childbirth were related to us. Almost all women told of losing children at birth and of abortions.

In Itá most births are attended by a *curiosa* (or *parteira*), as mid-wives are called. There are four professional midwives in town and but half a dozen others in the rural neighborhoods. These old women, who attend at the birth and who generally remain in the home caring for the mother and child for eight days, charge on the average $2.50 (cr. $50) for the first child and as little as $1.00 (cr. $20) for the succeeding births. During these days the midwife is fed, of course, and the husband is obliged to send a canoe to fetch her and later to return her to her home. Most midwives are old widows, such as Dona Joaquina Costa, who have had several children of their own and who live in the home of a relative during the short periods when they are without a client. Most of these midwives are also gifted with powers to "bless," and they know numerous prayers which are used like incantations to aid their clients. Midwives also advise their clients during pregnancy and on feminine hygiene during menstruation.

Women do not like to discuss menstruation, but the old mid-wives are remarkable repositories of knowledge about menstruation and other aspects of feminine hygiene. It was mainly from them that we learned about these aspects of Itá life. Men considered women to be unclean during menstruation, and sex relations during such days are considered dangerous to the health of the man.[11] Women are told not to take baths nor to wash their hair while menstruating, and they should avoid eating acid fruits such as oranges, lemons, and mangos. Above all, they should avoid streams

[11] Some men believe that they may contract gonorrhea during intercourse with a menstruating woman.

and rivers for fear of the *caruara*, a spider-like arthropod living near the water's edge. The smell of menstrual blood irritates the *caruara*, several midwives explained, which shoots the woman with invisible arrows as she passes. She will have painfully swollen legs and arms as a result. Morena Porto was once hit by the *caruara* during her menstruation, and she told us of the treatment which the midwife prescribed. She was told to rub herself with an ointment made of the leaves of several trees mixed with the oil from the nut of the *araticu* and *andiroba*. The midwife also "blessed" her (that is, touched her head while uttering a prayer) to drive the *caruara* away. Women also ask the midwife for herbal remedies against severe colic during menstruation and against excessive flow or abnormal suspension of the menses. For the latter, among other specifics, Dona Joaquina prescribes a brew made of *abuta* roots,[12] the pulp of a gourd,[13] and coffee leaves to be taken twice a day. Some midwives also know methods of anti-conception and methods of producing abortion, but most people feel that midwives are seldom successful at either. One of them told us that she knew a prayer which would *atalhar* (block) a woman. She had used this prayer for a woman who lived on the Igarapé Itapereira. The woman had had three twin births and did not want to conceive again. This midwife also prescribed teas made out of *carapanaúba* bark (*Apocináccas*),[14] green *ananás* (wild pineapple), the pulp of the gourd, and quinine bark to induce abortion in case her patient conceived in spite of her prayer.

Most midwives claim that they can predict whether a pregnant woman is carrying a male or female child. One of the four who live in the town of Itá told us that she could tell the sex of the child by the way the pregnant woman walked. "If she puts her left foot forward first as a woman does, then it is a girl, but if she starts on her right foot as a man does it is a boy." All midwives warn the

---

[12] Menispermaceas sp.

[13] The gourd known as *buchinha* (*Lufa operculata*). The pulp of the fruit is said to contain a strong alkaloid. See Paul Le Cointe, *Amazonia Brasileira: Arvores e Plantas Uteis* (São Paulo, 1947), p. 81.

[14] This bark is also said to contain a strong alkaloid. *Ibid.*, p. 123.

expectant mother and her husband (if they do not already know) not to touch the meat and the fish caught by others. They might cause the hunter or the fisher to have panema. She tells the pregnant woman to be careful in church, for the smell of incense will cause her to faint.[15] Pregnant women should not eat a "twin" banana (that is, two fruits joined) for fear that the birth will result in twins. During pregnancy, however, women may continue to work preparing farinha and even carrying heavy cans of water from the river. Except for the few restrictions and dangers mentioned above, pregnancy is considered a relatively healthy period.

As soon as the woman feels birth pains, her husband calls the midwife. When the midwife lives a considerable distance away, she often comes early to wait for the birth. Some women prefer to give birth in the hammock. They take a semi-sitting position with their legs dropped over the side. Often the midwife, or even the husband, supports the woman under her shoulders as she sits in the hammock, which is split underneath so that the midwife can secure the child from below as it is born. Most midwives, however, do not like their patients to use the hammock. They prefer a pallet prepared on the floor out of straw mats and sheets. Women have more support, they say, *para dar o puxo* (to give the pull), or to exert force at each contraction. As the birth pains come, the midwife massages the woman's abdomen and her thighs and makes her flex her legs. If the birth is difficult, she gives her teas and *garrafadas* (that is, preparations made out of various herbs, barks, and roots generally soaked in rum). During one difficult birth, Dona Joaquina spread a beaten egg mixed with sugar over the woman's abdomen and gave the woman the same mixture internally to give her strength. She uses a mixture of several palm oils with the leaves of wild plants as an ointment to relieve the birth pains.

Prayers and incantations are also used by the midwife to help a woman through a difficult birth. As soon as the child is born, the midwife cuts the umbilical cord "three fingers away from the child

[15] Fainting in church can therefore be quite embarrassing, especially for an unmarried girl.

and three fingers away from the mother" and ties it with a string. She anoints the ends of the cord with an oil of palm and rubs the child's navel with tobacco juice. Formerly the infant was not bathed at this time for fear of the "illness of the seventh day" (infection of the umbilical cord). Now it may be bathed in warm water. If a child is born "asleep" (seeming to be dead), the midwife takes some olive oil or any palm oil on her fingers and spreads it over the infant's throat and chest. Then, with a rattle or any two pieces of metal, she makes a noise to "awaken" the child. To cause the placenta to drop Dona Juaquina blows into the mouth of a bottle. Most mothers are wrapped with a long sheet just after the birth "to hold them in place," and to prevent *mãe de corpo* (prolapse of the uterus).

Following the birth there is a long period of convalescence during which the mother must respect numerous post-natal taboos. The convalescence differs in length, depending upon the sex of the child. It should be forty-five days for a male child and forty-two for a female. During the first eight days of this period most midwives advise their patients to remain in the hammock and, if possible, in a dark room. The remaining days should be spent at home avoiding heavy duties, if possible, and observing many dietary restrictions. During the first eight days, for example, she may eat chicken but not the variety with black legs and no feathers on its neck, which is common in Itá. She may eat a porridge made of rice flour and of manioc flour; and the large plantain, if it is well cooked, is not harmful. The mother should take mainly teas made from various medicinal herbs to drink. Even after the first eight days the mother must avoid certain foods which are felt to be strong or harmful, such as eggs, pork, citric fruits, beans, fish without scales, and most game. The meat of animals which are reproducers is considered harmful, especially those which might have been in rut when they were killed. But veal and the meat of castrated animals is considered less strong and not dangerous. During the entire period of convalescence women should not bathe in the river. After fifteen days or so, she is allowed to wash herself in a basin of water, but if she were to bathe in the river before the entire convalescence were over, she would be thought to be in danger of being impregnated by an electric eel or a large constrictor.

Some midwives advise husbands to observe eight days of convalescence after their wives give birth. During this time the father should not perform heavy work. He might cause the child to have "body aches," according to the midwives. But few men believe that this very modified form of couvade is really necessary, and few observe it.

Childbirths attended by midwives are not particularly clean or sanitary. Recently, the physician of the public-health service has been able to persuade at least those midwives who live in town itself to come to the health post for some instruction in elementary hygiene. He has asked them to boil water and to have the sheets, towels, and the abdominal binding of the mothers sterilized and to boil their scissors before using them. These new ideas, if the midwives in town may be believed, have been adopted. The health service has given each midwife a small handbag equipped with surgical scissors, gauze, adhesive tape, mercurochrome, and surgical thread. They are asked to report all births to the physician for purposes of vital statistics. One old midwife rebelled against these ideas. She was horrified when the physician suggested that a mother be given orange juice and eggs before the end of her forty-two days of convalescence, and she continues to follow the traditional concepts and methods. But the other midwives seem to be proud of the recognition given them. Recently they have called the physician more frequently to aid them with difficult births.

As in childbirth, most cases of illness or accident in Itá are treated by native practitioners and by traditional methods of folk medicine. There is a large daily attendance at the health post established in 1942 by the SESP where the physician now offers consultations each morning. Townspeople are getting the habit of going to the post whenever they are ill and even request the physician to come to their homes in the case of an accident or of grave sickness. People from the rural districts, even beyond the area included in the Itá community, come to the health post for consultation. There is no charge for the physician's services or for the medicines he dispenses; but, since the physician's primary function in the community is that of a public-health officer, and since he has two other towns in his district, he has relatively little time to give to medical assistance. Furthermore, despite the line of people waiting each morning for consultation at the health post, the SESP cannot reach the entire urban and rural population in this enormous district. Nor are the majority of the people in this area accustomed as yet to seeking medical care. Despite the presence of the physician and despite his growing importance, people still seek out their pagés or their *benzedeiras* (literally, "a blesser," but used to mean "one who blesses") and *rezadeiras* (literally, "a prayer," one who prays) for treatment of illness.

These practitioners, the blessers and the prayers, may be of either sex, but most of them are women. Like the pagé, they generally have some especially endowed power to cure. Their powers, however, manifest themselves in a milder form than those of the pagé. Such power is evident in successful diagnosis of illness and in successful treatments. Their treatments consist both of prayers, used as incantations, and of herbal medicines. Their prayers, which they know by memory and which most of them keep secret, are specifics for headachęs, colds, diarrhea, fevers, and other common diseases and ailments. Such prayers only have power for the particular practitioner who uses them. A few blessers are specialists. One of them is famous for the cure of snake bite. But most of them have an extensive knowledge of herbal remedies, and even numerous patent medicines available at the local stores, which will cure a large variety of diseases. In the town of Itá, there are at least a dozen of these practitioners, and there is always at least one in each rural neighborhood.

Many of the medicines prescribed by the blessers and prayers are common household remedies which may be applied by anyone with the knowledge. Women more frequently than men know the names and the uses of these plants. "Men always ask their wives," one man answered when we asked him to explain the medicinal value of a plant. In the back yard of almost any Itá home, a flat box set on stilts, called a *jirau*, may be seen in which a series of plants are growing. These plants, sometimes mistaken for decorative flowers, are medicinal herbs—in a sense the family medicine chest—which have been planted or transplanted to be handy in the case of need. In addition, in almost every Itá household there are bottles of medicines prepared from roots and barks of native trees soaked in rum. People also keep a sack of their favorite herbs, barks, and roots handy in the house. Others may even be purchased at the local stores and trading posts. There are the *urubu caá* (*Aristolochia trilobata*) leaves, peppermint leaves, *japana branca* bark (*Eupatorium ayapana*), locust-tree bark, *pracaxi* bark (*Pentaclethra filamentosa*), the sap of the *caxinguba* tree (*Ficus*), avocado-tree leaves, *manjericão* (*Ocimum minimum*) leaves, and literally hundreds of other plants, barks, and roots known to have medicinal properties. These medicines are used in a variety of combinations, depending frequently upon the training of the practitioner who prescribes it. In general, however, they are prepared and used as hot teas, as infusions mixed with rum, as medicines, as *suadores* (to bring on perspiration), as fumigations (to produce smoke which is thought to be curative), or as baths. Others are taken as tonics, and still others to produce vomiting and as purgatives.

An Itá blesser is able to prescribe literally hundreds of detailed recipes for these preparations. The leaves of the aromatic *manjericão* plant are used to make a tea to treat a common cold or a cough. The juice from the bark of the *pracaxi* tree mixed with a little water, passed through a piece of cloth, and left out at night to catch the dew is a strong emetic which is used to treat intestinal worms. To prepare one strong purgative "take nine seeds from the *piãoseiro* tree (*Jatropha cureas*), cut them in half, throw away the skin around the seeds, crush one-half of each seed, and extract the juice which should be taken with a small cup of coffee." For sore eyes "grate the root of *japuí* and mix it with maternal milk—or, if this is not available, with the white of an egg to be placed over the eyes."

Rheumatism may be treated with "a hot bath made of sugar-cane stalks or of *manjericão* leaves which have been left to soak in the sun for three days and to catch the dew three nights." Whooping cough is treated "with *aturiá* [16] leaves mixed with a few drops of kerosene." "Lizard fat mixed with a liquid formed by soaking corn cobs, orange and lime leaves and dried *sabugueiro* flowers (*Sambucus nigra*) in water" is a remedy for measles. All of these teas, emetics, purgatives, and baths in general require a convalescence during which one must avoid certain foods, exposure to sun or rain, and performance of heavy work. After taking the purgative of *piãoseiro* described above, one may not eat fish for two days nor should one be exposed to rain, sun, or dew. After any purgative the patient should avoid looking at any green foliage until after the first bowel movement. After most remedial baths, purgatives, and emetics, those foods classified as strong must be avoided. So intrenched is the idea in Itá that every medicine must have its rules of convalescence that the physician there has found it very difficult to persuade his clients that the medicines he dispenses need not involve special diets, rest, and other taboos.

Not all of these medicines are specifics for disease, but many of them may be taken as preventives, or to give strength to the individual for particular purposes. Women take baths into which they mix the *cumaru* bean [17] in order to make their husbands jealous. A preparation made from the *umaparanga* root will give good luck in business. There are also infusions taken to avoid the bad effects of the "evil eye" and to drive away the vampire bat. A hot bath of the house of a *cupim* (termites) mixed with sweet herbs from the forest is a preventive against witchcraft. Other teas and herbal medicine are taken to protect women during their long post-natal lying-in period and to prevent children from catching childhood diseases. There are several aphrodisiacs, such as the root or the bark

[16] A spiny plant with long leaves which grows on the low banks of the river (*Machaerium lunatum*).
[17] The tonka bean, *Coumarouna odorata* Aubl.

of the *marapuana* tree [18] mixed with rum or a powder made of the dried penis of the coati [19] taken in water. In addition to internal medicine there are plasters and methods of treatments. Yaws and tropical ulcers are treated, for example, by placing a plaster made of a baked lemon mixed with rust scraped from iron over an open sore. The milk of *apuí* plant (*Guttiferae*) mixed with black pepper forms a plaster for any sore arm or leg. Ulcers from syphilis are cured by salve made of silver nitrate (secured in the local store) and the white of an egg, or a piece of copper may be placed over the ulcer and tightly bound next to it.

Numerous formulas are also known for fumigations. People fumigate to cure a disease, to prevent catching a prevalent disease, to drive away *assustamento* (fright), to free individuals and objects of panema, and even simply to bring happiness into the house. A few traditional housewives "fumigate their homes each week." Dona Branquinha, the schoolteacher, does so each Saturday, and Dona Felicia Marajó, also an upper-class housewife, fumigates her house every Friday. They vary the formula according to the purpose. A formula for prevention of any disease which is epidemic is "the nest of [a certain] bee mixed with the seed of *Oxí* and the dried leaves of the *parapará* tree." This mixture is burned in a broken ceramic bowl. The fumigations, according to several people, should always begin at the front of the house, progressing room by room back to the kitchen, and afterward the ashes should be thrown in the direction of the setting sun. Fumigation is not as much used nowadays in Itá as it was in the past. Many people use it only for treatment of panema, but many formulas are known, and fumigation remains a traditional method of Itá folk medicine. Amulets and charms with powers to cure and to protect are also included in this body of belief. *Almofadas* (literally, "pillows") are formed by placing various formulas and objects in a small sack to wear around

[18] This tree is called *catuaba* (*Bignoniaceae*) outside Amazonas, and its bark is widely used throughout rural Brazil as an aphrodisiac or a "nerve" tonic.

[19] The coati, an animal resembling the raccoon, "never has a soft penis," people explain.

the neck. A "pillow" of *jacuratú* [20] feathers will protect children from illness, and the teeth of the alligator or the fresh-water dolphin protect children from the evil eye and from diarrhea. A bracelet made of the "Tears of Our Lady" (small red and black seeds of a tree) protects a child against animals which might steal its shadow, against diarrhea caused by teething, and other evils. This body of belief involving disease, misfortune, accidents, and magical danger is very vast indeed in Itá. The native practitioners—the pagés, midwives, blessers, and prayers—have a wider range of knowledge than the layman, and they have personal capacity to cure which is manifest in the power of their prayers. But all people in Itá (especially women) have a wide knowledge of their folk medicine. The preoccupation with medicines is a never ending interest to the people of Itá. It is an aspect of life emphasized in their culture.

VI

The world view of the people of Itá and other Amazon communities is in process of transition. The change from a magical folk to one which possesses a modern scientific view of the world is one that took place some time ago in many centers of Western civilization. It is still taking place in many out-of-the-way regions of the Western World. The process has reached a point in Itá equivalent to that reached in most Western communities many years ago. But the change which is occurring in Itá, while essentially the same, differs profoundly in many respects. With modern communications and with the technology which we have nowadays at our command, the process of change in Itá is more rapid and more drastic. It does not occur gradually. Itá children are accustomed to seeing airplanes as they fly overhead and as they land once each week on the Amazon River bringing mail, cargo, and passengers. They do not, however, know automobiles, and they ask what automobiles look like and how they run. The physician in Itá uses penicillin to treat syphilis, pneumonia, and other illnesses rather than lizard fat, roots, and

[20] A variety of the jacú (*Penelope jacquacu*), a large forest fowl.

leaves from plants, and he cures without the added help of prayers and incantations. From a concept that malaria is caused by taking a bath or drinking stagnant water, the people of Itá are suddenly told that the disease is transmitted by the anopheles mosquito and that their homes must be sprayed with DDT. A patient may be treated one day with a strong purgative made of barks and roots of the forest and the next day with a sulfa compound or with penicillin. In Itá medieval and aboriginal methods and concepts are replaced at once by the most recent twentieth century methods and concepts. They did not and will not experience the gradual growth of modern science.

The people of Itá, like human beings everywhere, are quick to recognize the advantages of such efficient and productive methods and instruments. They are delighted, for example, with the results of DDT. Not only has malaria almost disappeared in the town itself but the periodic spraying with DDT has cleared their homes of other insects. It is a pleasure nowadays to sit outside in the early evening. They are quick to realize that penicillin is a more effective medicinal than their own "home remedies." But they are slower to accept the scientific concepts which lie behind the spraying of their houses and other innovations.

A new element which is introduced into a culture does not immediately replace the older element. New methods and new ideas must be integrated into the matrix of the preexisting culture, and in the process the culture and the view of the world of the people are modified. New methods may be imposed from outside, but the change is never complete until the new methods are integrated into the conceptual scheme of the people concerned. The mayor of an Amazon town, for example, explained to a public-health officer that he would cooperate in the drainage work, the medication program for malaria, and in spraying with DDT "because it is my obligation to do what our government orders." But he assured the doctor that "malaria comes from drinking stagnant water." People in Itá listened to the physician and the visiting nurse attentively when they explained that their children caught hookworm from the earth through walking without shoes and playing in the dirt. They accepted the physician's vermifuge to rid their children temporarily of the worms but they did nothing to correct the cause of infection. As one woman said just after the physician's lecture, "My grandson has worms because he eats too much condensed milk" (of a highly sweetened variety); others insisted that hookworms resulted from eating foods which are "strong" or even from fright caused by forest animals.

There is an often repeated saying in Brazil: "Believe in the Virgin and run"; in other words, one should not rely upon faith alone. People in Itá follow this old adage. Some have accepted the new scientific ideas coming from the outside, but at the same time they fear to give up their traditional beliefs and practices. Many continue to have more faith in their native practitioners and medicines than in the physician. In a crisis they will "give him a try." Mariano Gomes, for example, who was the secretary to the municipal government a few years ago, boasted a secondary education. He was one of the most prominent supporters of the health post and of the benefits of modern medical science. But when Mariano became very ill, he went both to the physician at the health post and to Ascendino, a pagé, for treatment. The pagé came secretly to Itá to diagnose his illness. He said that Mariano was sick because of witchcraft, which "the doctor does not know how to cure." Cases of people with apparent faith in science resorting to magical procedures are exceedingly frequent. And most people in Itá seek help from their herbal remedies, from their native practitioners, and from the supernatural before they turn to science. One of the most frequent complaints of physicians practicing in the Amazon region is the state of their patients when they finally seek their help. They are dehydrated from the use of strong purges and from violent vomiting. They have been given numerous herbal remedies and they have lost strength from rigorous diets. For most people, for reasons of economics, distance from medical facilities, or, simply, lack of faith in science, modern medicine is a last resort.

Between the two systems, between folk traditions and science, there are bound to be conflicts. The doctors, aware of the clash between the two systems, have driven the pagés out of town to practice secretly in isolated rural areas. Without understanding the local concepts of dangerous foods and the necessity for convalescence after any medicine, physicians are irritated when their patients refuse to take citrus fruits, eggs, and other "strong" foods and refuse to give them to their children. The people are worried, even angry, when the physicians laugh at their superstitions and when they advise women to break their post-natal taboos exposing them to illness and supernatural dangers. The doctors do not always know of panema or of *caruara*, for example, and if they do learn of these concepts they are apt to thrust them aside as the ignorance of backward people. Engineers are angry when their Itá labor force refuses to work on August 1st and August 24th, unaware that these are believed to be *dias aziagos* (days bringing bad luck). By knowing the folk beliefs of the people with whom they are working, the physician, the engineer, or anyone bringing new ideas and methods into a folk society would be able to avoid many conflicts. With such knowledge, many new concepts may be explained in terms understandable to the people, and many old customs and beliefs may be replaced with greater ease.

Not until scientific theories of causation are integrated into the world view of a people will such new methods, techniques, and concepts based on science be fully accepted. Some procedures may be accepted as practical mechanically, especially when they are forced upon a people from the outside. People may enjoy greater benefits from these innovations, but until they understand for themselves the basis for such activities it is doubtful whether they will continue to make use of them once outside pressure is removed. In Itá the people are happy to have sanitary privies, periodic spraying with DDT, vaccination, and other facilities. But at this point it is doubtful whether they would even contemplate attempting to continue such services by themselves if the health service were discontinued. A public-health campaign must therefore include a program of health education which aims to modify the entrenched traditional beliefs in the causes and treatment of disease as well as teaches the necessity and benefits derived from maintaining public-health facilities. The beliefs concerning health and disease held by the people of Itá are part of their view of the world, which includes the cult of the saints, their belief in forest and water spirits, their faith in pagés and the midwives, their dependency on prayers and incantations, and their knowledge of herbal folk remedies. These many beliefs and practices fuse magic with empirical knowledge. It is still fundamentally a magical view of the world, even though scientific knowledge is encroaching upon magic with increasing velocity.

8. A COMMUNITY IN AN UNDER-DEVELOPED AREA

Improvement of social and economic conditions in the so-called under-developed areas of the world will call for the cooperation of a wide variety of specialists and for knowledge drawn from the whole range of modern science. Engineers, public-health officers, nurses, agronomists, educators, and other experts in applied sciences must be called upon. Studies and surveys will be necessary by economists, political scientists, sociologists, geographers, and specialists in other fields of the social sciences and the humanities. The intricate

257

problems involved cannot be solved by any single scientific discipline. Like other fields of knowledge, anthropology has an important contribution to make. It offers no panacea, but it has a point of view and a body of knowledge regarding human behavior which will be helpful to all those responsible in one way or another for programs of economic development and technical assistance.

Throughout this book a number of suggestions have been made that should be useful to administrators and technicians dealing with rural communities in the Amazon Valley. Yet some of the more important contributions of anthropology have not been made explicit. This book has dealt with the culture of Itá, and the most important contribution that anthropology can offer to programs of technical assistance is the anthropological concept of culture. "By culture," Clyde Kluckhohn has written, "anthropology means the total way of life of a people, the social legacy the individual acquires from his group. Or culture may be regarded as that part of the environment that is the creation of man." [1] The culture of Itá, like all human cultures, includes economic and religious institutions, the customs, habitual behavior, and attitudes of the inhabitants, and, in fact, all of those lifeways which they have learned as members of their society and which they transmit to their children.

The anthropological concept of culture has several important implications. Above all, "The concept of culture carries a legitimate note of hope to troubled men." [2] If the technological backwardness and the human misery of certain regions of the earth were due to the biological heredity of the people who inhabit them or to immutable barriers in climate, then planned programs to change such conditions would be doomed to failure. But since the primary reasons for technological backwardness and low standards of living are clearly social and cultural, programs of social and economic changes can be planned and realized, even though they may involve complex questions of national or international economics and politics. Again, quoting Kluckhohn, "It is men who change their cultures, even if

[1] Clyde Kluckhohn, *Mirror for Man* (New York, 1949), p. 17.
[2] *Ibid.*, p. 44.

. . . during most of past history . . . they have been acting as instruments of cultural processes of which they were largely unaware." [3]

From study of a variety of human cultures, the anthropologist has gained "a cross-cultural frame of reference." He has become aware of the force of each culture to determine individual and group behavior, of the wide range of cultural values, and of the different response in each culture to analogous human situations. Many of the people who participate either in planning or directly in the operations of technical-assistance programs in distant lands have previously lived and worked only within the confines of their own culture. Therefore they often accept the basic assumptions of their own culture as if these were universal. They often expect people of other cultures to react as they do in any given situation and to have the same incentives and values. They are often unaware of the behavior expected of them by foreign cultures. The "cross-cultural frame of reference" of the anthropologist tends to create an awareness of cultural differences and tends to free the planner of ethnocentrism.

A study of a variety of cultures also shows that in many respects all human cultures are similar. Everywhere mankind has the same biological necessities and functions. Each human culture has a different way of handling the same universal life experience—birth, infant care, education, courting, mating, procreation, illness, old age, and even death. All cultures have methods of ensuring at least minimal conditions of survival: they provide food and shelter, some means of defense, mechanisms of social control, and other absolute necessities of the individual and the group. Thus each human culture has an economic system, rules for regulating social relations, the family in one form or another, recreation, and a religion. Although cultures differ in content and emphasis, all conform to a basic plan determined by the universal similarity and needs of all men. The culture of Itá differs from that of small communities in Africa, Asia, India, Oceania, and the Middle East; yet Itá culture shares basic

[3] *Ibid.*, p. 43.

cultural processes and problems with other peasant cultures throughout the world. A thorough and objective study of one or more
cultures will help in an understanding of a new human scene in
which one may need to live and work.

Finally, one of the important contributions which anthropology
offers technical-assistance programs derives from its research methods and from its traditional subject of research. One of the main
strengths of social anthropology as a scientific discipline lies in the
intimate and detailed knowledge which the field investigator gains
of the limited population group of his study. Since his field methods
include detailed personal observations of daily life, participation in
the society being studied, and lengthy and repeated interviews with
a wide selection of individuals, his unit of research has generally been
limited in size. With few exceptions, anthropologists have carried
out their field research among groups of one or two thousand people.
Classically they have studied primitive bands and villages. This was
true of the writer's studies among Brazilian tribal Indians. The total
tribal group numbered no more than two thousand people, and
although certain villages were studied more intensively than others
it was possible to verify observations through firsthand acquaintance
with most of the villages in the tribal group.[4] To cite another case,
Raymond Firth's studies of the Polynesian Island of Tikopia, which
are models of anthropological research technique, involved only
thirteen hundred people concentrated in a few square miles.[5] Social
anthropology might almost be defined as "a science of the small
community."

Studies in these small communities have contributed much to our
knowledge of the nature of culture. In his studies of small tribal
groups, the anthropologist was required to be a student of tribal
economics, history, social and political structure, religion, literature,
and language. As a result, he has learned to see the culture in ques-

[4] Charles Wagley and Eduardo Galvão, *The Tenetehara Indians of Brazil.*
[5] Raymond Firth, *We, the Tikopia* (London, 1936), and *A Primitive Polynesian Economy* (London, 1939). In his *Elements of Social Organization* (London, 1951), p. 49, Firth points out that the social anthropologist normally deals
with small populations.

tion as an over-all system, and to view each aspect of life in functional relationship to all others. Anthropologists have learned that each culture has an integration and an internal harmony and that customs and beliefs, apparently strange and illogical when torn from their context, are more readily understood in terms of the total cultural system of which they are a part. The intimacy of the field anthropologist's research techniques makes him sensitive to minutiae of custom and behavior often ignored or overlooked by the more formal students of human cultures.

But when the anthropologist turns to the study of modern nations and complex civilizations, his research methods impose certain limitations. Within a tribal society each band or village is an approximate replica of the others. In such societies there is a minimum of specialization: all men may be herders or farmers, for example. In complex modern nations each community is a specialized unit of a larger and more complex social system. Each community has its specialized position in the larger society determined by economics, physical location, history, and numerous other variables which enter into the making of a modern nation. No one community may therefore be said to be characteristic of a nation, no matter how carefully it is selected. Each community contains only a limited segment of the total culture of a modern nation. Furthermore, in modern nations there are national and regional institutions, such as the legal and political system, and there are social groups cutting across communities which bind the communities into a larger society and which may be understood only on a national or regional basis.

Does this mean that the methods of research of anthropology cannot be adapted to the study of the culture of complex modern nations? On the contrary, a large list of studies of modern communities attests to the adaptability of the methods to complex societies, and all the studies have added significantly to our understanding of complex national cultures. These community studies have shown that it is not enough to know the formal structure of a national government, the trends of national economics, or other high-level aspects of national affairs. It is just as important to have an integrated picture of a culture as it functions in a particular community. Community studies tell us how national institutions function in a concrete situation. They provide us with an understanding of national problems in their local manifestation. Such community studies add another dimension to the formal and somewhat lifeless picture so often offered us by economists, political scientists, historians, and others.

II

Itá, as it has been said, is not an entirely typical Amazon town, and it differs in many ways from other rural Brazilian communities. Itá is a community of townspeople, farmers, and rubber collectors who inhabit a low, humid tropical environment of the Amazon. Itá farmers, for example, differ from those living in the semi-tropical and quasi-temperate areas of South Brazil, from those of the arid *sertão*, and those of the coastal northeast. They differ from the hired workers on the cacao, sugar, coffee, and tea plantations of Brazil and from the cowboys on the ranches both in the northeastern *sertão* and in the southern pampa. The methods used by a people to exploit their particular environment determine many aspects of their total culture. Furthermore, throughout Brazil there are communities in closer touch with the main economic and political centers of the country than Itá, and with better communications with regional and national markets. In such communities less of the traditional way of life is present. Influences from the large urban centers have been felt with greater intensity, and culture change has taken place with greater velocity.

Yet Itá shares many traditions with rural communities throughout Brazil. There are economic, social, religious, and political institutions present in Itá culture which derive from the fact that it is a unit of a national society and from the fact that it shares in Brazilian national culture. Numerous problems common to most of rural Brazil appear in a local form in Itá, and many of the positive values of Brazilian national culture, which should be cherished and protected in the face of social change, are present in Itá culture. A study of Itá, in this sense, is a study of the Brazilian Amazon and of rural Brazil.

The people of Itá are poorer than most Brazilians and they are somewhat more isolated from the great modern cities of the country. Perhaps for these reasons they have maintained many Brazilian traditions which the outsider has learned to respect and from which the world might learn much. Foremost among these traditions is the relatively peaceful form of race relations. Although dark skin is a symbol of slave ancestry and low social status throughout Brazil, in Itá, as in most of the country, physical race is far from an absolute barrier to economic and social mobility. Prejudice and discrimination based on race are mild in Itá when compared to most small towns of the world. In São Paulo, in Rio de Janeiro, and in other industrial centers racial discrimination seems to have increased in recent years. The legislative bodies of the federal government, reacting against a threat to traditional Brazilian values, have found it necessary to pass a law placing heavy penalties on racial discrimination.

In Itá, as in all of Brazil, more than 96 per cent of the people are Catholic. The community is not divided by religious sects. Brazilian Catholicism is noted for its flexibility, its adaptation to the Brazilian scene, and its incorporation of African and Indian religious beliefs.[6] But a trend toward a more orthodox form of Catholicism is general throughout Brazil. This trend has already been felt in Itá in the policy of the Catholic priest who prohibits "profane" festivals. Although Itá has but an insignificant Protestant minority, various sects of Protestantism are growing in other Brazilian communities. These sects have much to contribute, but outbreaks of anti-Protestant feeling have already caused religious strife in some rural Brazilian communities. Furthermore, spiritualism has been increasing by leaps and bounds in urban centers where people have

[6] See Roger Bastide, "Religion and the Church in Brazil," in *Brazil: Portrait of Half a Continent*, pp. 334–355.

lost their traditional Catholicism with its many community functions. There is a tendency, not yet felt with force in Itá, for the traditional religious homogeneity of Brazil to be broken.

Although economic instability in Itá works for a relatively smaller "family" than is traditional in Brazil, people still place a high premium upon extended family relations. There is a great effort to bring friends into the kinship structure through the *compadrio* relationship and through marriage. In a world in which the larger kinship unit seems to be disintegrating in favor of the limited conjugal family, the Brazilian tradition of warm and secure social relationships among the members of a large family group is to be valued. The Itá religious brotherhoods, which are a variation of the Third Orders which have founded and maintained hospitals, asylums, and other social-welfare institutions in Brazil, are important associations of Brazilian society which are now disappearing in other communities. The cooperative work parties, called *puxirão* in Itá, are widespread throughout the country, and wherever they are present they make work more enjoyable. Like most rural Brazilians, the people of Itá are open and overt. They are not suspicious of strangers. Rather, they are anxious to know about them and ready to extend their hospitality. Hospitality, almost to a point of ostentation, is a traditional Brazilian trait, and the elaborate politeness and the polished manners of the aristocracy are characteristic also of the simple country folk. These and many other traditions, institutions, values, and personality characteristics which are traditional to Brazil persist in Itá. Many of them are now being challenged by modern commercial civilization. Their loss would be a high price to pay for the benefits of modern technology.

In addition, many of the major problems of the Amazon Valley, even of rural Brazil, are also problems of Itá. In Itá people still make a living from slash-and-burn agriculture and from collecting forest products. The Amazon Valley still has a "colonial economy"; it has an economic system based on monoculture and production of raw materials for a distant market. Numerous studies of Brazil have pointed out the evils of monoculture. The economic history of Brazil is the history of a series of "booms" and "busts" based upon a one-crop system. There was the sugar boom on the northeastern coast in the sixteenth and seventeenth centuries, the gold boom in Minas Geraes in the eighteenth century, the coffee boom in São Paulo in the nineteenth and twentieth centuries, and the rubber boom in the Amazon Valley, as well as a series of minor one-crop booms in various parts of the country. In each case temporary prosperity was based upon the sale of one crop or product to the neglect of subsidiary food crops and industry. And after each boom there was a "bust" resulting from competition and from price variations on the world market. Throughout Brazil, there are numerous communities like Itá, which were once rich and prosperous when their sugar, their gold, or their rubber brought high prices. Today they are poor and backward; and today numerous other communities depend upon one or more commercial crops or on extractive commodities, as the basis of their livelihood. Like Itá, many of these rural communities do not produce enough food for their people, and the products upon which they depend for purchasing necessities fluctuate in price in accordance with sensitive changes in demand and international events. It is a precarious economic situation.

There is nothing inherently wrong with monoculture or production for a distant market. Theoretically, certain regions of the world might be producers of foodstuffs, of raw materials, or of manufactured products, and one might depend upon another to provide what it needs. Unfortunately, however, our present system of economic exchange does not operate with the efficiency, logic, and equability that such a logical plan calls for. It is a fact that the regions producing raw materials are generally poor in comparison to those producing finished goods. Brazil has undertaken a phase of industrialization which is aimed at freeing the country to some extent from dependence upon foreign manufactured goods. But the situation in such communities as Itá makes it clear that above all agriculture must be developed throughout the country to free people from dependency on distant markets for their basic foods.

Like most similar communities, Itá suffers from lack of transportation and communication with the major centers of the region and of the nation. Brazil has only half the railroad mileage and only three-fourths the motor-road mileage of France, a country less than a tenth as large. Even between the two great industrial centers of São Paulo and Rio de Janeiro, the railroad is slow and inadequate, and a modern motor road has only just been completed. Between São Paulo and the rich frontier areas of Santa Catarina and Goiás [7] the railroads are unable to handle the traffic in either direction. In many localities foodstuffs spoil for lack of transportation to a market where they are eagerly sought. In many isolated rural communities manufactured articles cost three and four times as much as they do in São Paulo or Rio de Janeiro. The Amazon River offers an excellent system of relatively cheap transportation for Itá and other Amazon communities, but most of the river boats in use today are old. One of the major problems of rural Brazil is transportation.

In most of rural Brazil the percentage of illiterates in the total population is approximately the same as that of Itá. Brazil is a country of great extremes and contrasts. The Ministry of Education Building in Rio de Janeiro is one of the most modern buildings in the world. In São Paulo and in Rio de Janeiro there are scientific laboratories and centers of higher education with learned professors and famous research scientists. But even primary education is not provided in many isolated rural areas, and where there are rural schools the facilities are poor and insufficient. There is a shortage of teachers in Brazil, and trained teachers do not want rural posts which generally pay less and offer fewer modern comforts. Even the sons and daughters of rural families who receive sufficient education to become teachers remain in the city, where economic advancement is easier. Most of rural Brazil lacks the minimal educational

[7] It was strange to hear a Brazilian farmer in the interior state of Goiás say that he wished he had never planted grapefruit. His trees were producing magnificent and delicious fruit. The local market for grapefruit, however, was limited, and he had so many that he was forced to pay workmen to bury rotten fruit to keep down the foul odor which blew toward his home.

facilities for its people. Brazil is potentially one of the world's richest nations, but it has not as yet made use of its greatest resource: its people.

Until recently the health situation in rural Brazil was notoriously poor. Even today, in many areas of the country, rural people are entirely without modern means of health protection. Since 1942 Itá has been better provided with health services and medical assistance than the majority of the rural communities. The single physician stationed there by the SESP combines the duties of a public-health officer and a clinician. Thus he is able to give only limited medical attention to the approximately 25,000 people who live in his district, which covers three municipalities. There has been a marked improvement in health conditions in the town since 1942, but in Itá, as throughout Brazil, health conditions are still below Western standards. Even in the Rio de Janeiro environs, the rate of death from tuberculosis was 317.5 per 100,000 in 1941, which is almost seven times the rate for the United States in 1940. The death rate from syphilis was 57.1 per 100,000, as against 8.0 per 100,000 in the United States.[8] In the Amazon cities of Belém and Manaus, these and other diseases are much more prevalent than in Rio de Janeiro, and the health conditions in most rural communities are even worse. The majority of Brazilian towns do not have water-supply systems, facilities for sewerage disposal, or other provisions for health protection.

An excellent group of Brazilian public-health specialists, who have been trained in Rio de Janeiro at the Instituto Oswaldo Cruz and in São Paulo at the Institute of Hygiene, as well as at foreign universities, are fully aware of the health needs of Brazil. They are fully capable of establishing and administering up-to-date public-health services, if given the chance. One public-health officer of a northern Brazilian state (a graduate of the University of Minnesota) pointed out the rather illogical situation in regard to water supply in the various rural communities for which he was responsible. Most of the people in the towns use water carried in five-

[8] Cited in T. Lynn Smith, *Brazil: People and Institutions*, p. 257.

gallon tins from a spring or a river. They use on the average one tin per day for which they pay five cents as a fee to the carrier. "If 400 families use water at this rate," explained the public-health technician, "this would amount to $20 a day or $7,300 per year. A simple water-supply system for a town of 1,500 to 2,000 people might be constructed for about $20,000. It would be paid for at this rate in less than three years." But numerous families in his communities could not afford five cents a day for water. Such communities do not have the credit or cash to construct a water system, even on this basis, unless they are given help by the federal government.

Brazilians are also aware of the need for medical assistance in the rural areas. While there is but one physician for each 8,000 to 10,000 people in the small towns and rural zones of the interior, there is one physician to each 500 people in the coastal cities. Students from rural zones go to the city to study medicine, and never return home. They elect to try their luck in the cities rather than practice in small towns which do not offer a lucrative income to a doctor. Unless the income of the majority of rural Brazilians is increased several times, they will not be able to support private physicians. Only by combining public health and medical care as a public service (as the SESP has done in Itá) will most rural Brazilians be provided with medical assistance.

The community of Itá is not the same as the *município* (county) of the same name.[9] The community (that is, the area within the social sphere of the town) has a population of approximately 2,000 people, while there are more than 7,000 in the entire county. The area of the community comprises less than one-third of the total area of the county. In this difference between the community and the formal administrative unit, the county, lies an important rural problem of Brazil. With poor communications, the county is generally too large for effective administration. Furthermore, there is little or no *esprit de corps* among the people of a county. Except

---

[9] *Município* is generally translated as "municipality," but it would be better translated as "county," since it is that unit of local government in the United States which it most approximates. See T. Lynn Smith, *op. cit.*, p. 748.

for the people of the *sede*, the town which is the center of the county and of its immediate neighborhood, there is little local patriotism or group feeling of belonging to the county. Residents of the county of Itá, who live at some distance from the town itself, seldom come to Itá and they seldom see a municipal official. The noted debility of local government throughout the country derives from this lack of social unity.

Most public services—such as schools, communications, health services, and justice—are, when they exist, furnished by the state or federal government. In the county people feel that such services should be provided for them. They have no idea of securing such services by cooperative effort. Politics within the county are apt to be tense, but rivalry is usually based on family loyalties or on blind adherence to state-wide political factions rather than on differences of opinion regarding any public policy. Nowadays the federal government grants the county small revenues, approximately $5,000 per year, in order to stimulate local public endeavors; and since the new constitution of 1945, the mayor and the *vereadores* (town councilmen) are elected officials. Despite these efforts, there is still very little community spirit in rural Brazil.[10] Compared to the situation in other areas of the world, locality groups provide little basis for community action.

In Itá, as in most of rural Brazil, there is a conflict between the city and the country. Most of the funds of the county of Itá have been spent to build the enormous town hall, to clean the streets, and to provide other benefits for the townspeople. The services furnished to the county by the state and federal governments benefit the town more than the rural zone. The owners of trading posts within the county, who are the only articulate rural dwellers, complain bitterly of the lack of schools and health protection, and grumble at the necessity of paying county taxes. The townspeople have at least a faint sense of belonging to a community, and they look on those from outside the area as outsiders and strangers.

[10] T. Lynn Smith, *op. cit.*, pp. 613 ff., points out the strength of the Brazilian neighborhood and the essential weakness of the community.

Moreover, the local political leaders are inevitably drawn from among the townspeople; thus the town controls the rural zones. The result is that, although villages, towns, and cities are not incorporated as separate governmental units as they are in the United States, the *sede* (municipal center) always gets the lion's share of government benefits. Throughout Brazil the rural people and inhabitants of small satellite villages feel an antagonism against town-dwellers and against their local government.

The population of the Itá community has an average density of only 0.5 people per square kilometer. Throughout Brazil there is a steady drain of workers from the country to the city. There is a steady movement of people from Itá and other rural communities of the Lower .Amazon to Belém and to South Brazil. Cities are growing rapidly at the expense of the rural zones.[11] Thus, in Itá, there is the perennial problem of *falta de braços* (lack of labor). Some Brazilians and foreign observers advocate immigration from abroad to solve the problem. A look at Itá, however, makes it clear that immigration must be combined with economic development if it is to be of any help to the rural zones. Immigrants might contribute to the development of the community through the diffusion of different methods of farming and the introduction of new crops. The Japanese who were settled near the town of Parintins on the Lower Amazon introduced the cultivation of jute, which is now becoming a major commercial crop in the Amazon Valley. But with the present system of agriculture, with the present crops, and with the present system of transportation it seems very doubtful indeed whether food can be provided for an additional population in most rural communities of Brazil. Furthermore, the commercial products do not furnish sufficient cash income to provide a decent standard of living for rural workers.

Few European immigrants would be content with the standard

[11] The growth of cities over rural population was especially striking between 1940 and 1950. While the rural populations increased 16 per cent (from 30,-814,500 to 35,997,700), the urban population spurted 60 per cent (from 10,421,-813 to 16,647,772). *Brazilian Bulletin,* Brazilian Trade Bureau (New York), July, 1951.

of living available in most rural Brazilian communities. Because the new industrial centers of Brazil offer better opportunity and a higher standard of living, most immigrants have chosen to settle in the cities.[12] Immigration tends only to accelerate the widespread rural exodus.

The population of Brazil is growing with incredible rapidity, but from an excess of births over deaths rather than from immigration from abroad.[13] Rural communities such as Itá share in this rapid natural increase of population, although, since they furnish population to the cities, their population may seem to be relatively stable or even to decrease. Brazil does not need immigration simply to increase the population. As a leading student of Brazilian population has put it, "The amount of $1,000,000 spent on a campaign to reduce infant mortality, mainly by educating mothers about the care and feeding of children, probably would increase Brazil's population far more than a similar amount expended for the subsidization of immigration." [14] For rural communities such as Itá, the remedy for the problem is not more people but a new economic and social orientation. The Amazon Valley and other "empty spaces of Brazil" are unexploited because the present economic system and subsistence methods offer a living to a limited population only. The most serious problem is not lack of labor but the doubtful capacity of Brazil's productive system to change fast enough to keep up with the growing population.

Except in limited areas of the country, the people of rural Brazil live in scattered homesteads near their fields, near pasture for their animals, and near the products which they extract.[15] In most cases their method of subsistence is the imperative which determines this settlement pattern. The slash-and-burn system of the Itá farmer makes it convenient for him to live isolated from others where he

[12] Kingsley Davis, "Future Migration in Latin America," *Milbank Fund Quarterly*, No. 1, 1947, pp. 44–62.

[13] The population increased 36 per cent between 1920 and 1940 and from 41,565,083 in 1940 to 52,645,457 in 1950.

[14] T. Lynn Smith, *op. cit.*, p. 789.

[15] *Ibid.*, pp. 404–405.

may seek virgin forest or high second growth each year for his garden. The Itá collector lives near his rubber trails. This scattered mode of settlement causes many difficulties for the educator, for the public-health officer, and for other administrators. It is difficult to establish schools in rural zones, for example, within easy access for the dispersed population. If schools were established in each Itá neighborhood, some families would have to paddle three to four hours a day to bring their children to school. Only a school bus (which in the case of Itá might be a school launch) would solve the problem, but under present circumstances the cost of such a service would be excessive. It is difficult to offer medical care and public-health facilities to these scattered homesteads. People must travel hours, even days, to the nearest doctor. Public-health physicians have difficulties reaching such scattered families for vaccination, for such measures as spraying with DDT, and for health instruction.

One possible answer to this difficulty would seem to be apparent in such neighborhood villages as Jocojó within the community of Itá. This small concentration of Amazon farmers has already been able to establish a school for its children. Jocojó is visited periodically by the public-health officer. It has a chapel, as well as ovens and other means for the fabrication of manioc flour. Because Jocojó farmers live near one another, cooperative work parties are more easily organized there than in the dispersed type of neighborhood. Even with their wasteful and destructive system of agriculture, the inhabitants are still able to find forest land for gardens within easy reach of their small village; yet if they made use of rich lowland soils rather than terra firme, agriculture would provide them with a more secure basis for their village system. In other areas of Brazil plow agriculture and other means of more intensive exploitation of the soil would offer a stable basis for the formation of villages like Jocojó. The concentration of the rural population into small villages of no more than two hundred to three hundred people would make the development of the Amazon Valley an easier task.

Another serious barrier to economic development in Brazil is the fixed system of socio-economic classes. In South Brazil class lines have become less rigid. Social and economic mobility have become freer with the development of industry and commerce and with the growth of an enormous government bureaucracy. In Rio de Janeiro, in São Paulo, and in other urban centers a middle class composed of government employees, technicians, workers in commerce and industry, and others has been formed. In these large urban centers a new upper class, which is based on economic and commercial controls, and whose ancestors arrived only a generation ago, is supplanting the old landed gentry.

In a large part of the Brazilian "interior" and in many of the cities of North Brazil, however, the traditional class system survives with few basic changes. The new commercial and industrial rich and many members of the professions have simply joined the descendants of landed gentry as members of the upper class of the region. In such isolated communities as Itá, this "aristocracy" is not present; but they make their presence felt by ownership of land and commercial enterprises, and through political influence. Furthermore, their absence does not mean that a rigid system of social distinctions is not present in Itá and other rural communities. Although few members of the Itá "whites" or First Class ever become members of the "aristocracy," even though they move to the city, they feel an identity with the regional upper class. Locally, the members of Itá's First Class make a rigid distinction between themselves and the lower strata—the farmers, the collectors, and the lower-class town dwellers. The upper strata of these rural Brazilian communities share with the aristocracy a "gentleman complex" which has been derived from the landed gentry of the past. The bureaucrats, the commercial families, and other members of the local upper class in rural communities are not generally anxious for social change. Education of the lower strata would threaten their dominant position. Throughout rural Brazil townspeople are apt to be pessimistic about the capacity of the caboclo, the *tabaréu*, or the *caipira* for education and social and economic advancement.

Finally, like the people of Itá, the view of the world of most rural Brazilians is mainly a magical world view. Throughout Brazil a cult of the saints, *romarias* (pilgrimages) to important shrines, vows to saints for cures and other crisis situations, belief in the powers of curers and blessers, and the use of herbal medicines is widespread. In some areas African magical concepts are strong, as in the northeastern coastal region; in others old Iberian belief predominates; while in the Amazon a strong residue of American Indian belief persists. But throughout Brazil supernaturalism and folk science are the main elements of the world view of the majority of the rural population. Though this world view is beginning to disintegrate under the impact of more modern ideology coming from the large cities, it still poses a barrier to social change. Not until a scientific view of the world supplants the present folk view of rural Brazilians will economic and social change be fully integrated into Brazilian life.

These Brazilian problems, and many others too numerous to be discussed here, cannot be solved by individual communities, although they are readily apparent on the community level. Each of them depends upon social and economic change within the region and within the nation—and even upon international events and relations. The people of Itá alone cannot modify the orientation of their economic system. They are caught in a commercial system and a credit system which have developed as a concomitant of the Amazon extractive industry. To change this, there must be changes throughout, from the exporter in Belém to the trader in the rural areas and the individual collector. The people of Itá alone cannot make themselves into a literate people. They need teachers and other aids from the outside. They cannot cure their ills without scientific knowledge and personnel, which they do not have. They cannot produce more food without knowledge and tools which must be furnished them by the more "advanced" centers of Brazil. A unity of community effort would certainly facilitate such changes and speed up their acceptance, but, in the main, social change must originate in regional life and in the nation. Thus, as the Amazon Valley undergoes change, Itá will change. As Brazil develops, the time will come closer when man will turn to the Amazon. Brazil will develop its great potentialities only as international events and policies create amenable circumstances.

III

The Brazilian Amazon is clearly an under-developed area. In the way of life of the people of Itá, we have a case study of how people eke out an existence in such areas. But what it means to live in an under-developed part of the world can only be understood when the way of life and standard of living is compared to one of the more favored areas of the world. Compared, for example, to that of Plainville, a small community of approximately the same size in the central United States, Itá seems exceedingly backward and primitive.[16] Yet a comparison between the two communities makes it clear that many aspects of the Itá way of life provide as much satisfaction for its people as does the way of Plainville. Moreover, it becomes apparent that many social processes which are taking place in Itá are also occurring in Plainville, and that many of the dangers which progress and reform might bring to Itá are already contemporary problems of Plainville. Itá in the Brazilian Amazon and Plainville, U.S.A., have analogous problems, and the way of life of each of these two distant communities reflects the problems of a nation.

Like Itá, the community of Plainville is also considered to be a "backward" and a "poor" community. Plainville is isolated and "behind the times" as compared to the average American town. It is not a county seat and it lies off the railroad in Woodland County between the "hill-billy" country of American culture and the rich farming lands of America to the north. The county had approximately 6,500 people at the time it was studied. Plainville is a center for trading and for social life and, as in Itá, the majority of its people

---

[16] The data from Plainville is drawn from the book *Plainville, U.S.A.*, by James West (New York, Columbia University Press, 1945). Except where direct quotes are included, page references are omitted.

are farmers living in the surrounding rural zone. The town of Plainville itself has only 275 people. Again, as in Itá, the townspeople are merchants, professionals, odd-jobbers, and wage earners, as well as a few retired couples, widows, and widowers. More of the poor town dwellers of Itá depend upon farming for a livelihood than do the townsmen of Plainville, but both are essentially farming communities.

Both communities have a scattered settlement pattern which is typical of America and which differs from that of small communities in Europe, where farmers so frequently live in a village and go out each day to work their fields. In Itá the farmer and the collector live along the river and along the banks of the tributaries; in Plainville "a network of roads—often impassable in muddy weather—also connects the individual farm . . . with neighboring farms, with its own trading center and with all the other towns in the county." [17] Through Plainville passes a new concrete highway which connects it to a large city some 135 miles away. A gravel road, running through Woodland County, is used to travel to the county seat. For Itá, the Amazon mainstream is the "road" to the outside—the only means of communication, except for the weekly airplane, to the other towns of the Valley and to the city of Belém. Within the Itá area the small tributaries furnish the main routes of travel from one place to another.

These streams and river provide Itá with an excellent natural system of communication, but the inhabitants lack adequate means of transportation both within the community and to the outside. In Woodland County farmers own 1,000 automobiles and approximately 100 trucks. "Trucks carry most of Plainville's produce and livestock to market centers and deliver to Plainville most of the merchandise sold there." [18] In addition, there is a railroad at Stanton only eleven miles west. In Itá people move about by canoe, paddling or setting out a simple sail when the wind is favorable. On the average of once a week, a river steamer touches for a few hours at the

[17] *Ibid.*, p. 13.
[18] *Ibid.*

Itá municipal dock; most of these river steamers burn wood which they spend hours loading at trading-post docks along the way. The average travel time for a river steamer is at least five days between Itá and Belém. There are no wheeled vehicles at all in Itá, and the complete dependency upon water transportation ties man to the riverbanks; thus the "interior," the area back from the streams, is uninhabited. The lack of overland transportation means that man exploits only a portion of the total community area.

Furthermore, Itá lacks means of communication with the outside. The telegraph station maintained by the Amazon Company, which was a British firm, no longer operates, and as late as 1948 the federal government had not yet established a radio station there as it had in most Amazon communities. Telephones are unavailable throughout the Amazon Valley except in Belém and Manaus. In Plainville, on the other hand, there have been telephones for forty years, and there is always a way of "phoning out" a telegram. Mail comes to Itá on the slow river boats and once a week by plane. It is deposited at the post office and people call to claim it if they are aware that there is mail for them.[19] In Plainville mail is delivered each day. The rural mail route, a service unknown in rural Brazil, serves 200 mail boxes accommodating 286 families in the rural zone. Plainville may be considered "isolated" for the United States, but modern means of communication and transportation bring this "backward" American community into intimate touch with the region and the nation.

In regard to other material improvements, the contrast between the two communities illustrates how little technical equipment the people of Itá have to cope with their natural environment. In Plainville only two-thirds of the people of the town have electricity, and nearly all the farms still use kerosene lamps. Only three homes in Plainville have bathrooms with flush toilets and hot running water; most houses, both in town and in the rural area, use

[19] A letter may lie in the post office for days or even weeks in Itá because the postmistress neglects to send word to the recipient to fetch it. Only people with regular correspondence would think to inquire regularly for mail.

outside privies. A "water bucket" placed on a table in the kitchen holds water both for drinking and for washing. The situation in Plainville is far below the average for most rural districts in the United States, but it is far above the situation in Itá. Although most Amazon towns nowadays have some form of electric light, the old wood-burning generator which used to give electricity to a few homes in Itá no longer functions. Everyone uses some form of kerosene lamp; most rural people have only a tin container with an open wick. In Itá most people simply take their drinking water from the river. There are but three wells in town, all of which are in very bad condition. And, until the public-health service constructed privies for most of the houses in town, everyone simply retired to the nearby brush for their necessities. The nearby river facilitates bathing. There are cabins built out over the river with steps leading down into the water which are used by several families for bathing. Almost everyone in Itá, however, goes to the river or a nearby tributary stream for a daily bath. People in Itá are remarkably clean. In fact, they are cleaner than the people of Plainville, where the stated ideal is "a bath once a week" and where "many men are said to go through the whole winter without a bath." [20]

The people of Plainville must heat their homes during the Temperate Zone winter, and the average dwelling in Plainville contains a wood-burning kitchen stove and a living-room heater. The people of Itá also burn wood, but only for cooking over their adobe ranges; no one in Itá owns a stove. In the summer, windows and doors are screened against flies in Plainville, more for comfort than for sanitation; but in Itá, with the almost year-round problem of flies and other insects, screens are found only in the health post. Wire screen is not available in local stores, and if it were it would be at a price far above the possibilities of an average Itá family.

Household objects, such as dishes, cooking utensils, silverware, water glasses, and other American "necessities" are available to the people of Plainville at a relatively cheap price in the hardware store, in the drugstore, and from Montgomery Ward. The stock of Itá

[20] *Op. cit.,* p. 36.

stores and trading posts offers little choice, and such objects are extremely expensive. An inferior water glass costs approximately thirty cents, and a cup and saucer, cheaper in quality than any found in an American five-and-ten, cost more than fifty cents.

Similarly, Plainville is clothed better and at a cheaper price than Itá. Few people in Itá buy ready-made clothes. Instead they buy a "cut" of cloth for a dress, a shirt, or trousers. From time to time an itinerant tailor comes to town to make men's suits for "dress-up" occasions. Although the cotton suits he makes are no more expensive in monetary terms than men's "dress-up" clothes in Plainville, the material is inferior, and only fifteen or twenty men can afford to pay the price. Furthermore, the cloth for a simple dress, for pants, or for a shirt is more expensive to the people of Itá than the finished product in Plainville, where an average everyday ready-made print dress could be had for $0.98 to $1.98 in 1940. Plainville women are able to study catalogues, examine advertisements and home pages in newspapers and magazines, and even to visit large stores in Metropolis; thus they dress in a fashion almost "indistinguishable from women anywhere" in America.[21] Although in Plainville the standard male uniform is overalls, they are able to purchase such clothes cheaper and of a better quality than those which Itá wives are able to sew for their husbands.

The people of Plainville are also better acquainted with the outside world than the people of Itá. Fifty per cent of the townspeople and 50 per cent of the farmers own radios in Plainville, while in Itá there are only two radios. Only two families receive the Belém newspaper, and few magazines ever reach Itá. In Woodland County a locally printed weekly newspaper has a distribution of one thousand copies; ten to twelve copies of a metropolitan newspaper and fifty copies of a newspaper from a large town come each day. Most farmers in Plainville subscribe to a farm paper, and many people read monthly magazines. Although Plainville is considered a "backward" community for America, better than 90 per cent of its people are literate, while Itá shares the high rate of illiteracy of all rural

[21] *Ibid.*, p. 39.

Brazil. One of the most crucial contrasts between the two communities derives from this difference. Eighty-five per cent of the children of Woodland County are enrolled in school. Buses bring children daily from a wide area to the Plainville consolidated school, which now offers eight years of elementary school and four years of high school. Fully 50 per cent of those eligible now go to high school, where, among other subjects, citizenship, music, and vocational agriculture are taught. In the entire municipality of Itá there are only eight small schools, and these offer a three-year elementary course to 299 children, which is approximately 20 per cent of the children between seven and fourteen years of age.[22] The people of Itá are deprived of one of the fundamental weapons of civilized Western man; namely, the ability to read and write.

In Plainville cultivation of the land is strictly speaking "agricultural," while that of Itá is "horticulture," or hand cultivation. Both Itá and Plainville have, generally speaking, "inferior land." There is an area of originally rather fertile prairie in the Plainville farming area, but over 50 per cent of Woodland County is rocky hill land. Itá has both fertile *várzea* which is potentially rich pluvial soil, but it is on the poor lateritic soils of terra firme that most of the staples are grown at present. As early as the second half of the nineteenth century, the prairie land of Plainville was cultivated by the plow with traction animals, and a single-row cultivator was used. Then came corn planters, steel cultivators, mowing machines, binders, threshers, and other mechanical aids—and more recently tractors (145 are owned in Woodland County) and combines. The technical equipment of the Plainville farmer also includes innumerable other tools and gadgets, such as cream separators, hoes, rakes, and incubators which may be seen in any Sears Roebuck or Montgomery Ward catalogues. The only semi-mechanical aid which a few Itá farmers have is the *caitetu*, a hand-propelled bicycle-type grater for preparing manioc flour. In other regions of Brazil, pack animals (the horse, the burro, or the ox) and a few oxcarts are common; but in Itá there are no traction animals at all. In the entire

[22] The data on school enrollments for Itá are for 1945.

community of Itá there is not a single plow. Power-driven farm machinery is only a far-off potentiality for the Itá farmer, and under present conditions it is not even considered as a possibility. The tools of the Itá farmer are an ax, a bush knife, and a hoe. As compared to the "backward" methods of farming in Plainville, it is quite clear that the people of Itá exploit their environment with little or no aid from modern technology. If the people of Plainville were forced to work their Temperate Zone land with the simple equipment available to the Itá farmer, theirs too would be a "depressed" community and their region an under-developed area.

Differences in standards of living between Plainville and Itá can hardly be calculated in monetary terms, although both are within the orbit of a money economy. Estimates of farm income for both communities are deceptive, since they generally omit many sources of real income, such as odd jobs, consumption of natural products, and foods raised for subsistence. Yet monetary income does indicate in general what these people are able to purchase in commercial goods. According to the census figures, in which the author of *Plainville, U.S.A.*, puts little faith, one-fifth of the farm families of Woodland County have an average income of $145 per year. The average cash income for the farmer families of Itá included in our own survey is on the average of $15 per month or $180 per year, slightly more than the lower fifth of Plainville but much lower than the next poorest group unit of 230 families in Plainville, which averaged $320 per year.[23] In both communities farmers generally buy "store" products such as clothes, manufactured items, kerosene, and other products. These products have always been higher in price in the Amazon region, if not simply in monetary terms, most certainly in relation to the income of the purchasers. All goods imported into the Amazon Valley come from long distances and pass through many hands. Itá farmers are thus able to purchase less with their meager funds than Plainville farmers.

[23] Furthermore, these estimates were made at different times: in 1939 and 1940 in Plainville, before inflation in the United States, and in 1948 in Itá, after inflation had already been felt in Brazil.

The important differences between the standard of living in the two communities, however, cannot be expressed in terms of money. Both the farmers of Plainville and of Itá, like small farmers everywhere, live simultaneously "in two separate economic systems, a 'monetary economy' and a 'subsistence economy.' "²⁴ In Plainville almost everyone has a garden—even the doctor. A local businessman also keeps hogs and cows. In addition, farmers have chickens and other domestic fowls. They have eggs, milk, butter, vegetables, fruits, and meat which they produce for their own consumption. "The majority of [Plainville] farmers raise most of what they eat." ²⁵ In addition, "canned foods" prepared by the housewife herself add to most Plainville diets throughout the winter months. "A woman prides herself on having from 100 to 400 jars (quarts and half-gallons) of 'stuff put up.' " "Stuff" includes green beans, tomatoes, preserved fruit, jams, jellies, cucumber pickles, and other products of the family garden or orchard. In addition, twenty to fifty bushels of potatoes are stored in a cellar or " 'holed up' outside the house in a straw-lined pit." ²⁶ In Plainville the meat staple is pork raised at home and cured either by the traditional method of smoking or with the new commercial "liquid smoke." Although experts consider Plainville diets to be generally deficient, food is relatively abundant in most homes. Plainvillers put great value on food. Except in a few extreme cases, it would be difficult to classify the "worth" (financial position) of farming families in Plainville by the food they eat. The patterns of Plainville farm economy, despite its close relationship to the commercial world, are still oriented toward subsistence to a large extent.

The farmers of Itá also produce or derive from their natural environment much of their food. Even in the town, many families have fruit trees and perhaps a few chickens in the back yard. And even a few upper-class town dwellers have gardens planted by hired labor. Most Itá gardens are planted mainly in manioc, but bananas

²⁴ *Op. cit.*, p. 40.
²⁵ *Ibid.*, p. 41.
²⁶ *Ibid.*, p. 37.

and other local fruits are planted near the houses. People hunt and fish to add to their diets. But the cultural tradition of the Amazon region does not emphasize subsistence farming. The tradition of planting a variety of products for home consumption which is (and must have been in the past) so highly developed among the Portuguese and other European peasants seems to have been lost in the transfer of European elements to the Amazon Valley. A colonial economic system aimed at extracting natural products for the foreign market seems to have smothered the European tradition of mixed farming.

Most Itá farmers generally have a few scraggly chickens whose eggs may sometimes be found in the nearby bush and which are often so wild they must be shot if one wishes one for eating. Few people have ducks. They complain that the constrictor snakes and alligators eat them. Few pigs are seen in the rural districts, although pork is a highly desirable fresh meat. Though it is difficult to find natural pasture for cattle in the tropical forest, it is not impossible to prepare an area for pasture. Yet only two or three farmers have cattle, and these are sold generally in the town for meat. The only milk an Itá farmer ever consumes is in condensed form, and the only butter he eats comes salted in tins. Both of these foods are prepared thousands of miles away in southern Brazil. A few farmers plant—somewhat as an afterthought—beans, squash, peppers, and watermelons in their manioc gardens, and a few others plant maize and other quick-growing crops in the low flooded land in the summer. But in Itá little effort is made to raise a variety of crops or to have farmyard animals for family consumption. The emphasis of the farmer is to produce for market—to have a surplus of manioc for sale after his own needs are met. Some sell manioc flour to the trading post, only to buy flour later in the year when their own plantations are exhausted. This emphasis of the rural economic system toward a commercial market reaches its extreme, of course, among the rubber collectors, many of whom depend entirely upon the sale of their products for credit to purchase food.

Furthermore, few methods are known in Itá for the preservation or storage of foods, although this would seem to be all the more important in the tropics. Manioc flour may be kept for months if it does not mildew. Meat and fish are salted and dried in the sun. A few *doces* (fruits cooked in sugar) will last for many days. But, in Itá generally, people eat fruits and vegetables only in season and before they spoil. They eat fresh meat, when it is available at all, soon after it is butchered. Nothing like the canning complex or the smoke curing of pork of Plainville exists in Itá. There is a period of abundance of oranges, of bananas, of papaya, and of native forest fruits, and a period when people do without fruit. Fish are plentiful during the dry season, but during the rains people buy salted dried fish or commercially canned sardines from the stores. The Itá rural inhabitant depends far more upon purchased food than the farmer of Plainville.

In addition, as compared to Plainville, the Itá farmer has little or no support from the "outside," that is, from the state or federal government. Although there is considerable resistance to "reform" in Plainville, a county agent of the A.A.A. teaches modern agriculture, and the Farm Security Administration office makes loans "averaging under $500" to farm families. During the depression, approximately twenty years ago, before the anthropologist studied Plainville, the Social Security office dispensed direct relief to Plainville farmers and directed people to the WPA, the CCC, and the NYA, all of which were in operation in the community. In addition, there are in Plainville Home Economic clubs and 4H clubs, the former for housewives and the latter for farm children, which have been organized through the efforts of the county agent. There was once a weak attempt, supported by the state of Pará, to form a farmer's cooperative in Itá, but it failed rapidly. From time to time, funds are set aside by the state or in the municipal budget to aid agriculture, mainly through the distribution of a few hand tools and perhaps some seeds to a few farmers. No serious attempt, however, has ever been made to extend government credit to Itá farmers, who continue to seek credit from year to year from local commercial men. And the small Amazon farmers do not have at present any way of securing modern knowledge about agriculture. In fact, it might be said that they do not know that better agricultural methods exist.

In Plainville, according to the anthropologist James West, a series of trait complexes have twice " 'revolutionized' the local society." [27] The first was the "plow that broke the prairie" (about 1870), and the second was the automobile (about 1912). It is doubtful whether either of these trait complexes would produce the same results in Itá, for the river system calls for modern boats, not cars, and the plowing of the inferior terra firme soils would probably result in quick leaching. But the fact remains that analogous technological changes have not taken place.

A third trait complex, which might again "revolutionize" Plainville society, is scientific agriculture. According to James West: "One evening in 1940, the county agent and the vocational agriculture teacher agreed without argument to the following proposition [regarding Plainville]: 'If these people would just believe what we tell them about farming and practise it, the scale of living for the whole county would double in five years.' " [28] James West makes it quite clear that there is considerable resistance to scientific agriculture in Plainville and that, far from making full use of the help which comes from "outside," Plainvillers are somewhat hostile to "new ideas" and "book farming." Co-existent with modern agriculture and techniques, numerous practices and beliefs out of the past persist in Plainville regarding planting, castrating livestock, gardening, and other exploitative techniques. There is widespread "criticism of the government's efforts to instruct the people how a better living can be made out of their mediocre land." [29] Many of of the new ideas about agriculture, and the manner in which they have been introduced, run counter to local values and institutions. There are conflicts between "old ways" (local and traditional) and "new ways" (from outside), between "youth" and "old age," be-

[27] *Ibid.,* pp. 218 ff.
[28] *Ibid.,* p. 218.
[29] *Ibid.,* p. 11.

tween "field farming" and "book farming," between "old-time religion" and "cold religion" or "no religion." The innovators, the county agent and others, have not made full use of local leadership. "The county agent, aside from ignoring the lower class and its leaders, makes little or no effort to win the influence of merchants, lodge members, or ordinary school teachers." [30] James West suggests that the churches and the preachers would be powerful in the process of introducing scientific agriculture. This conflict results, according to him, "from a partial breakdown, through soil depletion and newly felt wants and needs arising from too rapid impact with the outside world, of a 'traditional' social, religious and technological system." [31] Plainville is faced with the problem of achieving a new integration in the face of increased influences from outside. As the author of *Plainville, U.S.A.*, writes, "Reform brings many hazards."

The impact of modern agriculture and other new influences might be even more disruptive to Itá society. The changes which are under way in Itá are from a community way of life in which technology, social institutions, and religion have altered little in the hundred years before the twentieth century. It is a change from illiteracy to literacy, from a magical world view to an acceptance of science, and from a traditional folk way to a Brazilian variety of modern Western culture. Only a hint of this process which is to come to Itá may be seen in the public-health program already under way. The physician has clashed with the pagés, although he is unable to supply fully the services which they furnish. There is a conflict between the use of herbal remedies and modern medicines. And, in the sphere of religion, there is already a clash between the orthodox Church and traditional religion over the powers of the local brotherhoods and over the local festivals. These and the numerous other conflicts are already apparent, but they will multiply many times as social change reaches into education, agriculture, nutrition, and other spheres of life. Some of these conflicts are inevitable. But many conflicts might be avoided by realizing that the new concepts

[30] *Ibid.*, p. 218.
[31] *Ibid.*, p. 220.

introduced into Itá society must be integrated with the existing
way of life, and that in the process of change many values and
institutions of the traditional way of life must be retained if Itá
society is not to be totally disorganized. There is the danger that
Itá will lose its rich cultural traditions in exchange for second-rate
participation in modern industrial and commercial society.

IV

The difference between the Itás and the Plainvilles of the world
is not simply a question of climate, of natural resources, of soils.
Nor is it a question of the race of the people who inhabit these
communities. Tropical climate presents many difficulties to human
life, but none that are insurmountable where adequate technical
equipment is available. Certain areas of the world have advantages
over others; they have superior soils for the production of crops
desirable at the moment on the world market or they have natural
resources made useful by available technological equipment. But
the main factors which make for the difference between those communities which furnish only a bare minimum existence and those
which provide more amply for human needs are, in a broad sense,
social and cultural. Included are not only the technology, the economics, the social organization, the religion, the value system, and
other aspects of the culture, but also the relationship of the community to national and international centers of economic and political power.

Out of the history of the Amazon region emerges the reasons for
its present "backward" condition. The contemporary society and
culture of such communities as Itá are the product of this historical
process. Since the sixteenth century the Amazon region has been a
colonial area, first of Portugal and then, in another sense, of Brazil
itself. For over three centuries it has been a producer of raw materials for distant markets without an adequate return from such
products. During the first century of European rule, there was
little in the area to lure settlers and colonists. The Portuguese were

looking for quick wealth and not for a new land in which to build their homes. The Amazon Indians were relatively few in number, and thus the Amazon was not an ever-flowing source of slaves as was Africa. The cultural traditions of the Amazon Indian were well adapted to the tropical environment, but technically and socially their culture was so simple that it had little to teach the newcomers beyond how to survive in the new land. A few native products, such as hardwoods, cinnamon, chocolate, *urucú*, and rubber were found to be desirable on the European market. Thus an extractive economy was established which has persisted to the present day. The native peoples were enslaved as collectors and, as in all slave societies, physical labor soon became identified with low social status. A slaveowning aristocracy, made up of European newcomers and their descendants, was formed.

With the end of slavery, and while the region was extraordinarily prosperous, owing to its monopoly on wild rubber, debt obligations replaced legal slavery. A commercial system based on credit developed, and the colonial class system was reinterpreted in terms of distinctions based on wealth from rubber. The new aristocrats, the rubber barons, were interested only in continuing the export of extractive products, and they were content to retain the old native system of cultivating the soil. They found it cheaper to use human labor than to introduce labor-saving devices. They found it easier to educate their children abroad than to establish educational institutions at home. They looked for comfort and diversion in Rio de Janeiro, Paris, and Lisbon rather than make an attempt to create comfort and diversion at home. They did not fix their roots in the Amazon, but looked upon it instead as a temporary abode where wealth might be accumulated in order to live elsewhere.

After the rubber debacle, many of these regional "aristocrats" moved away, but many were stranded and forced to live as best they could in the region. The highly crystallized class system and the emphasis upon an extractive economy to furnish raw materials for a foreign market continued. Brazil nuts, palm oils, rosewood oil, and other forest products supplanted rubber. Just as the Indian slave was the lowest rung in the class hierarchy of colonial society, the rural caboclo is today looked down upon by the descendants of the colonial aristocracy and of the rubber barons and even by the growing urban class. Both literate urbanites and the white-collar class of the Amazon small towns apply the term "caboclo" to the illiterate and semi-literate agriculturalists and collectors of the rural zones. A rigid system of class discrimination based on economic, familial, and educational criteria has persisted throughout the region. The Amazon Valley continued as a colonial area of the world. *Never in its history has the best of Western technology been available to the people of the Valley. Never has Amazon man had the use of knowledge and skills available in more advanced regions for the exploitation and control of the physical world.* The lack of technical equipment, the emphasis upon an extractive economy, a rigid class system, and other social and cultural factors have combined to keep the Amazon a backward area. These factors have always been greater barriers to change than the Amazon climate or soil, or the so-called tropical diseases. There are man-made barriers, and not immutable barriers which would make the development of the Amazon Valley impossible.

Since 1940 Brazil has shown a new interest in the Amazon Valley. In his famous "Amazon address," President Getulio Vargas announced in 1940: "Nothing will prevent us from accomplishing in this spurt of effort which is the twentieth century the highest task of civilized man: the conquest and the domination of great valleys of equatorial torrents, transforming their blind force and extraordinary fertility into disciplined energy. The Amazon, with the fecund impulse of our will, of our effort, and of our work, will not remain simply a chapter in the history of the earth but, on the same basis as other great river systems, will become a chapter in the history of civilization." Vargas' statement was in a sense a forerunner of Truman's "Fourth Point" and of the technical-assistance programs of the United Nations. Although limiting his aim to the internal development of his own country, President Vargas promised the full extension of modern technological skills and knowledge to an under-developed area of Brazil.

The Brazilian Government has since taken several positive steps toward this ideal. In 1942 the Serviço Especial de Saúde Pública (SESP), which has been mentioned frequently throughout this book, was established by accord with the Institute of Inter-American Affairs, an agency of the United States Government. Specialists in public health—physicians, engineers, nurses and others—were brought to the Amazon region from the United States and from South Brazil. The SESP already has a magnificent record in improving health conditions throughout the Valley. Since that time, the Instituto Agronômico do Norte has been expanded, and the former Ford Plantations on the Tapajoz River are now a gigantic experimental station for the institute. In addition, the federal government has founded agricultural colonies on the Amazon—one near Monte Alegre in the Lower Amazon and another upriver on the Rio Solimões. Three new federal territories have been carved out of the enormous states of Amazonas and Pará, Amapá, Rio Branco, and Guaporé. Into these three new territories and the older Territory of Acre federal funds have been poured. Under federal administration and primed with federal funds, these distant areas are developing rapidly. Modern agriculture is being stimulated, natural resources are beginning to be exploited. In the new capital "cities" of these federal territories, modern facilities are being installed, and transportation has been improved between them and Belém and Manaus. In order to finance these ventures in the Amazon, the Brazilian Constitution of September 18, 1946, set aside "no less than 3 per cent of the federal tributes" for use in the Amazon region during a period of at least twenty years. Since 1940 new influences have been felt. A period of rapid culture change is imminent, and it is hoped that such change will not be haphazard and uncontrolled.

It must be stated, however, that the Amazon region will probably not be the region of Brazil to develop most rapidly. There are other areas in western Santa Catarina, Goiás, and southern Mato

Grosso which have greater immediate potentialities. They have more fertile soils and are closer to the great metropolitan markets. Despite federal aid to the Valley of the São Francisco River and the great Amazon Valley, these southern frontiers will undoubtedly be populated and well exploited before Brazilians turn to solving efficiently the problems of the Amazon region. Yet the immense area of the Amazon Valley, with its enormous potentiality, remains not only an important Brazilian frontier but also a New World frontier. It is the most extensive sparsely inhabited area of the world. The development of such a region with modern technology is one answer to the horrid specter offered by neo-Malthusians who warn of the exhaustion of the world's food supply in the face of a growing population.

The "conquest" of the Amazon Valley, when it does take place, as well as the development of similar tropical regions of the earth, will call for the adaptation of standard techniques and of technological equipment to new conditions. Nutrition, agronomy, modern engineering, and other applied sciences have developed for the most part during the last century in countries which have a temperate climate. Our most advanced technology is, therefore, aimed at controlling and exploiting the Temperate Zone. When civilized man has lived in the tropics, he has tried to do so as if he were still in the Temperate Zone. The architecture of homes, for example, in Belém and Manaus, cities situated almost on the equator, follows patterns established in the United States and in Europe. In these cities people dress (or try to dress) as people do in Temperate Zone cities. Pictures of Amazon gentlemen of the upper class taken at the beginning of the century show them wearing black woolen frock coats, stiff shirts with wing collars, and silk ties. Students of engineering, agronomy, and medicine study books written by Temperate Zone authors. The tropics call for an adaptation of our Temperate Zone way of life. Basic scientific knowledge and engineering skills are applicable in the tropics, but the difference in soils, in heat, in sunlight, in rainfall, and other climatic factors will call for modification of applied methods. A whole new field of applied science must be developed for tropical conditions. "There seems to be a whole new science involved in adaptation of technologies," says a Carnegie Endowment for International Peace report on technical assistance. "But for lack of time and funds, the United Nations' approach has been piecemeal." [32] What will be necessary for the development of the Amazon Valley and for raising living standards of such communities as Itá is a Tropical Zone technology equivalent to our present Temperate Zone technology.

A new technology, however, will not be enough. Human factors will have to be considered in the "conquest" of the Amazon and of similar areas of the world. These human factors are present in the society and the culture of the peoples who inhabit these areas, as well as in the nature of their relations with newcomers. The development of the Amazon Valley will mean the modification of local society and of traditional culture. A knowledge of this society and culture will be as crucial to technical-assistance programs as the potentialities of the physical environment and the presence of an adequate technology. The direction of social change in a society and the effect of innovations need to be predicted within the range of our ability to do so, for there are dangers in technical assistance. Rapid change forced upon a people may disorganize their social systems and their traditional culture to the point where more is lost than gained. The world has seen many cases of primitive and peasant groups turned into miserable agricultural laborers, miners, and factory laborers—into people deprived of their traditional institutions and values without the possibility of full participation in the new society.

Innovations sometimes set up chain reactions in a society, as the automobile caused a series of changes in Plainville and other North American communities. The introduction of modern agriculture in the Amazon Valley would undoubtedly bring a series of far-reaching modifications in Itá society and in the society of the whole region. For example, modern agricultural practices would undoubt-

---

[32] *Implementation of Technical Assistance*, by Peter G. Franck and Dorothea Seelye Franck (International Conciliation, February, 1951), No. 468, p. 76.

edly cause changes in the present vague concepts of land tenure; low-lying floodlands would tend to be more valuable than terra firme. And, as elsewhere, with an emphasis upon agriculture, titles of ownership with legal sanctions would tend to replace the present titles granting the right to exploit only native products. Modern agriculture would modify Amazon settlement patterns. Larger numbers of people would concentrate near the better bottom lands of the river. Modern agricultural methods would turn the emphasis of the Amazon economic system to more stable and permanent exploitation of the region. Potentially, too, it might disrupt the Amazon credit hierarchy which binds the collector to the trader and the trader to the exporter.

Social change must be sought on many fronts at once. Because of such chain reactions, disequilibrium and disorganization may easily be caused by rapid changes in but one sphere of life. Without equivalent changes over a wide front, programs in one specific direction are often doomed to ultimate failure. Until education is available and until the economic system is subjected to basic improvement, the program of SESP in Itá for better health conditions will have only limited results. Without more education to understand the cause of disease, and without better diets, permanent improvement of health conditions in Itá is impossible. The doctors may be able to "keep their fingers in the hole in the dike," so to speak, by preventing serious epidemics through vaccination, use of DDT, and other mechanical means, but the people of Itá will continue to have bad health and low resistance to contagious disease. Disease will continue to spread because of their lack of knowledge of the scientific mechanism of contagion and disease transmission. Furthermore, improvement in health alone would actually be dangerous to Itá. A lower death rate without providing an increase in food supply would lead to actual starvation. Without modification of the subsistence methods and improvements in transportation, a larger population in the Amazon resulting from better health conditions would mean simply a larger number of underfed; without better educational facilities, it would mean a larger percentage of illiterates. Any program for the development of the Amazon Valley or for similar under-developed areas must envisage and include a wide scope of inter-related problems. Such programs must recognize that in society, health, economics, religion, educational processes, recreation, values, morals, and so forth, are but convenient categories. A society and the culture by which it lives is an integrated system. Change in one sphere evokes changes in the whole system.

Improvement of the situation of one group within a society means change for all groups. As the situation of the Amazon caboclo is improved, the position of the small-town upper-class (the commercial men, the bureaucrats, and so on) and the position of the regional aristocrats will be affected. It must be recognized, therefore, in planning technical-assistance programs, that certain groups within a society will not desire change. The status quo is or appears favorable to them, and for want of vision they feel that change challenges their present favorable position. If technical-assistance programs are to have any value for the people of under-developed areas, care must be taken not simply to reinforce the status quo. To avoid this danger, the planners of such programs must have a knowledge of the social system of the societies in question and of the functions and the needs of the various groups who together form the society. Only in this way will such programs "increase productivity of material and human resources and a wide and equitable distribution of such increased productivity, so as to contribute to higher standards of living for entire populations." [33]

It is inevitable that change will and should come to the Amazon region and to other similar areas. Social anthropologists have often argued "cultural relativity." They have pointed out that progress, good and evil, success and failure, and beauty and ugliness are values relative to the particular culture in which they are found. It is difficult, they say, to judge one way of life as superior or inferior to another. One people, as in India, places a high value on the development of religious and philosophical speculation; another values

[33] Economic and Social Council Resolution, United Nations, No. 222 (IX), p. 14.

technology, as in Europe and the United States. This point of view is sound when it teaches us to understand, to respect, and to tolerate other ways of life. Yet when a culture, through lack of technological equipment and for reasons of social organization, fails to provide for the material needs of man beyond a mere survival level, that society and culture must be judged inferior.

Change is in order in such technologically inferior societies. This does not imply, of course, the obliteration of a way of life or the passing of judgment on a total society. Each culture contains patterns and concepts of tremendous value to the people themselves which, if lost, would cause irreparable evil to the functions of the society and loss to our world heritage. The traditional folk culture of the Amazon region, built as it is out of generations of experience in that particular environment and derived from three cultural heritages, contains much of great beauty and value which will be necessary in the future and which must be retained. It is to be hoped that a new Amazon culture will be formed combining the productive powers of modern technology and science and the efficiency of modern industry with the many positive values of the present way of life. If the new Amazon culture is achieved, it will be as expressive of the region as that described in this book.

9. ITÁ IN 1974
by Darrel L. Miller

In recent years, world attention has been focused on the great Trans-Amazon Highway and settlement project in the Amazon region of Brazil.[1] Articles in newspapers and magazines around the world have appeared featuring the Trans-Amazon Highway, and its effects on the world's largest tropical forest and one of the world's least settled areas. Indeed, the Brazilian federal government has been pouring money into the development projects in the two northern states of Pará and Amazonas since 1970; however, communities along the Amazon River itself have largely been by-passed by these development projects. They remain, in a sense, traditional river communities when compared with river communities along the Tocantins, Xingú, and Tapajós rivers which lay in the path of the highway and whose populations have doubled or tripled since 1970.

The cities of Manaus and Santarém along the Amazon are now connected by roads to the Trans-Amazon Highway. Santarém, a small river city of 30,000 in 1962, has grown to over 90,000. Much of this growth has been attributed to the coming of the Santarém-Cuiabá Highway which crosses the Trans-Amazon 200 kilometers south of Santarém. Goods can now be trucked from Pôrto Alegre in Rio Grande do Sul to Santarém and even Manaus over a period of several days instead of the several weeks it takes by ship. However,

NOTE: The research on which this chapter was based was supported by the Tropical South American Program of the University of Florida, which is directed by Charles Wagley.

[1] My wife, Linda, and I visited Itá and the Trans-Amazon Highway as part of a summer research project during June, July, and August, 1974, thirty-two years after Charles Wagley's initial visit to the Amazon Valley and twenty-six years after his field research in Itá.

296

the highway is impassable during the rainy season from December through June. Herein lies one of the major benefits of the highway to the traditional river communities. During the rainy season there is an increase in river traffic carrying goods to cities along the highway such as Altamira on the Xingú and Itaituba on the Tapajós.

The highway not only provides improved transportation for the Amazon region, but it also has opened up lands for colonization by people from all over Brazil—people from land-poor and coastal states as far away as Rio Grande do Sul and Santa Catarina. Communities have grown up where only jungle existed four or five years ago. There is an air of optimism and a sense of excitement. The frenetic and booming activity of communities along the highway contrasts greatly with the slow, easy pace of life in Itá.

In spite of the fact that the highway has by-passed Itá, there has been a doubling of the population between 1948 and 1974. The town has grown from three streets to five streets and from slightly more than 600 people to a population of 1,300. During our first few days we noted many differences. The old fort has been restored complete with several old cannons found nearby. A *ginásio* has been built next to the church. Although it is not functioning due to a lack of quali-fied teachers, its two modern buildings attest to the concern of some members of the community for a better education for their children. Several new public buildings have been built along First Street in-cluding the state tax collector's office, state police post, a health post, and the *prefeito's* or mayor's house. A new hospital is being built on the site of the SESP health post. In various places all over town, new houses are being built.

There are still very few motor vehicles in Itá, but in 1948 there were none at all. We counted ten, all of which were trucks or utility vehicles. There is one road in the *município* which runs from Itá to a small settlement on an *igarapé* twenty kilometers away. Part of Second Street and soon, all of First Street, will be paved. The chief means of transportation in Itá today is the bicycle, which was un-heard of in 1948. Two bicycle rental stores rent by the hour. Young and old alike rent bicycles for errands or pleasure. The bicycle has in large part replaced the evening promenade. The hours between 5:30 and 7:00 P.M. are dangerous ones for pedestrians.

Each evening at dusk the electricity is turned on. It continues until 10:30 or 11:00 P.M. First, Second and Third Streets are lit by streetlights. The percentage of houses with electricity drops as one moves away from the river with First Street having the greatest percentage and Fourth and Fifth Streets having none at all. The monthly rate per household is slightly less than two dollars. Water is available to all houses at approximately the same rate. Eighty-five per cent of the houses in Itá are hooked up with the water system, but owing to non-payment only 57 per cent actually have running water. Those without running water borrow from a neighbor, get it from a well, or carry it from a nearby stream or the river.

Our first few weeks were spent talking with many of the older residents who had known "Doutor Charles" and Dona Cecilia, and Eduardo and Clara Galvão during their first visits. We were welcomed by Dona Dora who, at eighty-two years, is still quite active in the community and in the family business even though she never goes more than a few steps from home. She asked us out onto the veranda-dining room, and we were served the usual *cafezinho*. She wanted to know about the Wagleys and their family. Then she introduced us to her brother-in-law and her two nephews, one of whom is an elementary school teacher while the other helps with the store. She reminisced about how things were twenty-six years ago and how much different Itá was now. She cited many of the things we had noticed upon our arrival—the town was bigger, there was regular electricity, the hospital, *ginásio*, etc. On this and on subsequent visits we noted that the family business was centered on lumber instead of rubber. The store was very poorly stocked and was of little importance nowadays. Several other stores had much more merchandise and did more business. Dona Dora pointed out that they were far more concerned about their land-holdings with cattle and lumber and that this took up most of their time. As with the other informants who had helped Wagley and his associates, she well understood what an anthropologist wanted and needed to know. She answered our questions readily and pinpointed major changes which she felt would be of interest to us.

Due to her age Dona Dora was unable to provide us with our meals, but we were able to visit with her often, and she proved to be a valuable source of information. As in any other small community, news travels fast and Dona Dora had ready access to the grapevine. We had no need of a daily newspaper to find out what was going on.

Dona Dora, with from 250 to 300 godchildren, knew many people in town, but the recent growth in population made it almost impossible to keep up with everyone. In our questionnaire, over 50 per cent of the people in our sample of fifty houses indicated that they had been born either in the rural area surrounding Itá or one of the other surrounding *municípios*. This indicates that a large portion of the increase in population has been the first step in migration from rural to urban areas—a phenomenon noted in several studies of population patterns in Latin America. Not only was the population of the town increasing owing to migration, but the entire *município* was growing owing to an increased birth rate. The *município* increased in population by 25 per cent from 14,000 in 1960 to 18,800 in 1970.

All but a very few of those who recently moved to Itá lived on the Third, Fourth, and Fifth streets. Many of them are fairly well off financially; but because there were simply no vacant lots or houses along two streets, they built or bought houses away from the river. Wagley noted that the farther away from the river a family lived, the poorer it generally tended to be. Because of this lack of room on the first two streets we noted a slight deviation from this pattern. On Fifth Street in particular there were families with kerosene refrigerators, sewing machines, and good furniture who indicated that they ate well. These families included three *compradores*, or businessmen, who deal in lumber. There are also three small stores in this area. As noted above, electricity is not available to many sections of the Fourth and Fifth Streets. This coupled with the poor quality of the streets themselves and the lack of *movimento* as compared to First and Second streets still makes this a less desirable area in which to live and accounts for the high percentage of poor families living in palm thatch huts or *barracas*. Almost all of these families have moved from the interior within the last five years.

In addition to Dona Dora, we discovered that Dona Branquinha, the former school teacher and religious leader, was alive and well. She had moved to Belém for awhile, but had returned to Itá with her son, who was now the manager of the local sawmill. Her son proved to be very helpful in aiding us in our study of the sawmill and the lumber industry in general. He is also very active in local politics and is leader of the political party called ARENA II. (There is also an ARENA I and the MDB, Movimento Democratico Brasileiro, which does not have a faction in Itá.) At the house of Dona Branquinha we met the federal deputy for that district and the candidate for the state legislature when they were in town.

We also met with others frequently mentioned in this book including Juca, the storyteller and leader of the *Boi Bumba*, who is now retired but still did some work as the director of the men who worked for the *município* for a daily wage. José Marajo, also retired, was of enormous help in making contacts with some of the newer residents of the community. He had studied to become an *advogado* (a licensed attorney though not a law graduate) and assisted in court cases when the judge was in town. Oswaldo, who was born in Portugal, and his wife Dona Diquinha had three successful businesses—a bar, bakery, and pharmacy. Dona Joaquina had retired as a midwife and lived alone as all the members of her family had moved away to Santarém. We also talked with many others whose family names appeared in this book. Many had heard their mothers and fathers tell about the Americans who had come to Itá. With these people as a basis, we began our look at Itá twenty-six years later.

The economic base of Itá has changed greatly since 1948. Rubber gathering, which was on the wane in 1948, has been replaced almost entirely by lumbering. The export of Amazonian hardwoods gave a tremendous lift to Itá. World and domestic markets for veneers, plywoods, and lumber in general brought about a lumber "boom" in the late 60's and early 70's. In 1969, a company from the south of Brazil built a sawmill on the outskirts of Itá. The mill, however, has been plagued by management difficulties and has never fully been in operation. The sawmill employs only fifteen workers from the town. Hope in the community that an American company will buy the sawmill and put it into full operation still runs high. However, Itá is still far upriver and until forests nearer to Belém are exhausted, hope for a functioning sawmill in Itá are dim. Most logs, except those heavier than water, are towed downriver to one of the many sawmills which dot the riverbank from Belém to Breves.

The extraction of hardwoods from Itá is centered on the large island which forms a part of the *município*. Landowners, both large and small, have made substantial profits in recent years. The rubber gatherer–rubber trader system which was long the backbone of the economy in this region of the lower Amazon has been replaced by a similar system involving logs. The key to the logging cycle is the sawmill and lumber companies. Representatives from these companies fly into Itá periodically and offer contracts to local landowners or commercial men known as *compradores de madeira* (buyers of wood). The landowners or the *compradores* sign a contract which indicates that they will deliver a certain quantity of a type of wood to the sawmill or their representatives by a specified date, payment upon delivery. The local landowners hire laborers to cut the trees, to help move the logs to the river, and to chain the logs together into large rafts which will be towed to the sawmill behind small boats called *motores*.

The *compradores* follow a similar process. They, however, act more as middle men between the small landowners of the interior of the municipality and the lumber companies. The *comprador* usually has several landowners with whom he deals regularly. He sub-contracts with them to provide a certain amount or all of the wood for which he has contracted. The *comprador*, of course, pays a small landowner much less than the going price for the logs. The small landowner cuts the trees and delivers them to the river or to an *igarapé* where the *comprador* chains them together and tows them to the sawmill or to a central collection point until he has all he needs to fill a contract. The *comprador* then reinvests his profit into buying more logs or uses the profits to buy stock for his store in Itá. Most *compradores* are also small store owners and choose to invest in their stores rather than the fluctuating lumber market.

Raimundo Costa is a typical *comprador*. He is middle-aged with a wife and seven children. He owns a wood-frame house in the *bairro* at the end of Second Street. Next door and connected to his house is a small store which is stocked with soft drinks, beer, flashlights, batteries, hammocks, canned foodstuffs, and some small novelty items. Raimundo explained to us that he liked to put his profits back into the store because it was safer. Eight months ago, he explained, he lost much of his income when the government put restrictions on the export of logs. Prices fell and he was unable to solicit contracts from the lumber companies. His most recent contract was dated April, 1974.

Virola and *andiroba* are the two types of woods he deals in. Sometimes the company may call for *muiritinga* or *sucupira*. The first three kinds of wood belong to a category he called *branca*, or white. They are used in making plywood. *Virola*, before the export limit, was selling for 80 cruzeiros per cubic meter; now it is at 47 cruzeiros per cubic meter. The last type of wood, *sucupira* is a hardwood, or *pesada*. It is used for veneers or lumber. It is presently selling for 100 cruzeiros per cubic meter but was as high as 170 cruzeiros last year.

Raimundo's suppliers live on the big island of Itá. There are six small landowners from whom he buys. He owns his own boat which he uses to pick up the rafts and bring them to a collection point in front of the town. He especially likes to deal with an American company because it has its own boat which tows the rafts to the sawmill. Raimundo essentially acts as a middleman between the small landowner on the big island and the representatives of the lumber companies. The small landowner is often unwilling or unable to cope with these business dealings himself.

Raimundo deals with three lumber companies, all of which have sawmills located along the Amazon between Itá and Breves, a small river town about twenty hours upriver from Belém. After our visit to Itá, I was able to visit one of the sawmills near Breves. Most of the sawmills are foreign-owned by American, West German, or Japanese interests. Such was the case with this company. I contacted company officials in Belém and was flown to the sawmill in a company plane.

The sawmill operated two distinct sections—the sawmill itself and the plywood mill. *Andiroba* and some *sucupira*, hardwoods, are used strictly at the sawmill for cutting into boardlengths for export. *Sumaúma*, *virola*, and *muiritinga*, all soft woods, are used in the manufacture of plywood. Logs of each type are cut in the *município* of Itá.

The sawmill identified eight major suppliers from Itá. Six of the eight are large landowners and the remaining two are *compradores*. There are several smaller suppliers, but the company has not dealt with them since the government ban on exports and the drop in prices. Approximately 16 million cubic meters of lumber were extracted from the *município* of Itá during the first seven months of 1974. This has meant a profit to the landowners and *compradores* and an increase in state tax revenues.

For those residents of Itá who are not involved in the commercial life of the community, there is a very limited job market. The large landowners and the *compradores* do require a small number of loggers who are employed on a daily basis. Recently, the national government has passed a law restricting the export of logs. Lumber may only be exported in the form of plywood, veneer, or cut boards. This law has caused the export of lumber to drop. At the same time, the local sawmills have been unable to handle the greater volume of logs. With the reduced demand, prices have dropped considerably. *Macacáuba*, for instance, has dropped 70 cruzeiros per cubic meter since January of 1974. The lower prices have caused most of the large landowners to hold back their timber until sawmill capacity has increased and world demand for Amazonian hardwoods returns. However, for the unskilled laborers of Itá, this means fewer jobs. Thus, Itá still depends in large part on the "vagaries of distant markets and government policies" as it did when Wagley first went there in 1953.

There are two other means of livelihood for the unskilled—work for the municipal government or horticulture. During the summer of 1974, the *município* had several projects underway for which workers were paid a daily wage of less than two dollars. Such projects include the construction of a new hospital; the paving of First Street; the cutting of the grass in public places, such as the riverfront park; the restoration of the fort; and the care of the municipal market. Jobs with the municipal government are steady but, as almost everyone pointed out, one's family can hardly eat one good meal a day on less than two dollars a day.

Agriculture in the Brazilian Amazon region has traditionally been slash-and-burn. These techniques have not changed and are still practiced to a large extent in the *município* of Itá. In 1962, a road to the interior was completed and some new land was opened up for agriculture. This caused a temporary increase in yields according to several farmers in that area; but after ten years or more of cultivation, the soils along the road are considered almost as poor as the land nearer town. The size of the manioc tubers was generally the smallest we had seen in this region of the Amazon. Only one store in Itá still buys manioc from local farmers. The other stores either do not sell manioc or they buy their supplies in Santarém. Rice and vegetables are grown in very small quantities. Thus, agriculture as a means of earning money or of exchange is very poor in Itá. Food is usually grown only for family consumption.

In general, the amount of foodstuffs grown in Itá is not sufficient to support the community. However, in the area of meat production, Itá has made great strides. The *município* itself has gone into the cattle business. Municipal employees raise the cattle, butcher it at a *município*-owned slaughterhouse and then market it to the public at a reasonable price. The current *prefeito* has followed through with his campaign promise to make meat available every day. When he is in town, an animal is butchered almost every day. Needless to say, this policy has made him extremely popular. The beef supplements the traditional sources of meat and protein—pork, chicken, eggs, and fish. It is interesting to note that there were five fish corrals in and near Itá in 1948, but we found none in use during our visit.

For other items, the people are even more dependent on the store owners because of failing crop yields and increases in population. Due to inflation, store owners must pay cash for supplies for their store. The need for cash has, of necessity, extended down to the customers. Stores in Itá have signs posted which advise the customer that nothing can be bought on credit. For good friends, however, some store owners will still extend credit; but this accounts for very little of their total business.

Inflation and the resultant inability of the store owners to grant credit has spelled the end of the traditional patron-client relationship as exemplified by the rubber trader and rubber gatherer. When talking about his economic problems today the average citizen of Itá cites the lack of a patron to help him through his difficulties. Many of the former rubber gatherers have moved to town after their patron sold his land or simply discontinued trading in rubber. But the community of Itá cannot possibly provide patrons for all those who seek one. Even in the town, the traditional customer-storekeeper relationship has broken down. Purchases are made by cash so that the storekeeper can buy stock for his store when representatives of the wholesalers from Belém stop in Itá. One of the newer stores even has a "cash and carry" slogan painted on the outside.

In short, inflation and national economic policies have made the search for a patron and the concommitant security he provides a very difficult one. This search is largely based on conditions over which the client has negligible control. The complimentary needs and resources which hold the patron-client relationship together are lacking. Should there be a resurgence in the lumber market, the patron-client relationship might well reappear.

The traditional store which traded in a few staple goods over a counter in the front room of the family's house is still the most common of the twenty stores which Itá now contains. However, new merchandising techniques have begun to appear. There are three stores which are specialized—a pharmacy and two dry goods stores, none of which existed in 1948. The other stores sell a great variety of goods from foodstuffs to clothing. The two dry goods stores have comparatively large stocks and generally lower prices on most items than the smaller *mercaderias*. Their success lies in the modern merchandising technique of greater volume at lower prices. Other store owners have not begun to react to this new threat. The lower prices are already attracting customers from the smaller stores. One store owner told us that he may start giving limited credit in an effort to keep some of his better customers.

A descendant of one of Itá's original Jewish families is the owner of one of these successful new stores. He began his career as a *comerciante* with almost no money, but he managed to take a correspondence course in repairing radios and record players. He opened a radio repair shop seven years ago. With his profits from the radio shop he began to buy bicycles which he rented out for one cruzeiro per hour. He then became interested in photography and set up a small studio for taking pictures for the Brazilian *carteira de identidade* (official identity card). In February of 1974, he moved his place of business to a building in the center of town just behind the town hall, installed a small generator, and began making his own ice cream. The daily gross from his business now averages 1,000 cruzeiros per day.[2] With the profits he hopes to build his own business complex complete with a hotel on a lot bordering the main plaza.

As a result of such enterprising businessmen, the citizen of Itá now has access to many of the pleasures formerly only available in large cities such as Santarém and Belém. He can buy all sorts of patent medicines at the drugstores and beer, soft drinks, and canned food items at any of the several stores. Paperback books, magazines, cosmetics, household goods, and factory-made clothing are also available, admittedly not in great variety, but nonetheless available.

Itá has contact with the outside world not only through manufactured goods but also through the telegraph office, which was reactivated during our visit. There is also a possibility that mail service will begin again with some regularity. News comes in via the radio. Radio stations from Belém, Manaus, southern Brazil, and other countries

[2] About 125 U.S. dollars at the 1974 rate of exchange.

can be heard by radio owners. A questionnaire which we administered to 50 households revealed that approximately 30 per cent of the people in Itá own radios; and for those who do not have them, there is music from several stores or the radio of a neighbor. During our visit President Nixon resigned. Even without a radio, we learned of it. The day following the resignation, someone flew in on one of the air taxi flights and brought a newspaper with the whole story. There has even been talk of a television relay tower so that Belém stations could be beamed into Itá.

Transportation to Belém and Santarém is provided on a more or less regular basis by FAB (Forca Aerea Brasileira) air taxi twice a week, and by the many river boats which pass by Itá. There is also a state-owned launch which can provide emergency transportation if necessary. One thing that the community does lack, however, is a radiotelephone for immediate contact with the outside world.

In spite of all these possibilities for travel and communication, Itá remains isolated for the vast majority of its citizens. Travel, except possibly by small boat, is costly. FAB flights have only a few vacancies which are usually reserved for government functionaries or the sick. Without a road there is no inexpensive bus travel. Juca, for instance, had not been out of Itá in twenty or thirty years (he could not remember exactly how long it had been). And even with the radio and an occasional newspaper, Juca found it hard to believe that Americans had actually been to the moon. While we were in Itá, one of the store owners bought a cash register. Many people came to the store just to watch the machine, for they had never seen one before.

We attempted to ascertain, by using our short questionnaire, whether socio-economic status of a family could be determined by the distance they lived from the river. In Wagley's original study he found this to be true. Yet, as noted above, we found some deviation from this pattern. Later in the summer we found the answer to the deviation which confirmed the findings of our questionnaire.

We first examined the structure of the homes along each of the streets. There are four basic types of walls or sides—cored brick, wood, daub-and-wattle, and palm thatch—and two types of roofs—tile and palm thatch. Of course materials such as cored brick,[3] tile, and wood can be expensive and must be purchased with cash. Daub-and-wattle and palm thatch are free for the taking. We found that all of the cored brick and tile structures (we excluded all public buildings) were on First and Second Streets. Wood-frame and tile houses predominated on Second Street. On Third Street, wood-frame houses with palm thatch roofs were in the majority as they were on Fifth Street. Palm side and palm thatch roofs were prominent on Fourth Street. However, except for cored brick structures on First and Second Streets and palm thatch *barracas* on Third, Fourth, and Fifth Streets, all types of houses appeared on every street. In general, we concluded that the better houses tended to be closer to the river except in the case of Fifth Street, where the houses were roughly equivalent to those on Third Street. As noted above, lack of building room and the fact that the new road runs off Fifth Street, account for this slight difference.

We also noted other factors of material well-being such as whether the house had electricity, a radio, a kerosene refrigerator, and how many times each week the family ate meat. There was no electricity after Third Street. All houses on First Street had electricity. After the first two streets, radios and refrigerators were scarce with the exception of a few families on Fifth Street. The number of times a week a family ate meat was indicative, too, of a family's economic situation. The results of this questionnaire singled out the families who were regularly employed or large landowners, such as Dona Dora. Again, the pattern indicated decreasing economic well-being the farther one lived from the river. We concluded that Wagley's findings were still valid with the exception of some families on Fifth Street.

Of the four classes identified by Wagley in Chapter 4 of this book —*Gente de Primeira, Gente de Segunda, Gente do Sítio,* and *Caboclos da Beira*—we found that there was little reference to social classes using these terms. The only term in current usage is caboclo, which is used by the upper classes when speaking of the lower classes

[3] A type of hollow, baked-mud brick which is very fragile.

and by the different lower-class groups—farmers, day laborers, rural residents—when referring to each other. Only Dona Dora and Dona Branquinha remain as representatives of the old *gente de primeira* in Itá. Nowadays, the amount of money one has and whether one owns a business or is in a position to hire workers is most significant. There are no definite ethnosemantic categories, but we noted with some frequency the use of the term *empregado* (employee) as opposed to the class of store owners, government officials, wealthy landowners, and those dealing successfully in the lumber market who were referred to by their position or by name and the title of respect in the region, *"Seu"* (*Senhor*).

Again, we chose to do an inventory of three representative families on three different streets and three different economic levels. The first family we chose lived on First Street in a cored brick side and tile roof house. They were neither the wealthiest nor the poorest in what we termed the upper class. Because of the greater availability of manufactured goods, we were unable to do a complete inventory. Our purposes were served by looking primarily at the furnishings of the house. They included a living room suite (sofa and chair), four end tables, several framed religious pictures on the wall, two metal and plastic lawn chairs, a dinette set with matching chairs, twelve straight-back chairs, a china closet, a kitchen table, a refrigerator, a gas stove, and a bed and dresser in each bedroom. They own two radios, one of which was in the store next door.

The second family lived on Second Street in a house with a daub-and-wattle side and palm thatch roof. They fall somewhere in the middle of the "middle" class group. Household furnishings consisted of a bookcase with some books, a dining room table, five folding chairs, a long wooden bench, a framed religious picture on the wall, a kerosene refrigerator, and a charcoal stove. The family slept in hammocks. They owned a radio which did not work.

Finally, the third family which was near the middle of the low-income group lived in a palm thatch *barraca* on Fourth Street. The house had only two rooms and a kitchen under an overhang in the back. Inside, there were three wooden folding chairs and a long bench. The kitchen had a rough wooden shelf which held a small charcoal stove. The family slept in hammocks. There were families in this low-income group which only had hammocks and a charcoal stove made of rocks and a wire grate.

From the results of our questionnaire and from just visiting families in all parts of Itá, we felt that the economic situation (as evidenced by material possessions) of the upper economic strata is better than twenty-six years ago. However, the plight of the lower-class families, a group which includes over two-thirds of the population of Itá, is much the same as twenty-six years ago with little hope of immediate improvement.

Education in Itá is no longer the haphazard operation it was in 1948. The primary school has now been fully integrated into the state educational system. As of April 30, 1974, there were 356 children attending the primary school. The school, which has not yet changed over to the new educational reform, consists of five series or grades. Children begin school at the age of seven. There were 195 children enrolled in the first series, 59 in the second, 46 in the third, 33 in the fourth, and only 21 in the fifth. Generally speaking, if a child fails a grade he may repeat that grade only once. If he does not succeed the second time, he will not be allowed to continue unless the school decides that it has enough space to accommodate him. There is, therefore, a tremendous drop-out rate between the first and second series. In the first series a child must learn to read and write. In addition to the difficult academics of the first year, all children who attend the school must have a uniform. If the child's family is poor and cannot afford the uniform, he is unable to go to school. Sometime the *município* provides a limited amount of money to buy uniforms for indigent children but, according to the school principal, this helps only a very few of those children who are in need of uniforms.

There is, fortunately, a solution for those who do not make it in the regular system. The elementary school itself provides instruction at night in a program called *ensino supletivo*. As of April 30, 1974, there were thirty-nine students enrolled ranging in age from twelve to twenty-five years. There is no instruction at night for the first series, only the second and third.

After a student has completed the fifth series in Itá, he must attend the *ginásio* in Belém or Santarém. This is, of course, an expensive proposition. A family must be relatively wealthy or have relatives in one of those cities who are willing to board the child. The only families who had children in a *ginásio* or *colégio* in Belém or Santarém were families who lived on First Street, i.e., the wealthier people in Itá. The granddaughter of Dona Branquinha was attending the federal university in Belém.

Part of the problem in providing adequate education in Amazon areas, such as Itá, is obtaining teachers with the proper educational backgrounds. Native sons or daughters of Itá, if they are educated in a *ginásio* or *colégio* in the city, are not likely to come back. The government does not provide special compensation to teachers from urban areas who agree to teach in rural, isolated communities. As a result, well-trained teachers for the primary schools and "certified" teachers for schools above the *ginásio* (fifth through eighth years) are not to be found in Itá. Primary teachers need only have a primary education themselves in order to be able to teach. In Itá, only one teacher, Dona Dora's nephew, has even completed the *ginásio*. Most, according to the principal, have only completed primary or have one or two years of *ginásio*.

The case of the *ginásio* in Itá is a different story. Itá had an Austrian priest in the early 60's who planned to build a *ginásio* with the money from the festival of São Benedito. At that time, the priest was fortunate enough to obtain a promise from an order of nuns in Manaus which agreed to staff the school with the necessary teachers. When the school building was actually completed in 1972, however, the number of nuns in the order had dropped from approximately 300 to 89. The order was able to supply only two teachers. For this reason the school has never been opened. While we were there, a group of interested students began circulating a petition to the Secretary of Education and Culture in Belém which asked for teachers to staff the already completed and furnished *ginásio*. Only people who had completed the fifth year of primary were able to sign the petition. There were in excess of eighty signatures when we saw the petition. João da Silva, for instance, had completed two years of *ginásio* and then had moved to Itá when his mother remarried. In Itá he was unable to continue his education because of the expense involved in sending him to Belém. He is now working as a bricklayer at the new hospital. He expressed his frustration to us saying that "there is no way to advance oneself here (Itá)." One can only "drink, dance, and ride a bicycle."

One bright spot in the educational picture is that the *município* of Itá is participating in the literacy program called "Movimento Brasileiro de Alfabetização" (MOBRAL). The MOBRAL program is funded by the federal government and is put into operation by the state secretary of education. MOBRAL consists of two levels. The first level is the six months beginning MOBRAL and is the basic literacy program. It is equivalent to completion of the first grade in the regular school regimen. After completing the basic MOBRAL program, the student can elect to go to the higher level called Educação Integrada (Integrated Education) which lasts one year. Upon completion of this program, the student has the equivalent of a primary education and may take an exam and enter the *ginásio*. Of course, in Itá this last step is impossible.

The MOBRAL programs are largely composed of adults. Regulations state the minimum age is sixteen. There are twenty-five MOBRAL centers in the *município*. In the town of Itá, there are forty-nine students enrolled in the literacy program and ninety-six enrolled in Educação Integrada. Literacy classes meet almost every night. Attendance is poor because of conflicts with home life. Mothers have children to take care of and fathers are tired after a hard day's work. However, Educação Integrada is well attended the three nights a week it meets. Educação Integrada has its own building which was recently completed along First Street. Both programs attempt to use texts which are self-motivating and of general interest to the students. Some of the beginning MOBRAL units deal with proper diet, medical care, proper sanitation, and the evils of alcohol.

After completing Educação Integrada, what advantage does it give the average citizen of Itá? There are no job opportunities in Itá, so being able to read and write makes little difference. In larger cities the government has coupled a job training program (SENAC) with the MOBRAL program; but there is no possibility of establishing this type of program in most traditional communities in the Amazon Basin, simply because these communities do not have the economic base to provide employment. Many times we heard people say that education was the answer to their problems and that they wanted their children to attend school and do well. Doing well in school or completing the MOBRAL programs, though, leaves one right where he started or encourages him to move off to the city where jobs are plentiful.

The educational programs in Itá gave us a clue to the large amount of federal and state money spent on programs in the Amazon. As Joaquim Gonçalves, the secretary of the *município* said, "We live in a consuming state which is supported by the states in the south." The main function of the *prefeito*, or mayor, of the *município* was to procure the money from the proper government agency and to allocate it according to the governmental guidelines which are passed by the municipal council. The *prefeito* can stray from the following guidelines by only 4 per cent. Twenty per cent of the budget must be allocated to education. Ten per cent to health, at least 30 per cent to capital expenditures and 40 per cent to miscellaneous areas including welfare. In discussion with me, several state officials expressed disfavor about the projects undertaken by the *município*, such as construction of a riverfront park including the bulkheading of the river bank in front of the park or the current project which was the paving of First Street. This latter project will cost the *município* about $28,000. These projects are in accordance with past projects, as Wagley has pointed out concerning the building of the town hall. The budget money does provide for fifty-six paid positions including twenty-five teachers, a public health nurse, and the various municipal employees from *prefeito* to secretaries.

This year's budget totalled $78,000. Next year's budget will be almost double, $157,000. The money comes from two sources. The first source of money is the União do Estado which is a federal program designed to assist *municípios* in the poorer regions. A second federal program, called the Fundo Rodoviaria, draws from the federal highway funds. The exact amount of money these two programs provide is not public information; but subtracting the total of the second source of municipal income from the total budgeted, I estimated that the federal government provided $52,000 or 67 per cent of the municipal budget in 1973.

The second source of income comes from the state in the form of tax revenue on all items extracted from the *município* such as lumber, rubber, jute, etc. The tax, called the ICM or Imposto Circulação de Mercadoria, is administered by a state office in Itá, the *coletoria*. In the case of the lumber companies, they pay the state a 15 per cent tax on the purchase price. Tax money from the lumber companies accounted for approximately 50 per cent of the ICM collected by the municipality of Itá. Sixteen per cent of the tax money collected is returned to the *município*. The accounting is done on a monthly basis. For the month of June, 1974, the municipal coffers received $3,074. The ICM accounts for 33 per cent of the municipal revenue. In 1973, the *município* received $25,143 out of a total budget of $78,000.

During July of 1974, the state government instituted a new ICM tax. The new tax will be levied on store owners according to their yearly gross intake. There are no exact means of determining the gross intake of most of the stores in Itá, except for the one store with a cash register. In order to levy the tax, the government makes an estimate of the store's sales. Usually, the estimate is high and several of the store owners we talked to did not know what they were going to do. Gustavo Rodrigues received a tax-payment booklet in the mail which stated that the estimate on his yearly intake was $857.00 (6,000 cruzeiros). His monthly payment would be $10.00 (70 cruzeiros). Gustavo cannot read. He received the payment book in the mail but did not open it because he did not know what he was supposed to do. We visited him on the day he found out that he was in arrears in his payments. We opened the package and attempted to explain to him what it was all about. He was dumbfounded by the monthly payment. Since much of his trade is barter or credit (an exception in Itá), he only made a small amount. Talking with the *coletor* proved to be of no help since Gustavo could not prove exactly what his yearly intake was; the government figure stood. When we left, he was still pondering his fate.

Another area in which there is a large amount of state and federal support is health. Charles Wagley's initial visit to the Amazon concerned this very problem. At that time malaria and intestinal parasites plagued the Amazon Basin. To help combat these diseases and to provide adequate health care in general, Wagley helped to establish the SESP post in Itá. SESP no longer functions in the area around Itá. Other agencies have taken over its function. SESP left a health post which was built during World War II, and the local government continued to support a public health nurse. At times there was a SESP doctor who lived in Itá. But there has not been a physician in the community since the early 1960's.

For the past ten years, health care in the region has been very precarious. The inability of SESP to recruit a doctor for Itá and later SESP's total withdrawal from the area have made health care one of Itá's major problems. The state provides transportation to Breves or Belém in the case of an emergency and would periodically send out a doctor to examine a suspected case of malaria, hepatitis, or the other infectious diseases. The only regular doctor to visit the town was an Argentinian doctor who worked on a small boat provided by the Assistência Social Adventista. The boat would dock at Itá once every three months for several hours. Those who heard he was coming and made it to the dock on time could get treatment. Those who could not were simply out of luck.

Recently, a new governmental organization, FUNRURAL, in conjunction with Assistência Adventista has begun construction of a new hospital on the site of the old SESP health post. When completed, according to the former *enfermeiro*, the FUNRURAL organization and the state will provide two or three new doctors to staff the hospital. However, they will undoubtedly have a problem of attracting doctors who are willing to live in Itá or even to visit on a regular weekly or bi-weekly basis. Like the town of Breves which has a hospital and only one doctor, Itá, an even smaller community, may end up with a hospital and no doctors.

Current health problems are handled by the *enfermeira* or public health nurse. The former *enfermeira* who retired after 37 years, six months, and one day of service stayed on to assist the new *enfermeira*. She is the daughter of a local family and received her training at a hospital in Belém. In addition, she and two assistants were trained in a midwife program. The *enfermeira* can give vaccinations, dress minor wounds, and pull teeth. The health post is adequate, but has a very low stock of medicines and supplies. The health post has an old dentist's chair, a recovery room, and an examination room. There is also an office of SUCAM, the public health service, where records are kept but the office itself is unstaffed. For those who can afford to buy them, patent remedies are available at the pharmacy.

An alternative to health care as provided by the health post and by the state, is the traditional folk-health remedies provided by the *pagés, benzedeiras,* and *rezendeiras*. A *pagé* who practices near or in the town of Itá is subject to arrest. There are, as a result, few practicing *pagés* in Itá. There is supposedly one who practices in the nearby rural areas but we were unable to confirm this. There are, however, old women *benzedeira* who use herbs and chants to cure the sick. There are also some SESP trained midwives in the interior. When the baby brother of the current *enfermeira* was sick with a high fever, a *benzedeira* was called in for the cure. Unfortunately, we were unable to watch the cure which she administered, but the baby recovered. Many people still grow their own herbs for medicinal purposes. Herb gardens and herbal cures abounded; most of them concerned colds and/or stomach aches. Were a doctor available in the community, we feel sure that he would be consulted, but in the absence of formal medical care, the people have no alternative but to return to the old methods used before doctors ever came to the Amazon.

The city's water service was originally established by SESP. The source of the city's water in 1948, before the water service (SAA or Serviço Autônomo de Água) was established, was the Amazon River. Water had to be carried by hand from the river to the houses, and people came to the river to bathe and do laundry. The public water now comes from seven drilled wells south of the city. Five of the wells are functioning and two are held in reserve. The water is filtered three times before it is pumped in plastic pipes to residences. Residents are proud of their water, especially since it does not have to be boiled or refiltered before it is drunk.

Jorge Martins, secretary of the water authority, pointed out that the peak period of dysentery during the year was the festival of São Benedito when thousands of people would descend on the community. At that time, visitors and even townspeople would drink, bathe, cook, and launder using the river water. Since the construction of the water system, dysentery has been sharply reduced even during the festival.

The festival of São Benedito is still the highlight of the year in Itá. Itá now has an Italian padre who lives in the community. He had read Wagley's book and was quite eager to help us in comparing the past with the present. When asked how the festival of São Benedito had changed over the years, he began by pointing out that the church itself participates only in the religious aspects of the festival and not in the profane. The crowd at the festival in 1973 ranged from 2,000 to 6,000 depending on the day and type of activities. Dona Dora still offers a quadrille. There are several public dances, a dramatization and traditional folk dances. There are no elaborate preparations as before, nor is there a formal *folia*. He also noted that during the last three years, all the houses were full and the waterfront was lined with many boats. There were a total of sixty boats in the river procession last year.

In spite of the padre's disdain for the "profane," the festival of São Benedito is a financial bonanza for the church. The current padre, who has been in Itá for three years, enumerated the uses of the money earned at the festival's auction of donated items. During his first year, the *ginásio* was completed. During the second year, it was furnished. And from last year's money, he is planning to build a new *barraca do Santo* behind the *ginásio* which can be used as a meeting hall. It will have a large kitchen and serve as a center for the yearly catechism meetings. Toward the end of our visit, workers began tearing down the old *barraca* along the river and clearing the area behind the *ginásio* in preparation for construction of the new *barraca*. In addition to all these special projects, the money from the festival makes the parish one of the few self-supporting parishes in the state.

As before, there is still very little participation in the festival of St. Anthony held on June 13. There was no money available for the festival this year, so only a mass was celebrated. The padre admitted that the festival of St. Anthony could hardly be called a festival nowadays.

The church is still unable to render much service to those who live in the interior. The padre is kept busy with the townspeople and has no time to travel to the interior on a regular basis. In an effort to provide some religious instruction to the people of the interior, the church sponsors a catechism session each year for representatives of the many small neighborhoods and settlements within the *município*. This year's session was attended by almost two hundred people. They meet each day during the week for instruction and special projects concerning all manner of religious subjects. Each evening there was a mass. To help the padre conduct the session, the Bishop of the Xingu,[4] and two other priests came. The total cost of the session was 5,000 cruzeiros ($750). The catechists themselves provided 1,500 cruzeiros ($225) worth of goods and money, and the parish paid the remainder. Dona Dora and the *prefeito* each provided a steer for the catechists' meals. An additional steer was provided by an anonymous donor who pledged it as a *promessa* to São Benedito. Part of the money went to provide the catechists with printed materials to be taken back to their neighborhoods for use by those who

[4] The Bishop, Dom Eurico Krautler, is the same German priest who visited Itá regularly in 1948. He now admits that his concept of Catholicism in 1948 was severe and states that he learned much by reading this book. In 1974, the Bishop was most helpful to the anthropologists working in the Amazon.

were unable to attend the session. Each neighborhood has a "library" where the local citizenry can read the materials or purchase them for a small amount.

The townspeople, of course, have ready access to mass and the catechism sessions held each week. In addition, the church sponsors a program held at the *ginásio* developed and distributed by FASE (Fundação de Assistência Social e de Educação). The program is centered on community and family problems and how to cope with them. The two resident nuns are responsible for these sessions which are held periodically throughout the year. One of the nuns also operates a small kindergarten downstairs in the *ginásio*. There is also a special room for a youth group which holds meetings, dances, and parties. These special activities were a result of the padre's opinion that the church should play a major role in the community. Our own observations confirmed that the nuns and the padre were very visible in the community and well liked.

Protestants form a very small minority in Itá. There is one church, the Assembly of God, which holds services in a tiny church along the waterfront. According to the priest, the pastor who was there before the current pastor was very dynamic and had many converts, but the current pastor is not and the number of Protestants has dwindled. Protestant services are held many times throughout the week including twice on Sunday. The highest attendance we observed at a Protestant service was thirteen, and over half of them were children. The weekday services are often held in competition with the music from the dance hall two doors away. When the windows are open, passers-by stop to look in. There is usually a large gathering outside—larger than the one inside. The Protestant families live in an area behind the church. They are generally poorer and more recent residents in the community.

On the island of Itá, there is a larger community of Protestants. The padre delights in telling the story of the main sponsor of the Protestant church on the island who displays an image of São Benedito in his living room. The Padre maintains that the people in Itá are wedded to their saints and especially to São Benedito. There was not a Catholic home in Itá, which did not have a picture of São Benedito or another patron saint. Most homes in fact had several religious pictures. The influence of São Benedito still reaches up and down the river, as in the past, as is evidenced by attendance at his festival and the rockets fired off in his honor by almost every passing boat. And thanks to him, the Catholic church still plays an important role in the life of the community.

The festival of São Benedito is the largest festival of the year, but what do the people of Itá do throughout the year for entertainment and recreation? There are usually several private parties during the week, held at one of the four clubs or dance halls in town, which are an entirely new phenomenon since 1948. They generally attract the younger adults. The parties begin at about 9 P.M. Each hall is equipped with outdoor speakers which broadcast the music to the whole town. Things begin slowly with only a few girls dancing inside. The eligible men and the rest of the girls stand outside in two separate groups. *Cachaça* and rum begin to liven things up later in the evening. Many do not even come until eleven o'clock. The music is modern rock or a local dance called the *carimbó*. The festivities can last until two or three in the morning.

There are also private parties in the rural areas, but the people in town consider them wild affairs.[5] During our stay, a man was wounded at a party on the island and then brought to town in a canoe and laid on the dock. He subsequently died. The talk in the town the next day concerned the wild orgy on the island. José Marajo told me that these affairs always end that way, and that those caboclos would pull a knife at the drop of a hat.

Sports are very popular in Itá. On Sunday mornings there is usually a soccer game between the town's two adult teams followed by a match between two youth teams. In 1948, the people of Itá knew vaguely about national soccer but due to the lack of communication with the outside world were unable to follow it closely. There were

[5] Rural festivals, as described by Wagley and by Eduardo Galvão (*Santos e Visagems*, São Paulo, Companhia Editora Nacional, 1955), are said no longer to exist. We were unable to verify this. They may in fact be these "orgies" as described by the townspeople.

no organized soccer teams. The young men spent many afternoons during the week at Orlando's bar where there is a volleyball net. These games lasted two hours or more and were loud and hotly contested events.

The daily routine in Itá begins at 7 A.M. when Juca rings the bell behind town hall. Those who work for the *município* begin work at this time. By 7:30, all stores are open, the first session of school begins and the streets start to fill up with people buying the day's provisions and conducting whatever business they might have. The prefecture and the *coletoria* are also open by now. Between 8:00 and 10:00 activity is at its peak. Men from the governmental offices come out and talk in small groups from time to time. The *delegado* whose office is at the end of the street, often stays home and joins these groups. By 10:30 the day is getting hot and activity gradually slackens until 12:30 when everyone is inside for the midday meal. Stores close until 2:30. Even those who are working in their fields stop for a rest and a meal. The second session of school starts at 1:30. Until 3:00, the streets are largely deserted as most people are inside taking rests in their hammocks or visiting with their families during the heat of the day. In late afternoon the town gradually becomes alive again. People often come outside and just sit in the shade. The evening session of school begins at 4:30. At 5:00, Juca rings the bell to announce the end of the workday. By this time, people are out in force. They rent bicycles and ride around town or simply walk down the street to greet friends. Young couples and children crowd the park to watch the sunset or the boats. At 7:00, MOBRAL classes begin and families are finishing supper. During the evening hours there is some activity in the stores which all close by 10:00. Families sit in front of their homes and visit. Lights come on at dusk and parties begin at the dance halls. If it is Sunday night, vespers begin at 7:30. Lights are out by 11:00. The streets are deserted again, and the only activity in town is the party, should there be one.

We were fortunate enough to be in Itá during an election year. During our stay, one of the local parties headed by Dona Branquinha's son, Alberto Viana, held a rally which was attended by the federal deputy and the candidate for the state legislature. After a dinner with the candidates and the local politicians, we adjourned to the rally. When we arrived, there were a few people inside the dance hall which had been rented and about fifty others standing outside. These included many local citizens who are prominent in the party, ARENA II (Alianca Renovadora Nacional). The leader of the other faction, ARENA I, Joaquim Gonçalves, was conspicuously absent along with the current mayor who was said to have crossed over to ARENA I. Alberto Viana gave an opening speech after he had asked all of those standing outside to come in. He then yielded the microphone to José Marajó who was shy about speaking in front of a group. He spoke of party allegiance and how they would strive to better Itá.

These speeches were followed by other speeches from local politicians and then the visiting candidates. The crowd inside numbered 120 with another 110 outside. One comment made by Alberto Viana brought laughs from the audience. When he introduced the federal deputy he said, "a man of the party who has done so much for the development of your community." It is a generally held opinion that those in federal and state government do nothing for Itá except put on a small party like this one every four years. After the speeches, the bar opened and the music and dancing started.

The rally was the only politicking we saw in Itá. Elections for the mayor and the town council are held every four years. The last election was held in 1973 for municipal offices. The mayor has almost all governmental power in the *município*. The only function of the town council is to pass a budget at the beginning of each year. Politics no longer seems to be the heated and much discussed topic it was before the military take-over in 1964. We also felt that politics had never been the answer for Itá's problems.

At the end of the summer, we took our own leave from Itá saying goodbye to those who had known Wagley during his visits and those new friends we had made during our stay. Dona Dora, Dona Branquinha, José Marajó, Juca, Dona Joaquina and many others asked us to convey their *saudades* to the Wagley's and asked when we would come back.

We left with mixed feelings about the future of traditional river towns like Itá. The highway had by-passed them; what hope was there for a similar "boom" along the river? Many in Itá spoke hopefully of a road which might connect Itá with the Trans-Amazon Highway, but the community and the people themselves still depend heavily on the river and any new developments will more than likely rely on it too, whether it be the opening of the sawmill or a mineral deposit discovered nearby.

The whole of the Amazon, as the magazines and newspaper stories would have it, is experiencing a "boom" unparalleled in modern times. But there is another world represented by all the Itás located along the rivers of the Amazon Basin. They are poor communities with little or no industrial or agricultural base. Where there are industrial bases, such as lumber in Itá, they are still extractive industries dependent upon markets and conditions far removed from the Amazon region, much the same as when rubber was booming. But we still had to ask ourselves, had Itá changed? If so, was it for the better or worse?

Itá will soon have a new hospital and the people hope to have a full-time doctor to staff it. After a decline in health-care facilities since the withdrawal of SESP, they are looking to the hospital as the answer to adequate medical facilities. The average citizen of Itá also has better educational opportunities thanks to greater contact with the state education offices in Belém and the new literacy program, MOBRAL. However, the town is still hoping for a *ginásio* staffed with teachers. Communications with the outside world have improved with the telegraph service, semi-regular mail service, semi-regular transportation to Belém and Santarém, and radio contact with all areas of South America. There are increasing quantities and varieties of manufactured goods and services available. All of these features and the *movimento* or activity of the town makes Itá the first stopping place for those people who are moving from isolated areas in the interior and perhaps later to the big city. The "attractions" of Itá merely whet their appetites for life in the cities of Belém, Santarém, Manaus. The result of this migration to the town has been a doubling of the population in the past twenty years.

However, a concurrent increase in jobs and patrons has not occurred. Jobs are scarce. There has been a breakdown of the old patron-client relationship which has brought changes to the entire social structure. Several informants indicated that there is no longer a class system in Itá based on family background. The important factor is money and/or whether you were able to provide jobs to others. Our observations confirmed this. There are only two remnants of the old class system in Itá—Dona Dora and Dona Branquinha. They are still much respected, but the old system will die with them.

Are the people of Itá better off now than in 1948? Our answer must be somewhat equivocal. In a few respects the upper and middle income groups have more access to manufactured goods and to the outside world, but for the lower income groups things have changed very little. Each day is a struggle for enough to eat even if it is only enough manioc to fill the stomach. For this two-thirds of the population, increased contact with the outside world has only made their existence seem that much more miserable. With no prospects for a new industry or job markets in Itá, the outlook for their betterment is indeed dim.

In the original edition of this book, Wagley compared Itá with Plainville, U.S.A., a rural farm community in the Midwest studied by James West in 1939-1940. A comparison between the two communities in 1974 would reflect an enormous gap between the social and economic changes which have occurred in Plainville in the past twenty-six years and the changes which have occurred in Itá during the same period. Plainville has moved "into an urban sphere of interest, and its people have improved their standard of living many times over" (Wagley 1964:311).[6] Itá, on the other hand, has made little progress in the improvement of the standard of living for the

---

[6] Charles Wagley, *Amazon Town: A Study of Man in the Tropics* (New York, Alfred Knopf, 1964), p. 311.

vast majority of its citizenry. Itá remains a poor community by any standard.

Our experiences led us to much the same conclusion reached by Wagley in the 1964 edition of his book:

> The lethargy and backwardness of Itá, and all similar communities, is a threat to the world, not just to Brazil. People cannot continue to be illiterate, hungry, badly clothed, ill-informed, sick, and deprived of the minimum facilities of a modern community without seeking in desperation for some formula to provide them with rapid change during their lifetime. Today, Itá is in communication with the outside world and open to outside influences. The people of Itá want the things they have seen or have merely heard about.

REFERENCES

Agassiz, Louis, *A Journey in Brazil*. New York, 1896.

Album do Estado do Pará, compiled at the behest of Dr. Augusto Montenegro, governor (1901–1908). Paris, 1910.

Bastide, Roger, "Race Relations in Brazil: São Paulo," *Courier*, UNESCO, Paris, Vol. 5, Nos. 8–9, 1952.

———, "Religion and Church in Brazil," in *Brazil: Portrait of Half a Continent*, T. Lynn Smith and Alexander Marchant, eds. New York, 1951.

Bates, H. W., *The Naturalist on the River Amazon*. London, 1930.

Candido, Antonio, "The Brazilian Family," in *Brazil: Portrait of Half a Continent*, T. Lynn Smith and Alexander Marchant, eds. New York, 1951.

Castro, Josué de, *Geografia da fome*. Rio de Janeiro, 1946.

Costa Pinto, L. A., "Race Relations in Brazil: Rio de Janeiro," *Courier*, UNESCO, Paris, Vol. 5, Nos. 8–9, 1952.

Cunha, Euclides da, *Rebellion in the Backlands*, trans. Samuel Putnam. Chicago, 1944.

———, *À margem da história*. Pôrto, 1941.

Davis, Kingsley, "Future Migration in Latin America," *Milbank Fund Quarterly*, No. 1, 1947.

Deane, L. M., Freire Serra, W. E. P. Tabosa, and José Ledo, "A aplicação domiciliar de DDT no controle da malária em localidades da Amazônia," *Revista do SESP*, Ano 1, No. 4, pp. 1121–1139, Rio de Janeiro.

Denis, Pierre, *Brazil*. London, 1914.

Ferreira de Castro, José Maria, *The Jungle*, trans. by Charles Duff. New York, 1935.

Ferreira Reis, Artur Cezar. *Síntese da história do Pará*. Belém, 1942.

Firth, Raymond, *We, the Tikopia*. London, 1936.

———, *A Primitive Polynesian Economy*. London, 1939.

———, *Elements of Social Organization*. London, 1951.

Forde, C. Daryll, *Habitat, Economy and Society*. London, 1948.

Franck, Peter and Dorothea, "Implementation of Technical Assistance," *International Conciliation*, February, 1951, No. 468.

Freyre, Gilberto, *The Masters and the Slaves,* trans. Samuel Putnam. New York, 1946.

Galvão, Eduardo, The Religion of an Amazon Community, unpublished Ph.D. dissertation, Faculty of Political Science, Columbia University, 1952.

Gourou, Pierre, *Les Pays tropicaux.* Paris, 1948.

———, "L'Amazonie," *Cahiers d'Outre Mer,* Vol. II, No. 5, 1949, pp. 1–13.

Hanson, Earl Parker, *The Amazon: A New Frontier.* Foreign Policy Association Pamphlet No. 45, 1944.

Huntington, Ellsworth, *Civilization and Climate.* 3rd ed., New York, 1939.

James, Preston, *Latin America.* New York, 1942.

Kluckhohn, Clyde, *Mirror for Man.* New York, 1949.

Koster, Henry, *Travels in Brazil.* 2nd ed., London, 1816.

Ladislau, Alfredo, *Terra immatura.* Rio de Janeiro, 1933.

Le Cointe, Paul, *Amazonia brasileira: Arvores e plantas uteis.* São Paulo, 1947.

Leite, Serafim, *História da Companhia de Jesus no Brasil.* Lisbon, 1938.

Linton, Ralph, *The Study of Man.* New York, 1936.

Magalhães, Pedro de, *The Histories of Brazil,* trans. John B. Stetson, Jr. New York, Cortes Society, 1922.

Métraux, Alfred, "Les Migrations historiques des Tupí-Guaraní," *Journal de la Société des Américanistes de Paris,* Vol. 19, pp. 1–45, 1927.

Meyerhoff, Howard A., "Natural Resources in Most of the World," in *Most of the World,* ed. Ralph Linton. New York, 1949.

Mills, C. A., "Climatic Effects on Growth and Development with Particular Reference to the Effects of Tropical Residence," *American Anthropologist,* Vol. 44, No. 1, 1942.

Moog, Vianna, *O ciclo do ouro negro.* Pôrto Alegre, 1936.

Myrdal, Gunnar, *An American Dilemma.* New York, 1944.

Nash, Roy, *The Conquest of Brazil.* New York, 1926.

Pierson, Donald, *Negroes in Brazil.* Chicago, 1942.

Price, Grenfell, *White Settlers in the Tropics.* American Geographic Society Publication No. 23, New York, 1939.

Smith, Herbert, *The Amazons and the Coast.* New York, 1879.

Smith, T. Lynn, *Brazil: People and Institutions.* Baton Rouge, 1946.

Thomas, Gladwin, "Climate and Anthropology," *American Anthropologist,* Vol. 49, No. 4, Pt. 1, 1947.

Wagley, Charles, ed., "Race Relations in an Amazon Community," in *Race and Class in Rural Brazil.* Paris, UNESCO, 1952.

Wagley, Charles, and Eduardo Galvão, *The Tenetehara Indians of Brazil.* New York, 1949.

Wallace, Alfred Russel, *A Narrative of Travels on the Amazon and Rio Negro.* London, 1853.

West, James, *Plainville, U.S.A.* New York, 1945.

Index

A Selva (Ferreira de Castro), 93
Abaetetuba, 21
Aboriginal religious beliefs, assimilated by Christianity, 224–225
Acre, District of, 97; Territory, 290
Acre fino, 82
Adoption, 177, 179–184; attitude in United States toward, 183; its relation to poverty, 181–182; and usefulness of children, 179
Africa, 259; retarded tropical areas of, 2–3; "wet" tropics of, 3
African folklore, 217
Agassiz, Louis, 39
Agassiz, Mrs. Louis, 39
Agriculture, 14–16, 32, 61, 64–72, 100, 101, 264, 265, 271, 290, 304; necessity for modernization of, 101; primitiveness of, in Amazon, 64–72. See also Slash-and-burn agriculture
Agropolis, viii
Almanac do Pará, 48
Altamira, 28
Amapá Territory, formed, 290
Amazon, climate of, 10–11; collapse of rubber industry in, 49–51; debt-slavery system in, 93–94; potentiality of, 5–6. See also Amazon Basin, Amazon Indian, Amazon River, Amazon Valley, Amazonas, Amazonia, Brazilian Amazon
"Amazon Address," 289
Amazon Basin, lack of scientific and cultural factors in, 16–17; as underdeveloped area, 2–3
Amazon Cable Company, 58
Amazon Indian, cultural traditions of, 288; as source of slaves, 288
Amazon River, agricultural colonies on, 290; drainage system of, 3; flood plain, 15; as transportation system, 266
Amazon Telegraph Company, 277
Amazon Valley, agricultural potential of, 14–16; American Indian heritage

Amazon Valley (Cont.):
in, 32–33; basic reasons for backwardness of, 61–63; as colonial area, 287–288, 289; colonial economy of, 264–265; components of population of, in 1852, 39; economic structure of, rejuvenated by World War II, 53–55; effects of Indian culture on, 33–34; effects of rubber industry on, 45–49; effect of steady rains on, 11; effects of tropical seasons on man in, 10–11; factors in backwardness of, 287–289; festivals in, 188; folk beliefs in, 216–217; influence of rubber on, 90–99, 288–289; interest of Brazilian Government in, 289–291; lack of sanitation in, 12–13; lack of Western technology in, 289; lateritic soils of, 14; literacy in, 60; major problems of, 264–265; new technology and social approach for "conquest" of, 291–295; potential of alluvial lands in, 15; predatory economic pattern of, 60; rubber boom in, 265; rubber gathering in, 82–87; slavery in, 129, 288; trader-customer relationships in, 97; transportation in, 61; tribal divisions of, 33–34; tropical diseases in, 11–13
Amazonas, State of, 4
Amazonia, collapse of economic structure of, 50–51, 53; emigration of Jews to, 48; folklore in, 76–81; Iberian influence in, 39; influence of Tupían traditions on, 40–42; peonage, debt servitude and slavery in, 38; piecemeal subjection of, 34; slavery in, 36–37, 38
Amazonian Indian, assimilation of, 38–39
America, "wet" tropics of, 3
American Indian, beliefs of, 274; folklore of, 216–217; stereotype of, in Itá, 140–141
Ancylostoma, 12

329

Under-developed areas of world, discussion of, 2–3, 257
United Nations, 292; technical-assistance programs, 289–290
United States, 9, 21; American Negro in, 7; attitude toward adoption in, 183; forms SESP with Brazil, 55; population per kilometer, 3; social control in, 139, 142
United States Department of Agriculture, 18
United States Government, 53, 57
United States Rubber Development Corporation, 53
University of Michigan, 55
University of Minnesota, 267
Urutaí River, 96

Vargas, Getulio, 54, 289–290
Venezuela, 3, 14

Vieira, Antonio, 37
Virgin of Nazareth in Belém, shrine of, 221
von Humboldt, Alexander, 5–6
von Martius, Karl, 44, 45
Vows, in religious belief, 220–222

Wallace, Alfred Russel, 6, 41
West, James, his *Plainville, U.S.A.*, quoted, 276, 278, 279, 282, 285, 286, 324
World War II, 5, 31, 53, 89; effect of, on Itá, 57

Xingú River, 28, 82, 97

Yaws, 12